V I S U A L
ENCYCLOPEDIA
OF ANIMALS

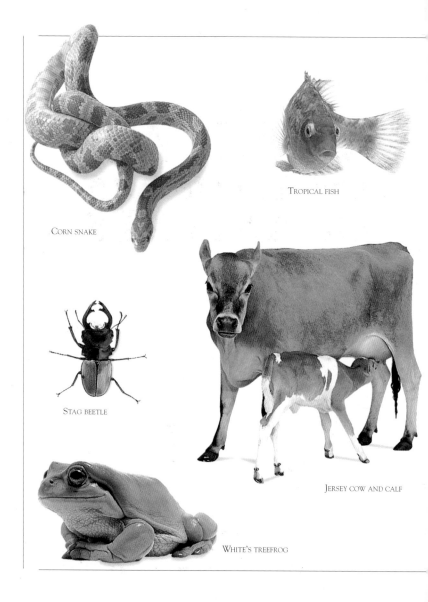

Corn snake

Tropical fish

Stag beetle

Jersey cow and calf

White's treefrog

VISUAL
ENCYCLOPEDIA
OF ANIMALS

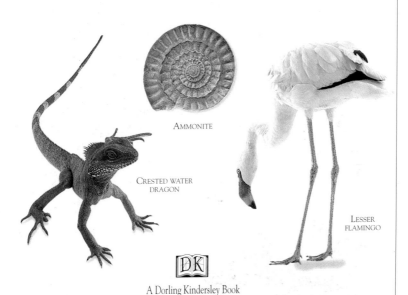

AMMONITE

CRESTED WATER
DRAGON

LESSER
FLAMINGO

DK

A Dorling Kindersley Book

Dorling Kindersley

LONDON, NEW YORK, SYDNEY, DELHI,
PARIS, MUNICH and JOHANNESBURG

Writers and consultants:
David Alderton, Steve Brooks, Dr. Barry Clarke,
John Farndon, Mark Lambert, Laurence Mound,
Scarlett O'Hara, Barbara Taylor, Steve Parker,
Joyce Pope, David Taylor

Project Editor Lucy Hurst
Managing Editor Jayne Parsons
Managing Art Editor Jacquie Gulliver
Production Kate Oliver

First published in Great Britain in 1999
as "Pockets Animals of the World" by
Dorling Kindersley Ltd., 80 Strand, London, WC2R 0RL

Original edition produced for Dorling Kindersley by
PAGE*One*, Cairn House, Elgiva Lane, Chesham,
Buckinghamshire, HP5 2JD

2 4 6 8 10 9 7 5 3

A CIP catalogue record for this book is available
from the British Library.

ISBN 0-7513-139-71

Colour reproduction by Colourscan, Singapore
Printed and bound in Italy by Printer Trento Srl

See our complete catalogue at
www.dk.com

CONTENTS

BIRDWING
BUTTERFLY

GREEN MANTELLA

TAWNY OWL

BIRDS 258

MAMMALS 366

ARMADILLO

GREAT DANE

HOW TO USE THIS BOOK

These pages show you how to use the *Visual Encyclopedi of Animals*. The book is divided into seven sections about the animal kingdom. There is also an introductory section about the origins of animal life, and how animals are classified. At the back of the book, there is a comprehensive index.

HEADING AND INTRODUCTION
Every spread has a subject heading. This is followed by the introduction, which outlines the subject and gives a clear idea of what these pages are about.

Label

Heading

Introduction

Muscular foot

Data box

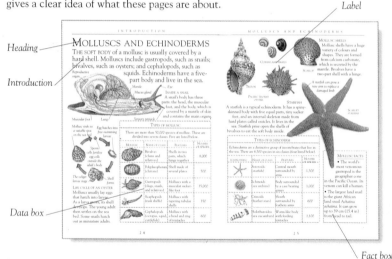

Fact box

DATA BOX
Some pages have data boxes, which contain detailed numerical information. This box gives data about types of mollusc.

FACT BOXES
Many pages have fact boxes. The information in these is related to the main topic on the page.

LABELS
For clarity, some pictures have labels. These give extra information about the picture, or provide clearer identification.

SECTION NAMES
Along the sides of the pages there are section names. The lefthand page gives the section, the righthand the subject.

SIZE INDICATORS
In some sections of this book, you will find clear symbols next to photography. These indicate the average size of an animal.

Size indicator

REAR-FANGED SNAKES
SNAKES WITH FANGS in the back of their mouth are found in both the Old and New Worlds and, as with other groups of snakes, they vary greatly in colour, size, and habitat. They are not as efficient as front-fanged snakes at injecting venom, and so most species are harmless to humans. Large rear-fanged snakes, however, can be dangerous.

CORAL MIMIC
The false coral snake preys on lizards, small mammals, and other small snakes. It is found in the forests of Central America, from Venezuela to Costa Rica.

FALSE CORAL SNAKE

Colours resemble those of a

LIZARD HUNTER
The blunt-headed tree snake is found in trees and shrubs from southern Mexico to Bolivia and Paraguay. It is active by night and feeds mostly on lizards such as anoles and geckos.

BLUNT-HEADED TREE SNAKE

Gaping mouth is a warning to enemies

JOLE THREAT
When threatened, a parrot snake raises its head and opens its mouth, but rarely strikes. Slender and well camouflaged, it hunts lizards and amphibians in the dense foliage of the rainforests of Central and South America.

This snake often feeds on eggs laid on leaves by frogs

Camouflaged for life in the treetops

IN THE TREETOPS
HIGH UP IN THE RAINFOREST CANOPY it is light and warm and there is plenty of food, especially fruits, seeds, and insects. Bird life includes large bird predators such as eagles which patrol the treetops looking for prey. Canopy birds, such as parrots and toucans, climb well and have strong feet for grasping branches.

HARPY EAGLE
The huge harpy eagle is one of the most powerful birds of prey. It swoops into the canopy to seize monkeys (like this capuchin), birds, sloths, and reptiles. It can fly very fast through the branches.

Bare, orange-yellow face and bill

LADY ROSS'S TURACO
This African turaco lives in small, noisy groups, usually high in the canopy. Although clumsy fliers, turacos are good at running along tree branches. They make a great variety of cackling and croaking calls.

TOCO TOUCAN
This is the largest toucan, with a bill up to 19 cm (7½ in) long. The bill is hollow inside with supporting struts, so it is not as heavy as it looks. The colours help it to recognize other toucans and find a mate.

ORANGE-BILLED LEAFBIRD
This Asian leafbird helps to pollinate the forest trees as it feeds on nectar. It also spreads the seeds of plants in the mistletoe family by eating the berries.

The leafbird is good at mimicking other birds' songs.

GREAT INDIAN HORNBILL
The hornbills of Southeast Asia and Africa look like the toucans of South America because they live and feed in a similar way. They are named after the horny casques on their bills. No-one knows what these bony growths are for.

The casque is a thin layer of skin and bone over a honeycomb structure.

Annotation

Caption

ANNOTATION
Pictures often have extra information around them, which picks out features. This text appears in *italics*, and uses leader lines to point to details.

INDEX
There is an index at the back of the book that alphabetically lists every subject. By referring to the index, information on particular topics can be found quickly.

CAPTIONS
Each illustration in the book is accompanied by a detailed, explanatory caption.

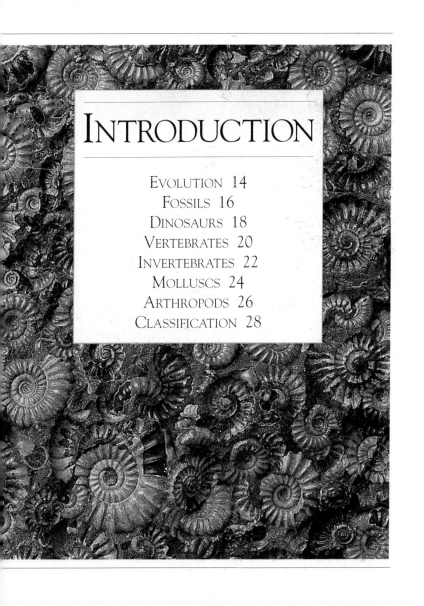

INTRODUCTION

INTRODUCTION

EVOLUTION

SINCE LIFE appeared 3.8 billion years ago, millions of different creatures have come and gone. As habitats changed, some species survived by adapting, while others died out quickly. This gradual turnover of species is called evolution.

PORPOISE'S FRONT FLIPPER

"Finger" bones form a powerful flipper for swimming

Two sets of short "arm" bones

ADAPTATION

Evolution works by slowly adapting existing features to suit different purposes. Although they look very different, humans and porpoises both have two "arm" bones and five "finger" bones.

Two sets of long bones make up the arm

Five sets of finger bones make up hand

HUMAN ARM

LIFE FORMS THROUGH THE AGES

By working out when certain rocks formed, and then studying the fossils found in them, paleontologists – who study the life forms of the past – have built up a remarkable picture of the way species have changed since the dawn of the Cambrian period 590 million years ago (mya). Little is known of Precambrian life forms as very few fossils remain.

PRECAMBRIAN	PALEOZOIC	
	Cambrian	Ordovician

4600–590 mya
Single-celled life forms, such as bacteria and algae, appear, then soft multi-celled life forms, such as worms and jellyfish.

590–505 mya
No life on land. Invertebrates flourish in the seas. First molluscs and trilobites.

505–438 mya
First crustaceans and early jawless fish appear. Coral reefs form. Sahara glaciated.

HOW EVOLUTION WORKS

According to Darwin's theory of evolution, animals and plants developed over millions of years, surviving according to their ability to adapt to a changing environment. Darwin's theory challenged the accepted 19th-century view that life forms did not change after being created by a deity (god).

CHARLES DARWIN (1809–1882)

The theory of evolution was developed by English naturalist Charles Darwin after studying the animals of the Galápagos Islands. He published his findings in 1859 in his book On the Origin of Species.

EVOLUTION OF THE HORSE

Eohippus
This hare-sized creature browsed in woodland.

Mesohippus
Over millions of years, Eohippus evolved into a larger grazing animal.

Merychippus
As early horses adapted to grassland, they developed longer limbs to escape from predators.

Modern horse
The horses of today are highly developed grazers, with long legs for running and keen senses.

Silurian	Devonian	Carboniferous	Permian
438–408 mya First jawed fish. Huge sea scorpions hunt in the sea. Small land plants colonize the shore.	*408–355 mya* Age of sharks and fish. Insects and amphibians appear on land. Giant ferns form forests.	*355–290 mya* Warm swampy forests leave remains that will turn to coal. First reptiles.	*290–250 mya* Reptiles diversify, conifers replace tree ferns. Mass extinction as Earth turns cold.

FOSSILS

THE REMAINS of living things preserved naturally, often for many millions of years, are called fossils. Most fossils are formed in rocks; however, remains can also be preserved in ice, tar, peat, and amber. Fossils tell us nearly all we know about the history of life on Earth.

Spider trapped inside resin

SPIDER IN AMBER
Amber is fossilized tree resin that may also preserve trapped insects.

AMMONITES BECAME EXTINCT 65 MYA

Fossilized shell

KINDS OF FOSSIL
Most fossils form on the sea bed, so shells and sea creatures are the most common. Fossils of land animals and plants are more rare. Footprints, burrows, or droppings may also be preserved.

MESOZOIC			CENOZOIC	
Triassic	Jurassic	Cretaceous	Tertiary	
			Palaeocene	Eocene
250–205 mya Mammals and dinosaurs appear. The climate warms and seed-bearing plants dominate.	205–135 mya The age of the dinosaurs. The first known bird, Archaeopteryx, appears.	135–66 mya First flowering plants. Period ends with a mass extinction that wipes out dinosaurs.	66–53 mya Warm, humid climate. Mammals, insects, and flowering plants flourish.	53–36 mya Mammals grow larger and diversify. Primates evolve.

1 ANIMAL DIES
The body of a dead animal lies decaying on the surface of the land.

2 REMAINS SINK
Gradually, the body becomes covered with sand or mud.

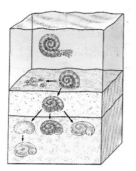

FOSSILIZATION AT SEA
Dead organisms sink to the sea bed and are buried. As the sediment turns to rock, their remains are either chemically altered or dissolve to leave a cavity, which may fill with minerals to form a cast.

3 BONES ALTER
Over time, the bones are altered, and the sand and mud turn to rock.

4 FOSSIL IS EXPOSED
Eventually, weather and erosion expose the fossil at the surface.

Oligocene	Miocene	Pliocene	Quaternary	
			Pleistocene	Holocene

36–23 mya
First human-like creatures appear. Hunting birds thrive. Some mammals die out.

23–6.3 mya
Climate cools, and forests shrink. Deer-like hoofed mammals flourish. First hominids.

6.3–1.6 mya
Cold and dry. Mammals reach maximum diversity. Many modern mammals appear.

1.6m–10,000 ya
Ice Ages. Homo sapiens evolves. Mammoths and sabre-toothed tigers die out.

10,000 ya to present
Humans develop agriculture and technology. Human activity threatens many species.

DINOSAURS

FOR 150 MILLION YEARS the Earth was dominated by giant reptiles called dinosaurs, including *Seismosaurus*, the largest creature ever to walk on land. Then, 65 million years ago, all the dinosaurs mysteriously died out.

Light bones for flying

Wings of skin

Furry body

PTEROSAUR
While dinosaurs ruled the land, giant reptiles, like Pterosaur, flew in the air.

DINOSAUR GROUPS
Scientists divide dinosaurs into two orders according to the arrangement of their hip bones. Saurischians have lizard-like hips and include both plant and meat-eaters. Ornithischians have bird-like hips and are all plant eaters. The two orders are divided into five subgroups.

Muscular tail balanced the front of the body

Long neck for browsing in treetops

Ruff

Horn

SALTASAURUS

STYRACOSAURUS

Sauropods (Saurischians) were huge, long-necked four-legged plant eaters.

Marginocephalians (Saurischians) had a bony ruff and horns for self-defence.

TYRANNOSAURUS

STEGOSAURUS

CORYTHOSAURUS

Thyreophorans (Ornithischians) were spiny-backed plant eaters.

Theropods (Saurischians) were two-legged meat eaters.

Ornithopods (Ornithischians) had a horny beak and bird-like feet.

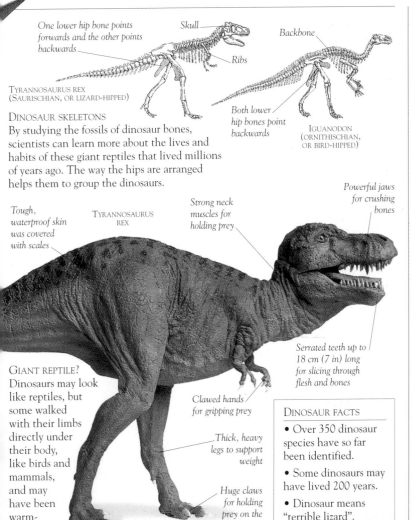

One lower hip bone points forwards and the other points backwards

Skull

Backbone

Ribs

TYRANNOSAURUS REX
(SAURISCHIAN, OR LIZARD-HIPPED)

Both lower hip bones point backwards

IGUANODON
(ORNITHISCHIAN, OR BIRD-HIPPED)

DINOSAUR SKELETONS

By studying the fossils of dinosaur bones, scientists can learn more about the lives and habits of these giant reptiles that lived millions of years ago. The way the hips are arranged helps them to group the dinosaurs.

Powerful jaws for crushing bones

Strong neck muscles for holding prey

TYRANNOSAURUS REX

Tough, waterproof skin was covered with scales

Serrated teeth up to 18 cm (7 in) long for slicing through flesh and bones

Clawed hands for gripping prey

GIANT REPTILE?
Dinosaurs may look like reptiles, but some walked with their limbs directly under their body, like birds and mammals, and may have been warm-blooded.

Thick, heavy legs to support weight

Huge claws for holding prey on the ground

DINOSAUR FACTS

• Over 350 dinosaur species have so far been identified.

• Some dinosaurs may have lived 200 years.

• Dinosaur means "terrible lizard".

VERTEBRATES

ONLY ABOUT three per cent of all animals have backbones, and these are called vertebrates. There are more than 40,000 different species of vertebrate, divided into classes of mammals, birds, fish, reptiles, and amphibians. Their sense organs and nervous systems are well developed, and they have adapted to almost every habitat.

GORILLA SKELETON

BACKBONE
Vertebrates have a skeleton of bone, with a backbone, two pairs of limbs, and a skull that protects the brain. Inside are the heart, lungs, and other organs.

REPTILES
Lizards, snakes, crocodiles, and geckos are reptiles. They all have a tough, scaly skin. Young reptiles hatch from eggs, and look like tiny versions of their parents. This chameleon is a type of lizard.

Spines along backbone give protection from attack

Scaly skin

Female frog lays eggs, called frogspawn

MADAGASCAN CHAMELEON

Male fertilizes spawn

ANIMAL REPRODUCTION
In vertebrates, offspring are created when males and females come together and the male's sperm join the female's eggs. This is called sexual reproduction, and usually involves mating. A few animals are neither male nor female, and they reproduce asexually.

Prehensile tail for holding on to branches

SENSES

Mammals and other vertebrate animals have senses to help them find their way, locate food, and avoid enemies. For land animals, such as this caracal, sight, hearing, and smell are the most important senses. Sea creatures rely more on smell and taste to escape danger and find food.

Sharp eyesight for hunting, even at night

Long, sensitive ears pick up even the faintest sounds

Strong sense of smell

Sharp teeth

CARACAL

TWINSPOT WRASSE

FISH

With streamlined bodies covered in slippery scales, these vertebrates are perfectly suited to life in the water.

Scales covered in slimy mucus

BIRDS

The only animals that have feathers are birds, and most of them are powerful fliers. Birds have a beak, or bill, instead of teeth, and all reproduce by laying eggs.

COUNT RAGGI'S BIRD OF PARADISE

RED-EYED TREE FROG

Large eyes spot prey

AMPHIBIANS

Frogs, toads, newts, and salamanders are amphibians. These vertebrates spend part of their lives in water and part on land. They all reproduce by laying eggs.

Long legs for jumping

PORCUPINE

Spiny quills protect body

MAMMAL

A mammal is usually covered in fur or hair. It gives birth to live young, which it feeds with milk.

Fur helps keep body warm

INVERTEBRATES

NINE-TENTHS of all animals are invertebrates, which means they have no backbone. They include jellyfish, sponges, starfish, coral, worms, crabs, spiders, and insects.

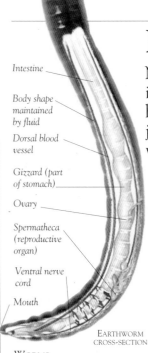

Intestine

Body shape maintained by fluid

Dorsal blood vessel

Gizzard (part of stomach)

Ovary

Spermatheca (reproductive organ)

Ventral nerve cord

Mouth

EARTHWORM CROSS-SECTION

Hard shell to protect soft body

Soft body

Eyes on stalks

MOLLUSCS

These soft-bodied invertebrates are often protected by a hard shell. Most molluscs, such as squid and octopuses, clams, mussels, and scallops, live in water, but some, like snails and slugs, live on land.

WORMS

A worm is an animal with a long soft body and no legs. There are many different kinds, including flatworms, tapeworms, earthworms, roundworms, and leeches.

STARFISH AND URCHINS

Starfish, sea urchins, and sea cucumbers are all echinoderms. All are predators, and most have sucker-tipped "tube feet" through which they pump water to move along and feed. The five broad arms of a starfish can wrench open a shellfish to suck out the contents.

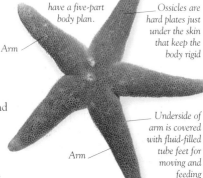

Echinoderms have a five-part body plan.

Ossicles are hard plates just under the skin that keep the body rigid

Arm

Underside of arm is covered with fluid-filled tube feet for moving and feeding

Arm

LIFE CYCLE
Each invertebrate has its own life cycle, but most species lay eggs. Some go through several larval stages, while others hatch as miniature adults.

Buds break away as free-swimming adults

Jellyfish

Fertilized larva

Polyp divides into eight-part buds

Larva grows into a polyp

SPIDER

ARTHROPODS
Insects, spiders, and lobsters are all arthropods. They have jointed limbs and a tough external skeleton.

CROSS-SECTION OF A JELLYFISH

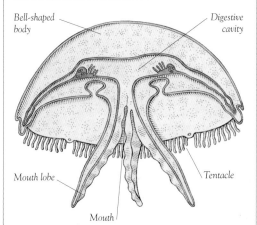

Bell-shaped body

Digestive cavity

Mouth lobe

Tentacle

Mouth

Jellyfish, anemones, and coral are all kinds of coelenterate – sea creatures with a mouth surrounded by tentacles. These tentacles usually carry a sting to stun or kill prey. Some coelenterates, called polyps, always attach to solid objects, such as a rock; others, called medusas, move by contracting their bell-shaped bodies.

SPONGES
These primitive sea creatures feed by drawing water into the holes in their soft bodies and filtering out any food.

INVERTEBRATE FACTS
• Up to 500 million hookworms may be found in a single human.

• Roundworms are probably the most numerous animals on Earth.

23

MOLLUSCS AND ECHINODERMS

THE SOFT BODY of a mollusc is usually covered by a hard shell. Molluscs include gastropods, such as snails; bivalves, such as oysters; and cephalopods, such as squids. Echinoderms have a five-part body and live in the sea.

Reproductive organ

Mantle

Mucus gland

Eye

INSIDE A SNAIL
A snail's body has three parts: the head, the muscular foot, and the body, which is covered by a mantle of skin and contains the main organs.

Muscular foot *Lung* *Sensory tentacle*

Mollusc sinks to a suitable spot on the sea bed

Egg hatches into free-swimming larvae

Sperm cells fertilize egg cells outside the adult's body

The veliger larvae stage *Shell forms*

LIFE CYCLE OF AN OYSTER
Molluscs usually lay eggs that hatch into larvae. As a larva grows, its shell develops. The young adult then settles on the sea bed. Some snails hatch out as miniature adults.

TYPES OF MOLLUSC			
There are more than 50,000 species of mollusc. These are divided into seven classes. Five are listed below.			
MOLLUSC	NAME OF CLASS	FEATURES	NUMBER OF SPECIES
	Bivalves (clams and relatives)	Shells in two parts, which hinge together	8,000
	Polyplacophorans (chitons)	Shell made of several plates	500
	Gastropods (slugs, snails, and relatives)	Molluscs with a muscular sucker-like foot	35,000
	Scaphopods (tusk shells)	Molluscs with tapering tubular shells	350
	Cephalopods (octopus, squid, cuttlefish)	Molluscs with a head and ring of tentacles	600

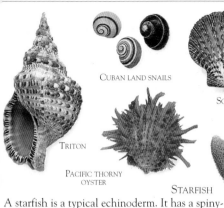

CUBAN LAND SNAILS

TRITON

PACIFIC THORNY OYSTER

SCALLOP

MOLLUSC SHELLS

Mollusc shells have a huge variety of colours and shapes. They are formed from calcium carbonate, which is secreted by the mantle. Bivalves have a two-part shell with a hinge.

A starfish can grow a new arm to replace a damaged limb

SCARLET STARFISH

STARFISH

A starfish is a typical echinoderm. It has a spiny-skinned body with five equal parts, tiny sucker feet, and an internal skeleton made from hard plates called ossicles. It lives in the sea. Starfish prise open the shells of bivalves to eat the soft body inside.

TYPES OF ECHINODERM			
Echinoderms are a distinctive group of invertebrates that live in the sea. There are 6,500 species in six classes (four listed below).			
ECHINODERM	NAME OF CLASS	FEATURES	NUMBER OF SPECIES
	Asteroids (starfish)	Central mouth surrounded by arms	1,500
	Echinoids (sea urchins)	Body surrounded by a case bearing spines	1,000
	Crinoids (feather stars)	Mouth surrounded by feathery arms	600
	Holothuroidea (sea cucumbers)	Worm-like body with feeding tentacles	1,100

MOLLUSC FACTS

• The world's most venomous gastropod is the geographer cone in the Pacific Ocean. Its venom can kill a human.

• The largest land snail is the giant African land snail *Achatina achatina*. It can grow up to 39 cm (15.4 in) from head to tail.

25

ARTHROPODS

ARACHNIDS, CRUSTACEANS, and insects are part of the arthropod group of invertebrates. Insects are by far the largest of these three groups. All arthropods have a jointed body with a tough body case. The case is shed as the animal grows.

The egg is laid in a silk sac to protect it

Spiderlings resemble the adult spider

Spiderling moults

LIFE CYCLE OF A SPIDER
Arachnids such as spiders lay eggs that hatch into tiny versions of adults. They moult several times before they are mature.

IMPERIAL SCORPION

Poison gland
Sting
Heart
Intestine
Cephalothorax
Pedipalps – a pair of pincers for feeding
Abdomen
Spiracle – air hole

INSIDE AN ARACHNID
The body of an arachnid is divided into a front and middle part (cephalothorax) and a rear part (abdomen). Arachnids have four pairs of walking legs.

TYPES OF ARACHNID

The class Arachnida includes spiders, mites, and scorpions. It contains 73,000 species, which are grouped into ten orders. Six orders are listed below.

ARACHNID	NAME OF ORDER	NUMBER OF SPECIES	ARACHNID	NAME OF ORDER	NUMBER OF SPECIES
	Scorpiones (scorpions)	2,000		Uropygi (whip scorpions)	60
	Solifugae (camel spiders)	900		Opiliones (harvestmen)	4,500
	Acari (mites and ticks)	30,000		Araneae (spiders)	40,000

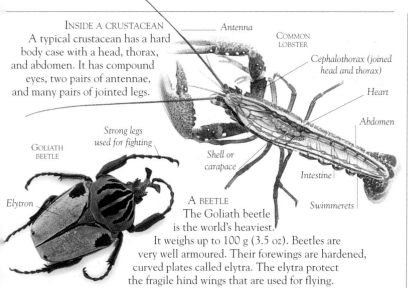

INSIDE A CRUSTACEAN

A typical crustacean has a hard body case with a head, thorax, and abdomen. It has compound eyes, two pairs of antennae, and many pairs of jointed legs.

Antenna

COMMON LOBSTER

Cephalothorax (joined head and thorax)

Heart

Abdomen

GOLIATH BEETLE

Strong legs used for fighting

Shell or carapace

Intestine

Elytron

Swimmerets

A BEETLE

The Goliath beetle is the world's heaviest. It weighs up to 100 g (3.5 oz). Beetles are very well armoured. Their forewings are hardened, curved plates called elytra. The elytra protect the fragile hind wings that are used for flying.

TYPES OF CRUSTACEAN

There are more than 55,000 species of crustaceans divided into eight classes. These include the four classes below.

CRUSTACEAN	NAME OF CLASS	FEATURES	NUMBER OF SPECIES
	Branchiopods (fairy shrimps, water fleas)	Small animals of freshwater and salty lakes	1, 000
	Cirripedia (barnacles)	Immobile animals with a box-like case	1,220
	Copepods (cyclopoids and relatives)	Small animals often found in plankton	13, 000
	Malacostracans (shrimps, crabs, lobsters)	Many-legged animals, often with pincers	30, 000

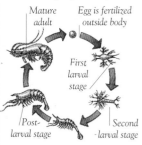

Mature adult

Egg is fertilized outside body

First larval stage

Post-larval stage

Second larval stage

LIFE CYCLE OF A SHRIMP

Crustaceans usually lay their eggs in water. Once hatched, the egg begins its first larval stage. After two more larval stages, there is a final post-larval stage before adulthood.

CLASSIFICATION

BIOLOGISTS HAVE identified and classified most species of vertebrates (animals with backbones), although it is likely that new species of fish await discovery. Invertebrates have not been so well documented, and there may be many species to be identified.

Springtails	Lice
Bristletails	Thrips
Diplurans	Booklice
Silverfish	Zorapterans
Mayflies	Bugs
Stoneflies	Beetles
Webspinners	Ants, bees, wasps
Dragonflies	Lacewings and
Grasshoppers,	antlions
crickets	Scorpionflies
Stick and leaf insects	Stylopids
Grylloblattids	Caddisflies
Earwigs	Butterflies and moths
Cockroaches	Flies
Praying mantids	Fleas
Termites	

INSECTS
(Insecta)
1,000,000 species

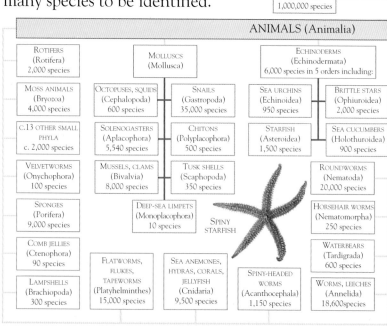

ANIMALS (Animalia)

ROTIFERS
(Rotifera)
2,000 species

MOSS ANIMALS
(Bryozoa)
4,000 species

C.13 OTHER SMALL
PHYLA
c. 2,000 species

VELVETWORMS
(Onychophora)
100 species

SPONGES
(Porifera)
9,000 species

COMB JELLIES
(Ctenophora)
90 species

LAMPSHELLS
(Brachiopoda)
300 species

MOLLUSCS
(Mollusca)

OCTOPUSES, SQUIDS
(Cephalopoda)
600 species

SOLENOGASTERS
(Aplacophora)
5,540 species

MUSSELS, CLAMS
(Bivalvia)
8,000 species

DEEP-SEA LIMPETS
(Monoplacophora)
10 species

FLATWORMS,
FLUKES,
TAPEWORMS
(Platyhelminthes)
15,000 species

SNAILS
(Gastropoda)
35,000 species

CHITONS
(Polyplacophora)
500 species

TUSK SHELLS
(Scaphopoda)
350 species

SPINY
STARFISH

SEA ANEMONES,
HYDRAS, CORALS,
JELLYFISH
(Cnidaria)
9,500 species

ECHINODERMS
(Echinodermata)
6,000 species in 5 orders including:

SEA URCHINS
(Echinoidea)
950 species

BRITTLE STARS
(Ophiuroidea)
2,000 species

STARFISH
(Asteroidea)
1,500 species

SEA CUCUMBERS
(Holothuroidea)
900 species

ROUNDWORMS
(Nematoda)
20,000 species

HORSEHAIR WORMS
(Nematomorpha)
250 species

WATERBEARS
(Tardigrada)
600 species

SPINY-HEADED
WORMS
(Acanthocephala)
1,150 species

WORMS, LEECHES
(Annelida)
18,600species

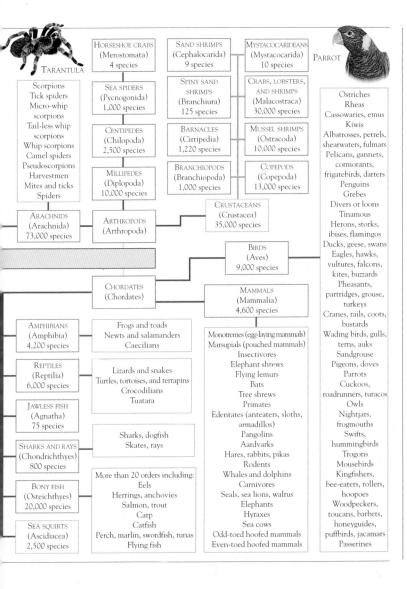

TARANTULA

HORSESHOE CRABS
(Merostomata)
4 species

SAND SHRIMPS
(Cephalocarida)
9 species

MYSTACOCARIDEANS
(Mystacocarida)
10 species

PARROT

Scorpions
Tick spiders
Micro-whip scorpions
Tail-less whip scorpions
Whip scorpions
Camel spiders
Pseudoscorpions
Harvestmen
Mites and ticks
Spiders

SEA SPIDERS
(Pycnogonida)
1,000 species

SPINY SAND
SHRIMPS
(Branchiura)
125 species

CRABS, LOBSTERS,
AND SHRIMPS
(Malacostraca)
30,000 species

Ostriches
Rheas
Cassowaries, emus
Kiwis
Albatrosses, petrels,
shearwaters, fulmars
Pelicans, gannets,
cormorants,
frigatebirds, darters
Penguins
Grebes
Divers or loons
Tinamous
Herons, storks,
ibises, flamingos
Ducks, geese, swans
Eagles, hawks,
vultures, falcons,
kites, buzzards
Pheasants,
partridges, grouse,
turkeys
Cranes, rails, coots,
bustards
Wading birds, gulls,
terns, auks
Sandgrouse
Pigeons, doves
Parrots
Cuckoos,
roadrunners, turacos
Owls
Nightjars,
frogmouths
Swifts,
hummingbirds
Trogons
Mousebirds
Kingfishers,
bee-eaters, rollers,
hoopoes
Woodpeckers,
toucans, barbets,
honeyguides,
puffbirds, jacamars
Passerines

CENTIPEDES
(Chilopoda)
2,500 species

BARNACLES
(Cirripedia)
1,220 species

MUSSEL SHRIMPS
(Ostracoda)
10,000 species

MILLIPEDES
(Diplopoda)
10,000 species

BRANCHIOPODS
(Branchiopoda)
1,000 species

COPEPODS
(Copepoda)
13,000 species

ARACHNIDS
(Arachnida)
73,000 species

ARTHROPODS
(Arthropoda)

CRUSTACEANS
(Crustacea)
35,000 species

BIRDS
(Aves)
9,000 species

CHORDATES
(Chordates)

MAMMALS
(Mammalia)
4,600 species

AMPHIBIANS
(Amphibia)
4,200 species

Frogs and toads
Newts and salamanders
Caecilians

REPTILES
(Reptilia)
6,000 species

Lizards and snakes
Turtles, tortoises, and terrapins
Crocodilians
Tuatara

JAWLESS FISH
(Agnatha)
75 species

SHARKS AND RAYS
(Chondrichthyes)
800 species

Sharks, dogfish
Skates, rays

BONY FISH
(Osteichthyes)
20,000 species

More than 20 orders including:
Eels
Herrings, anchovies
Salmon, trout
Carp
Catfish
Perch, marlin, swordfish, tunas
Flying fish

SEA SQUIRTS
(Ascidiacea)
2,500 species

Monotremes (egg-laying mammals)
Marsupials (pouched mammals)
Insectivores
Elephant shrews
Flying lemurs
Bats
Tree shrews
Primates
Edentates (anteaters, sloths,
armadillos)
Pangolins
Aardvarks
Hares, rabbits, pikas
Rodents
Whales and dolphins
Carnivores
Seals, sea lions, walrus
Elephants
Hyraxes
Sea cows
Odd-toed hoofed mammals
Even-toed hoofed mammals

CLASSIFICATION

INSECTS

WHAT IS AN INSECT?

THERE ARE AT LEAST five million insect species – they are the most abundant animals on earth. All insects have six legs, and their skeleton is on the outside of their body. This outer skeleton forms a hard, protective armour around the soft internal organs.

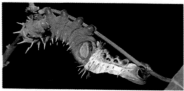

SHEDDING SKIN
A young insect is called a larva. As each larva feeds and grows, it must shed its hard outer skin, which is also called an exoskeleton. When the larva grows too big for its skin, the skin splits, revealing a new, larger skin underneath.

The antennae of insects can sense smells and vibrations in the air.

DISSECTED BEETLE

Eye

First part of thorax bears the front legs

Jointed front leg

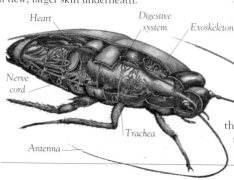

Heart

Digestive system

Exoskeleton

Nerve cord

Trachea

Antenna

INTERNAL ANATOMY
A typical insect breathes through holes in its sides and distributes air around the body in tubes called tracheae. It has a nerve cord which runs beneath the digestive system. The heart, a slender tube with several holes, pumps blood around the body.

INSECTS

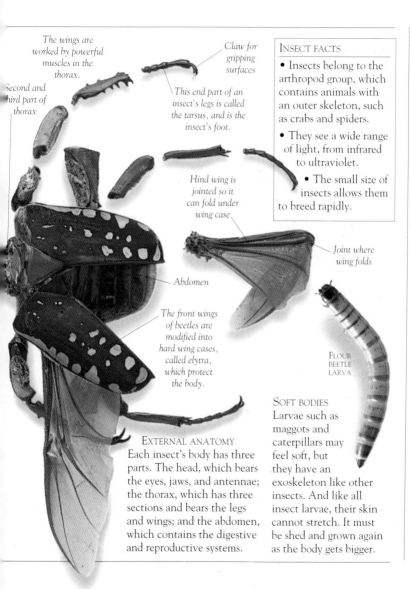

The wings are worked by powerful muscles in the thorax.

Claw for gripping surfaces

Second and third part of thorax

This end part of an insect's legs is called the tarsus, and is the insect's foot.

Hind wing is jointed so it can fold under wing case.

Joint where wing folds

Abdomen

The front wings of beetles are modified into hard wing cases, called elytra, which protect the body.

FLOUR BEETLE LARVA

EXTERNAL ANATOMY
Each insect's body has three parts. The head, which bears the eyes, jaws, and antennae; the thorax, which has three sections and bears the legs and wings; and the abdomen, which contains the digestive and reproductive systems.

SOFT BODIES
Larvae such as maggots and caterpillars may feel soft, but they have an exoskeleton like other insects. And like all insect larvae, their skin cannot stretch. It must be shed and grown again as the body gets bigger.

THE FIRST INSECTS

INSECTS WERE the first animals to fly.
They appeared 300 million years
ago – long before humans, and even
before the dinosaurs. The ancient
insect species are now extinct, but
some were similar to modern
dragonflies and cockroaches.

INSECT IN AMBER
Amber is the fossilized tree resin
which came from pine trees
over 40 million years ago.
Well-preserved ancient
insects are sometimes
found in amber. This
sweat bee is in
copal, which is
similar to amber
but not so old.

FLOWER FOOD
When flowering
plants evolved 100
million years ago,
insects gained two
important new foods –
pollen and nectar. Insects
thrived on these foods.
They pollinated the
flowers, and many new
species of plants and
insects evolved together.

FIRST INSECT FACTS

• The oldest known
fossil insect is a
springtail that lived
400 million years ago.

• Some of the earliest
insects seem to have
had three pairs of wings.

• The oldest known
butterfly or moth is
known from England
190 million years ago.

MODERN
EARWIG

*Fossil
earwig*

ROCK REMAINS
This fossil of an earwig
was found in 35-million-
year-old lake sediment in
Colorado, U.S.A. The
fossil shows how similar
in shape ancient earwigs
are to modern ones.

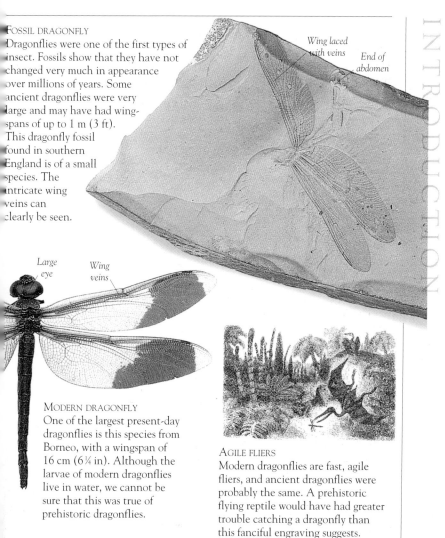

FOSSIL DRAGONFLY

Dragonflies were one of the first types of insect. Fossils show that they have not changed very much in appearance over millions of years. Some ancient dragonflies were very large and may have had wing-spans of up to 1 m (3 ft). This dragonfly fossil found in southern England is of a small species. The intricate wing veins can clearly be seen.

Wing laced with veins

End of abdomen

Large eye

Wing veins

MODERN DRAGONFLY

One of the largest present-day dragonflies is this species from Borneo, with a wingspan of 16 cm (6¼ in). Although the larvae of modern dragonflies live in water, we cannot be sure that this was true of prehistoric dragonflies.

AGILE FLIERS

Modern dragonflies are fast, agile fliers, and ancient dragonflies were probably the same. A prehistoric flying reptile would have had greater trouble catching a dragonfly than this fanciful engraving suggests.

35

TYPES OF INSECT

WE DO NOT KNOW exactly how many species, or types, of insect there are, since scientists constantly discover new insects. But we estimate that about five million insect species exist. Each belongs to one of about 24 groups, or orders, which are defined according to body structure and larval development.

Beetles, wasps, bees, and ants

About 400,000 species of beetles are described – they are the largest order of insects. Wasps, bees, and ants form the second largest order of insects, made up of about 200,000 species. The common feature in this order is a narrow "waist".

Jaws

STAG BEETLE

Hard wing cases meet mid-line.

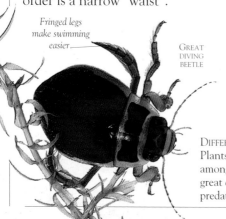

Fringed legs make swimming easier

GREAT DIVING BEETLE

BEETLES

WINGS AND JAWS
The front pair of wings in beetles is hardened and forms a strong shield over the folded hind wings. Some beetles, such as stag beetles, have greatly enlarged jaws which look like horns.

DIFFERENT FOODS
Plants, fungi, insects, and dead animals are among the wide variety of beetle foods. The great diving beetle lives in ponds. It is a fierce predator which hunts tadpoles and small fish.

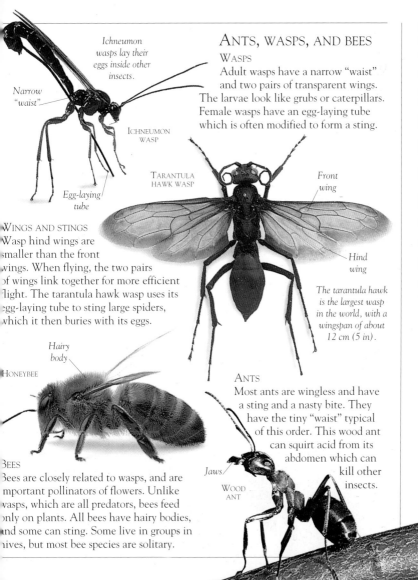

Ichneumon wasps lay their eggs inside other insects.

Narrow "waist"

ICHNEUMON WASP

Egg-laying tube

ANTS, WASPS, AND BEES

WASPS

Adult wasps have a narrow "waist" and two pairs of transparent wings. The larvae look like grubs or caterpillars. Female wasps have an egg-laying tube which is often modified to form a sting.

TARANTULA HAWK WASP

Front wing

WINGS AND STINGS

Wasp hind wings are smaller than the front wings. When flying, the two pairs of wings link together for more efficient flight. The tarantula hawk wasp uses its egg-laying tube to sting large spiders, which it then buries with its eggs.

Hind wing

The tarantula hawk is the largest wasp in the world, with a wingspan of about 12 cm (5 in).

Hairy body

HONEYBEE

ANTS

Most ants are wingless and have a sting and a nasty bite. They have the tiny "waist" typical of this order. This wood ant can squirt acid from its abdomen which can kill other insects.

Jaws

WOOD ANT

BEES

Bees are closely related to wasps, and are important pollinators of flowers. Unlike wasps, which are all predators, bees feed only on plants. All bees have hairy bodies, and some can sting. Some live in groups in hives, but most bee species are solitary.

Butterflies, moths, and flies

Two common insect orders are the two-winged flies and the butterflies and moths. Flies are distinctive because their second pair of wings is converted into balancing organs which look like drumsticks. Their young stages are maggots. Butterflies and moths have a coiled feeding tube, and their wings are covered in minute, flattened scales. Butterfly and moth larvae are called caterpillars.

BUTTERFLIES AND MOTHS

CATERPILLARS

Although caterpillars' bodies are soft, they have an exoskeleton like other insects. Caterpillars grow at a very fast rate. They feed on leaves and have sharp jaws for slicing vegetation.

Leaf-green colouring

Feathery antenna

MOTHS

There are 150,000 species of moth. Most moth species fly only at night. They are usually dull in colour and they often have feathery antennae. There are also many day-flying species, and some of these are brightly coloured.

POLYPHEMUS
MOTH

BUTTERFLIES

There are 15,000 species of butterfly. Most butterflies fly by day, have club-tipped antennae, and are brightly coloured. The scales which cover moths and butterflies sometimes produce colours by iridescence, which is the effect of sunlight shining on them to produce a display of many different colours.

Club-tipped antenna

SWALLOWTAIL
BUTTERFLY

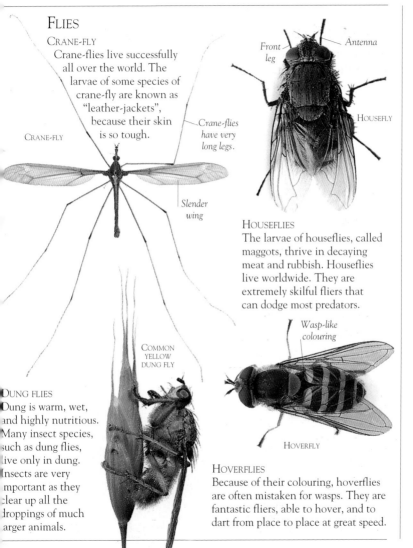

FLIES

CRANE-FLY

Crane-flies live successfully all over the world. The larvae of some species of crane-fly are known as "leather-jackets", because their skin is so tough.

CRANE-FLY

Crane-flies have very long legs.

Slender wing

Front leg

Antenna

HOUSEFLY

HOUSEFLIES

The larvae of houseflies, called maggots, thrive in decaying meat and rubbish. Houseflies live worldwide. They are extremely skilful fliers that can dodge most predators.

Wasp-like colouring

COMMON YELLOW DUNG FLY

DUNG FLIES

Dung is warm, wet, and highly nutritious. Many insect species, such as dung flies, live only in dung. Insects are very important as they clear up all the droppings of much larger animals.

HOVERFLY

HOVERFLIES

Because of their colouring, hoverflies are often mistaken for wasps. They are fantastic fliers, able to hover, and to dart from place to place at great speed.

39

Bugs and other types

There are about 67,500 species of bug – they are the fifth largest order of insects. Bugs have a feeding tube folded back between the legs, and most of them eat plant food. The many other orders of insects contain fewer species. Some of these orders are well known, such as fleas, cockroaches, dragonflies, and locusts.

BUGS

FEEDING TUBES

The mandibles (jaws) found in most insects are modified into needle-like tubes in bugs. The bug pierces food with the feeding tube and then sucks up juices.

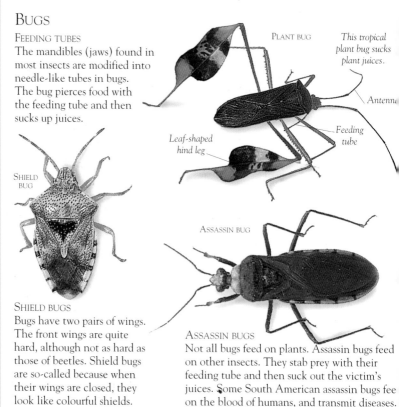

PLANT BUG

This tropical plant bug sucks plant juices.

Antenna

Leaf-shaped hind leg

Feeding tube

SHIELD BUG

ASSASSIN BUG

SHIELD BUGS

Bugs have two pairs of wings. The front wings are quite hard, although not as hard as those of beetles. Shield bugs are so-called because when their wings are closed, they look like colourful shields.

ASSASSIN BUGS

Not all bugs feed on plants. Assassin bugs feed on other insects. They stab prey with their feeding tube and then suck out the victim's juices. Some South American assassin bugs feed on the blood of humans, and transmit diseases.

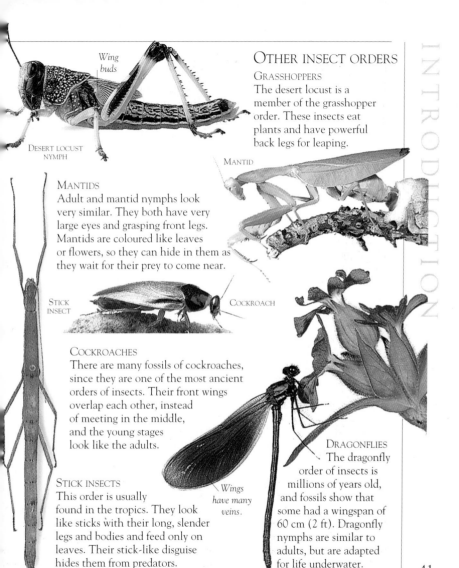

Wing buds

DESERT LOCUST NYMPH

OTHER INSECT ORDERS

GRASSHOPPERS
The desert locust is a member of the grasshopper order. These insects eat plants and have powerful back legs for leaping.

MANTID

MANTIDS
Adult and mantid nymphs look very similar. They both have very large eyes and grasping front legs. Mantids are coloured like leaves or flowers, so they can hide in them as they wait for their prey to come near.

STICK INSECT

COCKROACH

COCKROACHES
There are many fossils of cockroaches, since they are one of the most ancient orders of insects. Their front wings overlap each other, instead of meeting in the middle, and the young stages look like the adults.

DRAGONFLIES
The dragonfly order of insects is millions of years old, and fossils show that some had a wingspan of 60 cm (2 ft). Dragonfly nymphs are similar to adults, but are adapted for life underwater.

STICK INSECTS
This order is usually found in the tropics. They look like sticks with their long, slender legs and bodies and feed only on leaves. Their stick-like disguise hides them from predators.

Wings have many veins.

41

METAMORPHOSIS

INSECTS GO THROUGH several stages of growth before they become adults. This growing process is called metamorphosis. There are two types of metamorphosi complete and incomplete. Complete metamorphosis has four main growth stages – egg, larva, pupa, and adult. Incomplete metamorphosis involves three main stages – egg, nymph, and adult.

Incomplete metamorphosis

This growing process is a gradual transformation. The insects hatch from their eggs looking like miniature adults. These young insects are called nymphs. As they grow, they shed their skin several times before they reach the adult stage.

Clawed feet hook onto stem

Wing buds

Adult head

Adult head and thorax emerge

1 DAMSELFLY NYMPH
A damselfly nymph lives underwater. Paddle-like plates on its tail help it swim and breathe. It sheds its skin several times as it grows towards adulthood.

2 HOLDING ON
When the nymph is ready to change into an adult it crawls out of the water up a plant stem.

3 BREAKING OUT
The skin along the back splits open and the adult head and thorax start to emerge.

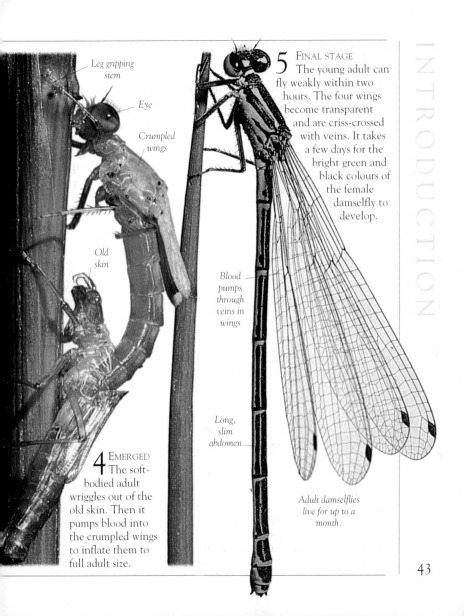

Leg gripping stem

Eye

Crumpled wings

Old skin

5 FINAL STAGE
The young adult can fly weakly within two hours. The four wings become transparent and are criss-crossed with veins. It takes a few days for the bright green and black colours of the female damselfly to develop.

Blood pumps through veins in wings

Long, slim abdomen

4 EMERGED
The soft-bodied adult wriggles out of the old skin. Then it pumps blood into the crumpled wings to inflate them to full adult size.

Adult damselflies live for up to a month.

INSECTS

Complete metamorphosis

The four main growth stages in a complete metamorphosis are egg, larva, pupa, and adult. The larva bears no resemblance to the adult it will become. The pupal stage is when the larva makes the amazing transformation into an adult. Insects such as wasps, butterflies, beetles, and flies undergo complete metamorphosis.

1 LAYING EGGS
Butterflies lay eggs near leaves which caterpillars can eat when they hatch. Newly hatched cater-pillars are too small to walk far to feed.

Egg

Eggshell

2 THE FIRST MEAL
When a caterpillar emerges, the first meal it eats is usually its own eggshell. The eggshell provides the caterpillar with valuable nutrients before it begins its diet of leaves.

Strong jaws slice food.

A caterpillar can increase its body weight by about 100 times in a few weeks.

3 GROWING
The caterpillar chews up hundreds of leaves and grows much bigger, shedding its skin several times. This growth prepares the caterpillar for the pupal stage of its life.

A pupa is also known as a chrysalis.

Silk thread holds pupa in place

A chrysalis often looks like a leaf for camouflage.

4 CHRYSALIS ACTIVITY
A pupa is like a busy factory. From the outside it looks still, but inside there is a great deal of activity. The caterpillar's organs turn into a milky liquid, and new butterfly organs grow rapidly in their place.

5 CHANGE COMPLETED
Once the metamorphosis is complete, the butterfly emerges from its pupa. It stretches its wet, crumpled wings. Before the butterfly is ready to fly, it must wait a couple of hours for its wings to expand and harden.

Empty pupa

Antenna

Wet, crumpled wings

Blood is pumped into the veins in the wings to open them out.

SWALLOWTAIL
BUTTERFLY

t takes about eight weeks for the swallowtail butterfly to grow from egg to adult.

6 BUTTERFLY
The fully developed butterfly leads a totally different life from the caterpillar. While caterpillars eat leaves in order to grow, butterflies spend their time sipping nectar from flowers and seeking a mate.

45

INSECTS

HOW INSECTS MOVE

INSECTS MOVE using muscles which are attached
to the inner surfaces of their hard outer skeleton.
Many insects walk, but some larvae have no legs
and have to crawl. Some insects swim, others jump,
but most adult insects can fly and in this way they
may travel long distances.

Legs

Insects use their legs for walking,
running, jumping, and swimming.
Many insects have legs modified
for a number of other purposes.
These include catching prey,
holding a female when mating,
producing songs, digging, fighting,
and camouflage.

LEGS FOR SWIMMING
The water boatman has long, oar-
shaped back legs, allowing the insect
to "row" rapidly through water. The
legs have flattened ends and a fringe
of thick hairs. The front legs are short
to grasp prey on the water surface.

LEG FACTS

• Fairy flies, which live
as parasites on the eggs
of water insects, can
"fly" underwater.

• Many butterflies walk
on four legs; the front
pair is used for tasting.

• The legless larvae of
some parasitic wasps
hitch a ride on a
passing ant in order to
enter an ant's nest.

1 PREPARING TO JUMP
The back legs of locusts are swollen and packed
with strong muscles for jumping. Before leaping, a
locust holds its back legs tightly under its body, near its
centre of gravity. This is the best position for the legs
to propel the insect
high into the air.

Wing

Long back
legs

Shorter
front legs

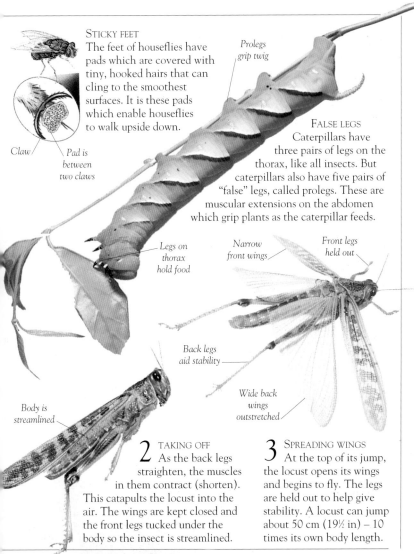

STICKY FEET
The feet of houseflies have pads which are covered with tiny, hooked hairs that can cling to the smoothest surfaces. It is these pads which enable houseflies to walk upside down.

Claw

Pad is between two claws

Prolegs grip twig

FALSE LEGS
Caterpillars have three pairs of legs on the thorax, like all insects. But caterpillars also have five pairs of "false" legs, called prolegs. These are muscular extensions on the abdomen which grip plants as the caterpillar feeds.

Legs on thorax hold food

Narrow front wings

Front legs held out

Back legs aid stability

Wide back wings outstretched

Body is streamlined

2 TAKING OFF
As the back legs straighten, the muscles in them contract (shorten). This catapults the locust into the air. The wings are kept closed and the front legs tucked under the body so the insect is streamlined.

3 SPREADING WINGS
At the top of its jump, the locust opens its wings and begins to fly. The legs are held out to help give stability. A locust can jump about 50 cm (19½ in) – 10 times its own body length.

47

Wings and scales

Insect wings are a wide variety of shapes and sizes. They are not used just for flying but also for attracting a mate or hiding from predators. Most insects have two pairs of wings, each with a network of veins to give strength. Flies have only one pair of wings – the second pair is modified into small balancing organs called halteres. Small insects have few wing veins since their wings are so tiny.

EXPERT FLIERS
Dragonflies are among the most accomplished fliers in the insect world. They can hover, fly fast or slow, change direction rapidly, and even fly backwards. As they manoeuvre, their two pairs of wings beat independently of each other.

WING FACTS

• The scales of butterflies and moths contain waste products from the pupal stage.

• There is a hearing organ in one of the wing veins of green lacewings for hearing the shrieks of bats.

• Many species of island insects are wingless because of the risk of being blown out to sea.

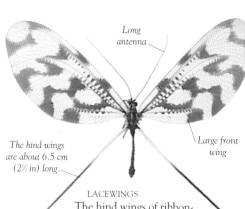

Long antenna

The hind wings are about 6.5 cm (2½ in) long.

Large front wing

LACEWINGS
The hind wings of ribbon-tail lacewings are modified into long graceful streamers. Scientists are not sure what these are for, but they may act as stabilizers in flight, or even divert predators from attacking the lacewing's body. The lacewing's mottled patterns probably help to conceal it in the dry sandy places where it lives.

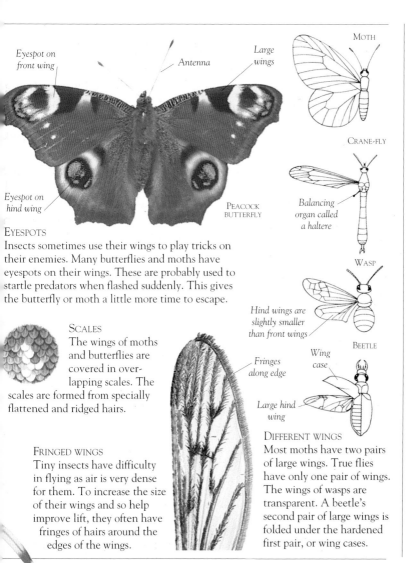

Eyespot on front wing

Antenna

Large wings

Moth

Eyespot on hind wing

PEACOCK BUTTERFLY

CRANE-FLY

Balancing organ called a haltere

WASP

Hind wings are slightly smaller than front wings

BEETLE

Fringes along edge

Wing case

Large hind wing

EYESPOTS

Insects sometimes use their wings to play tricks on their enemies. Many butterflies and moths have eyespots on their wings. These are probably used to startle predators when flashed suddenly. This gives the butterfly or moth a little more time to escape.

SCALES

The wings of moths and butterflies are covered in over-lapping scales. The scales are formed from specially flattened and ridged hairs.

FRINGED WINGS

Tiny insects have difficulty in flying as air is very dense for them. To increase the size of their wings and so help improve lift, they often have fringes of hairs around the edges of the wings.

DIFFERENT WINGS

Most moths have two pairs of large wings. True flies have only one pair of wings. The wings of wasps are transparent. A beetle's second pair of large wings is folded under the hardened first pair, or wing cases.

Flight

The ability to fly is one of the main reasons insects have survived for millions of years, and continue to flourish. Flight helps insects escape from danger. It also makes it easier to find food and new places to live. Sometimes insects fly thousands of kilometres to reach fresh food or warmer weather.

FLYING GROUPS
This African grasshopper has broad hind wings which allow it to glide for long distances. Locusts are a type of grasshopper which fly in huge groups when they need new food. Sometimes as many as 100 million locusts fly together for hundreds of kilometres.

WARMING UP
An insect's flight muscles must be warm before the wings can be moved fast enough for flight. On cool mornings, insects like this shield bug shiver, vibrating their wings to warm themselves up.

Vibrating wings

Elytra protect body

1 PREPARING TO FLY
This cockchafer beetle prepares for flight by climbing to the top of a plant and facing into the wind. It may open and shut its elytra (wing cases) several times while warming up.

2 OPENING THE WINGS
The hardened elytra, which protect the fragile hind wings, begin to open. The antennae are spread so the beetle can monitor the wind direction.

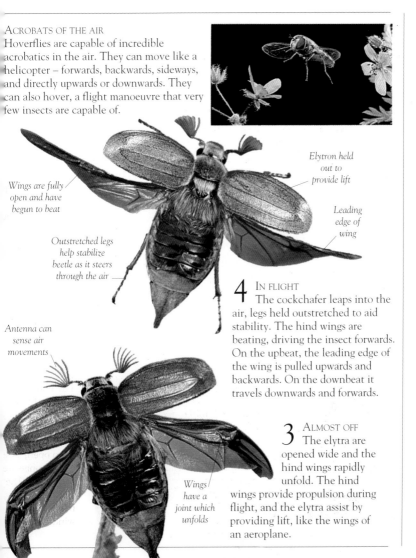

ACROBATS OF THE AIR
Hoverflies are capable of incredible acrobatics in the air. They can move like a helicopter – forwards, backwards, sideways, and directly upwards or downwards. They can also hover, a flight manoeuvre that very few insects are capable of.

Wings are fully open and have begun to beat

Outstretched legs help stabilize beetle as it steers through the air

Elytron held out to provide lift

Leading edge of wing

Antenna can sense air movements

Wings have a joint which unfolds

4 IN FLIGHT
The cockchafer leaps into the air, legs held outstretched to aid stability. The hind wings are beating, driving the insect forwards. On the upbeat, the leading edge of the wing is pulled upwards and backwards. On the downbeat it travels downwards and forwards.

3 ALMOST OFF
The elytra are opened wide and the hind wings rapidly unfold. The hind wings provide propulsion during flight, and the elytra assist by providing lift, like the wings of an aeroplane.

51

INSECT SENSES

INSECTS NEED to be fully aware of the world around them in order to survive. Although insects are tiny, they have keener senses than most larger animals. They can see colours and hear sounds that are undetectable to humans, as well as being able to detect smells from many kilometres away.

Sight

There are two types of insect eyes – simple and compound. Simple eyes can probably detect only light and shade. Compound eyes have hundreds of lenses, giving their owner excellent vision.

HEAD OF COMMON DARTER DRAGONFLY

SIMPLE EYES
Caterpillars never need to look far for their plant food – they are constantly surrounded by it. Because of this, they do not need sharp eyesight. They can manage perfectly well with a group of simple eyes.

GOOD VISION
The eyes of dragonflies take up most of their head. This allows them to see what is in front, above, below, and behind them all at the same time. Dragonflies use their sight more than any other of their senses to catch prey.

COMMON DARTER DRAGONFLY

Simple eyes

52

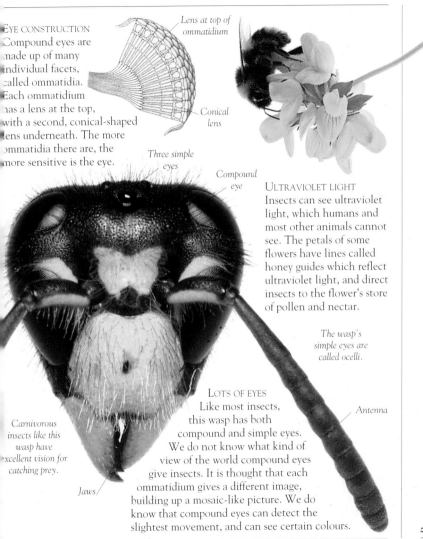

EYE CONSTRUCTION
Compound eyes are
made up of many
individual facets,
called ommatidia.
Each ommatidium
has a lens at the top,
with a second, conical-shaped
lens underneath. The more
ommatidia there are, the
more sensitive is the eye.

Lens at top of ommatidium

Conical lens

Three simple eyes

Compound eye

ULTRAVIOLET LIGHT
Insects can see ultraviolet
light, which humans and
most other animals cannot
see. The petals of some
flowers have lines called
honey guides which reflect
ultraviolet light, and direct
insects to the flower's store
of pollen and nectar.

The wasp's simple eyes are called ocelli.

Carnivorous insects like this wasp have excellent vision for catching prey.

Antenna

LOTS OF EYES
Like most insects,
this wasp has both
compound and simple eyes.
We do not know what kind of
view of the world compound eyes
give insects. It is thought that each
ommatidium gives a different image,
building up a mosaic-like picture. We
know that compound eyes can detect the
slightest movement, and can see certain colours.

Jaws

53

INSECTS

Smelling, hearing, and touching

The bodies of insects are covered in short hairs which are connected to the nervous system. These hairs can feel, or "hear", vibrations in the air due to sound or movement. Some hairs are modified to detect smells and flavours. Sensory hairs are often found on the antennae, but also occur on the feet and mouthparts

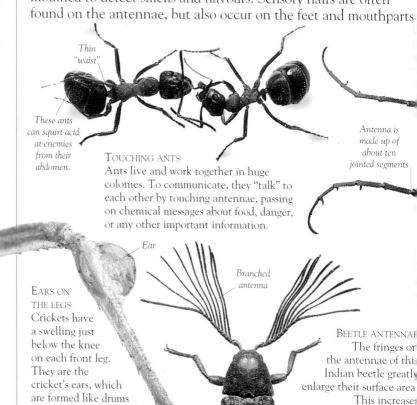

Thin "waist"

These ants can squirt acid at enemies from their abdomen.

Antenna is made up of about ten jointed segments

TOUCHING ANTS
Ants live and work together in huge colonies. To communicate, they "talk" to each other by touching antennae, passing on chemical messages about food, danger, or any other important information.

Ear

Branched antenna

EARS ON THE LEGS
Crickets have a swelling just below the knee on each front leg. They are the cricket's ears, which are formed like drums and pick up the mating songs of other crickets.

BEETLE ANTENNAE
The fringes on the antennae of this Indian beetle greatly enlarge their surface area. This increases their sensitivity to scents carried in the wind

54

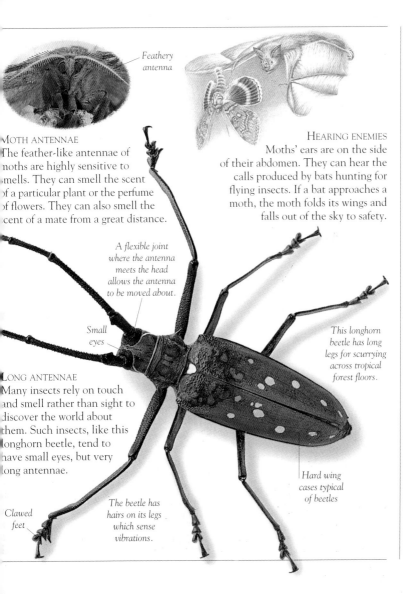

Feathery antenna

MOTH ANTENNAE
The feather-like antennae of moths are highly sensitive to smells. They can smell the scent of a particular plant or the perfume of flowers. They can also smell the scent of a mate from a great distance.

HEARING ENEMIES
Moths' ears are on the side of their abdomen. They can hear the calls produced by bats hunting for flying insects. If a bat approaches a moth, the moth folds its wings and falls out of the sky to safety.

A flexible joint where the antenna meets the head allows the antenna to be moved about.

Small eyes

This longhorn beetle has long legs for scurrying across tropical forest floors.

LONG ANTENNAE
Many insects rely on touch and smell rather than sight to discover the world about them. Such insects, like this longhorn beetle, tend to have small eyes, but very long antennae.

Hard wing cases typical of beetles

Clawed feet

The beetle has hairs on its legs which sense vibrations.

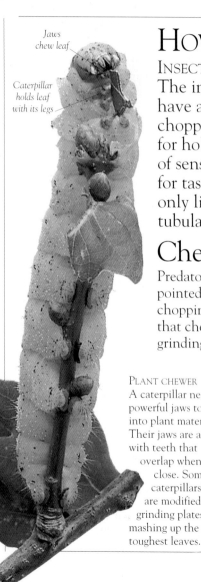

Jaws
chew leaf

Caterpillar
holds leaf
with its legs

HOW INSECTS FEED

INSECTS HAVE complex mouthparts.
The insects that chew their food
have a pair of strong jaws for
chopping, a smaller pair of jaws
for holding food, and two pairs
of sensory organs, called palps,
for tasting. Some insects drink
only liquid food and have special
tubular mouthparts like a straw.

Chewing

Predatory, chewing insects need sharp,
pointed jaws for stabbing, holding, and
chopping up their struggling prey. Insects
that chew plants have blunter jaws for
grinding their food.

PLANT CHEWER
A caterpillar needs
powerful jaws to bite
into plant material.
Their jaws are armed
with teeth that
overlap when they
close. Some
caterpillars' jaws
are modified into
grinding plates for
mashing up the
toughest leaves.

THRUSTING JAWS
Dragonfly larvae have pincers at
the end of a hinged plate folded
under the head. When catching
prey, the plate unfolds, shoots
forwards, and the pincers grab the
prey. Toothed jaws in the head
reduce the victim to mincemeat.

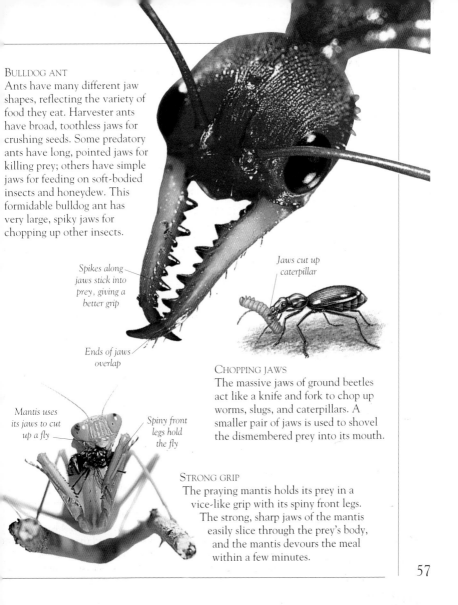

BULLDOG ANT
Ants have many different jaw
shapes, reflecting the variety of
food they eat. Harvester ants
have broad, toothless jaws for
crushing seeds. Some predatory
ants have long, pointed jaws for
killing prey; others have simple
jaws for feeding on soft-bodied
insects and honeydew. This
formidable bulldog ant has
very large, spiky jaws for
chopping up other insects.

Spikes along
jaws stick into
prey, giving a
better grip

Ends of jaws
overlap

Jaws cut up
caterpillar

CHOPPING JAWS
The massive jaws of ground beetles
act like a knife and fork to chop up
worms, slugs, and caterpillars. A
smaller pair of jaws is used to shovel
the dismembered prey into its mouth.

Mantis uses
its jaws to cut
up a fly

Spiny front
legs hold
the fly

STRONG GRIP
The praying mantis holds its prey in a
vice-like grip with its spiny front legs.
The strong, sharp jaws of the mantis
easily slice through the prey's body,
and the mantis devours the meal
within a few minutes.

57

Drinking

For many insects, the main way of feeding is by drinking. The most nutritious foods to drink are nectar and blood. Nectar is rich in sugar, and blood is packed with proteins. Some insects drink by sucking through straw-like mouthparts. Others have sponge-like mouthparts with which they mop up liquids.

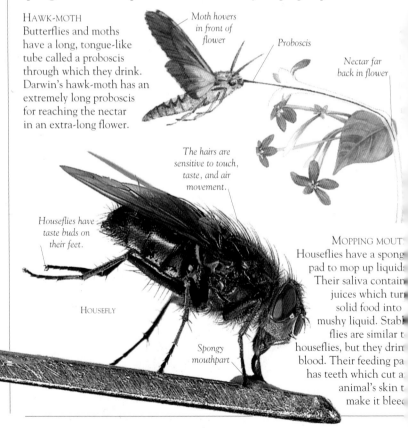

HAWK-MOTH
Butterflies and moths have a long, tongue-like tube called a proboscis through which they drink. Darwin's hawk-moth has an extremely long proboscis for reaching the nectar in an extra-long flower.

Moth hovers in front of flower

Proboscis

Nectar far back in flower

The hairs are sensitive to touch, taste, and air movement.

Houseflies have taste buds on their feet.

HOUSEFLY

Spongy mouthpart

MOPPING MOUT[H]
Houseflies have a spong[y] pad to mop up liquid[s] Their saliva contain[s] juices which tur[n] solid food into mushy liquid. Stab[le] flies are similar t[o] houseflies, but they drin[k] blood. Their feeding pa[rt] has teeth which cut a[n] animal's skin t[o] make it blee[d]

58

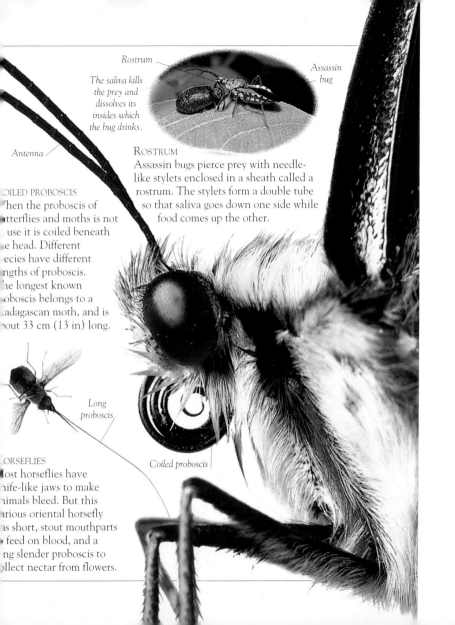

Rostrum

The saliva kills the prey and dissolves its insides which the bug drinks.

Assassin bug

Antenna

ROSTRUM

Assassin bugs pierce prey with needle-like stylets enclosed in a sheath called a rostrum. The stylets form a double tube so that saliva goes down one side while food comes up the other.

COILED PROBOSCIS

When the proboscis of butterflies and moths is not in use it is coiled beneath the head. Different species have different lengths of proboscis. The longest known proboscis belongs to a Madagascan moth, and is about 33 cm (13 in) long.

Long proboscis

Coiled proboscis

HORSEFLIES

Most horseflies have knife-like jaws to make animals bleed. But this curious oriental horsefly has short, stout mouthparts to feed on blood, and a long slender proboscis to collect nectar from flowers.

COURTSHIP, BIRTH, AND GROWTH

REPRODUCTION is hazardous for insects. A female must first find and mate with a male of her own species, and lay eggs where the newly hatched young can feed. The larvae must shed their skin several times as they grow. All this time the insects must avoid being eaten.

Courtship and mating

Males and females use special signals to ensure that their chosen mate is the right species. Courtship usually involves using scents, but may include colour displays, dancing, caressing, and even gifts.

COURTSHIP FLIGHTS
Butterflies may recognize their own species by sight, but scent is more reliable. Butterfly courtship involves dancing flights with an exchange of scented chemical signals specific to each species.

Butterflies find the scented chemicals, called pheromones, very attractive.

The light is produced by a chemical reaction.

GUIDING LIGHT
Glowworms are the wingl[e]ss females of certain beetle species. They attract male[s] by producing a light near the tip of their abdomen. Some species flash a distinctive code to attract the correct males.

MATING DANGER
Mating between some insect species may last for several hours, with the male gripping the female's abdomen with claspers. This keeps other males away, but the pair are vulnerable to predators at this time.

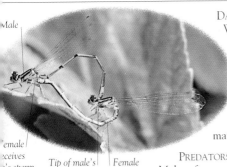

Male

Female receives male's sperm

Tip of male's abdomen grips female

Female

Female

DAMSELFLIES

When mating, a male damselfly grips a female's neck with the tip of his abdomen. She receives a packet of sperm from a pouch near his legs, and he continues to hold her neck while she lays eggs. This prevents other males mating with her.

PREDATORS MATING

Males of some predatory species, such as empid flies, give the female a meal of a dead insect when mating so they are not eaten themselves. Some males trick the female. They give an empty parcel, and mate while the female opens it.

MATING ASIAN
SWALLOWTAIL
BUTTERFLIES

Male

UNNATURAL BEHAVIOUR

It is often said that a female mantis will eat a male while he is mating with her. But this probably only happens when the mantises are in captivity and their behaviour is not natural.

Eggs and egg-laying

Insects use up a lot of energy producing eggs. To make sure this energy is not wasted, insects have many ways of protecting their eggs from predators. A few species of insect stay with their eggs to protect them until the larvae hatch. Some insects lay their eggs underground with a supply of food waiting for the newly hatched larvae. Most insects lay their eggs either in food, or near food, so the young larvae do not have to travel far to eat.

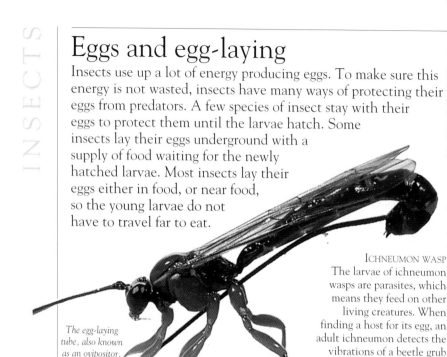

The egg-laying tube, also known as an ovipositor, drills into the wood.

The ovipositor is longer than the ichneumon's body.

ICHNEUMON WASP
The larvae of ichneumon wasps are parasites, which means they feed on other living creatures. When finding a host for its egg, an adult ichneumon detects the vibrations of a beetle grub gnawing inside a tree trunk. The wasp drives its egg-laying tube into the trunk until it finds the grub. An egg is laid on the grub, which then provides meat for the wasp larva when it hatches.

SUITABLE FOOD
Butterflies desert their eggs once they are laid. Different butterflies lay their eggs on different plants, depending on what the larvae eat. The Malay lacewing butterfly lays its eggs on vine tendrils.

Wasp carrying beetle to nest

Beetles are stored in underground nest

CARING EARWIGS
[fe]male earwig looks [ov]er eggs, licking [the]m regularly to [keep] them clean. [When] the nymphs [hatc]h, she feeds [them] until they [are bi]g enough to [le]ave the nest.

Earwig eggs

HUNTING WASPS
Most species of hunting wasp collect soft-bodied prey, such as caterpillars or spiders, for their grubs. But the weevil-hunting wasp collects adult beetles which it stings in the throat, and then stores in a tunnel as food for its larvae.

[Beet]le [in] [tunn]el

Beetles mould dung into balls

Beetle filling tunnel with dung as food for newly hatched grubs

[DUN]G BEETLES
[Ma]les and females of some dung [beetl]e species work together to dig an underground [tunne]l with smaller tunnels branching off it. A female [lays a]n egg in each of the smaller tunnels and fills them [with] animal dung, which the beetle grubs will feed on.

INSECT EGG FACTS

- Whitefly eggs have stalks that extract water from leaves.

- Tsetse flies develop their eggs internally and lay mature larvae.

- Green lacewing eggs have long stalks, making them difficult for predators to eat.

Birth and growth

As an insect grows from egg to adult it sheds its skin several times to produce a larger exoskeleton. Whilst this new skin hardens the insect is soft and vulnerable. Insects show many life-cycle adaptations to protect their soft young stages.

EGGS LARVA PUPA ADULT LADYBIRD

LADYBIRD GROWTH
Ladybirds and all other beetles go through a complete metamorphosis. An adult ladybird lays its eggs on a plant where small insects called aphids feed. Ladybird larvae eat aphids and shed their skin three times as they grow. The colourful adult emerges from the dull resting stage, or pupa.

APHIDS
Female aphids can reproduce without mati
They give birth to live
young rather than lay e
and each female may ha
about 100 offspring. Th
newborn aphids can giv
birth after only a few da

FROTHY PROTECT
Froghoppers are soft-bodied bugs l
aphids. A froghopper nym
produces a frothy liquid from
anus. The froth protects
nymph from drying out, a
also hides it fr
predate

*Frothy
hideaway*

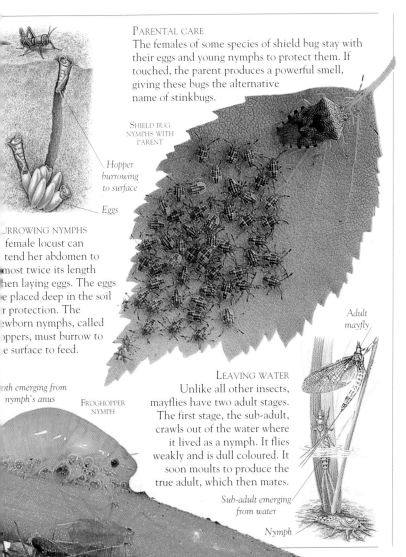

PARENTAL CARE
The females of some species of shield bug stay with their eggs and young nymphs to protect them. If touched, the parent produces a powerful smell, giving these bugs the alternative name of stinkbugs.

SHIELD BUG NYMPHS WITH PARENT

Hopper burrowing to surface

Eggs

[BU]RROWING NYMPHS
[A] female locust can [ex]tend her abdomen to [al]most twice its length [w]hen laying eggs. The eggs [ar]e placed deep in the soil [fo]r protection. The [n]ewborn nymphs, called [h]oppers, must burrow to [th]e surface to feed.

[M]oth emerging from [nymph's anus

FROGHOPPER NYMPH

LEAVING WATER
Unlike all other insects, mayflies have two adult stages. The first stage, the sub-adult, crawls out of the water where it lived as a nymph. It flies weakly and is dull coloured. It soon moults to produce the true adult, which then mates.

Adult mayfly

Sub-adult emerging from water

Nymph

65

Survival of the young

Predators eagerly hunt insect larvae since many are slow-moving, soft, and nutritious. To ensure survival, most insect species produ large numbers of young which grow rapidly. Most insect larvae ar defenceless and have developed special ways of hiding from predators. But many insect larvae are fierce predators themselves, consuming other creatures for nourishment as they grow.

Grub in pupal cell

Caterpillar rears up whe threatened

WELL HIDDEN
The larvae of chafer beetles live underground, safely hidden from most predators. The larvae, or grubs, may take many weeks to develop. They then produce a cell of hardened earth in which they will change into an adult.

Fearsome "face"

Sharp spines

True legs

Proleg

SPINY LARVA
Mexican bean beetle larvae eat leaves and develop rapidly. They are covered with long, branched spines which may deter birds and other predators from attacking them.

SCARY DISPLAY
Caterpillars are a favourite food of birds. Some caterpillars try to hide to stay safe. But if the puss moth caterpillar is threatened, it puts on a startling display which can frighten off birds.

WATER LARVA

Stone-fly larvae live in cold water and grow slowly, spending about three years as a larva. They are slow-moving and hide from predators under rocks and amongst plants.

SOFT BODIES

Young mantids are fierce predators. The body of some species resembles a flower. This disguise helps them to go unnoticed by prey, and also by predators such as birds.

NIGHT FEEDER

The mormon butterfly caterpillar feeds in the dark of night to avoid being seen by predators. In less than eight hours it will chew away a leaf which is more than twice its own length. During the day it rests as inconspicuously as possible.

For a more frightening, display, the caterpillar waves these "tails" as if they were stings.

Eye

Pink, flower-like body

Leg

Legs are striped pink and green

67

INSECTS

NESTS AND SOCIETIES

MOST INSECTS lead solitary lives, but some, particularly wasps, ants, bees, and termites, live in societies which are sometimes very ordered. There are queens, kings, workers, and soldiers. Each of these has particular jobs to do. Social insects live in nests which are often elaborate, where they protect each other and rear their young.

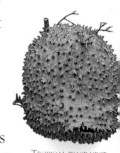

TROPICAL WASP NEST MADE OF CHEWED-UP PLANT FIBRES

The nest is cemented together with wasp saliva.

Wasps, ants, and bees

These insects produce a wide range of nests. Some are small with only a few dozen members, while larger nests may contain thousands of insects. Most have a single queen, and all the nest members are her offspring.

ANTS

A species of African tree ant builds its nest from fragments of plants and soil to produce a substance like dark cement. The ants live on a diet of honeydew which they get from aphids. The aphids feed on the sap of leaves in the tree tops and discharge the honeydew from their rear ends.

BEES

A bumblebee queen starts her nest alone in spring in a hole in the ground. She makes cells for her eggs of wax. She also makes a wax pot which she fills with honey for food.

The queen uses her antennae to measure the cells as she builds them.

A NEW START

European wasp colonies die out each ~~w~~inter. In spring a queen begins a new nest of ~~"p~~aper" made with chewed-up wood. She makes ~~f~~ew cells for her eggs, building walls around ~~th~~e cells to shield them.

Entrance hole

2 PROTECTIVE LAYERS
The queen builds more and more paper layers around the cells. The layers will protect the larvae from cold winds as well as from predators. The queen leaves an entrance hole at the bottom.

Finished nest

3 HARD-WORKING FAMILY
The first brood the queen rears become workers, gathering food for more larvae and expanding the nest. By summer, a nest may have 500 wasps, all collecting caterpillars for the larvae. A large nest may be as much as 45 cm (18 in) in diameter.

INSIDE THE NEST
The queen lays a single egg in each cell. When the larvae hatch they stay in their cell and the queen feeds them with pieces of caterpillar.

Termite nests

Termites have the most complex insect societies. Their elaborate nests, which may be in wood or underground, last for several years. Each nest has a single large queen and king, which are served by specialized small workers and large soldiers. Termites feed and protect each other, and one generation will help to raise the next generation of offspring.

QUEEN TERMITE
In a termite society, the queen lays all the eggs. She is too fat move, so the workers bring foo to her. The queen lays 30,000 eggs each day and, as she lays them, the workers carry them to special chambers for rearing

Layers of "umbrellas"

NEST DEFENDERS
Termite soldiers fight enemies that attack the nest. Most termite speci have soldiers with enlarged heads and powerful jaws. In some species each soldier's head has a snout tha squirts poison at invaders.

STRANGE NEST
The function of the "umbrellas" on this African nest is a mystery to scientists. The termite speci which builds this type of nest lives underground If an "umbrella" is damaged, it does not get repaired, but a new one may be built.

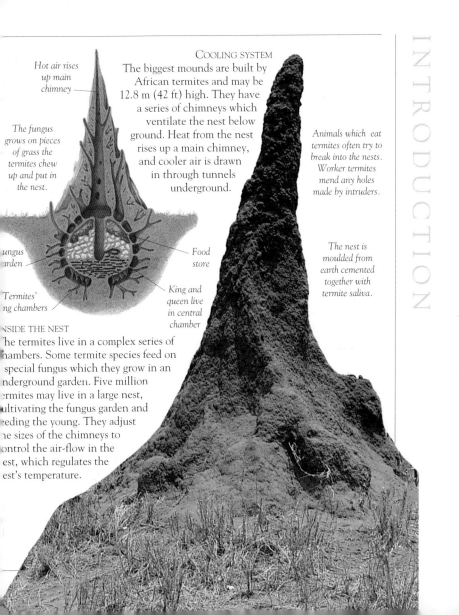

*Hot air rises
up main
chimney*

*The fungus
grows on pieces
of grass the
termites chew
up and put in
the nest.*

COOLING SYSTEM

The biggest mounds are built by
African termites and may be
12.8 m (42 ft) high. They have
a series of chimneys which
ventilate the nest below
ground. Heat from the nest
rises up a main chimney,
and cooler air is drawn
in through tunnels
underground.

*Animals which eat
termites often try to
break into the nests.
Worker termites
mend any holes
made by intruders.*

*ungus
arden*

*Termites'
ng chambers*

*Food
store*

*King and
queen live
in central
chamber*

*The nest is
moulded from
earth cemented
together with
termite saliva.*

NSIDE THE NEST

he termites live in a complex series of
hambers. Some termite species feed on
special fungus which they grow in an
nderground garden. Five million
ermites may live in a large nest,
ultivating the fungus garden and
eeding the young. They adjust
he sizes of the chimneys to
ontrol the air-flow in the
est, which regulates the
est's temperature.

HUNTING AND HIDING

SOME INSECT SPECIES are deadly hunters, killing prey with poisonous stings and sharp jaws. Insects are also hunted by a huge number of animals. To hide from predators, many insects have developed special disguises and patterns of behaviour.

Hunting insects

About one third of insect species are carnivorous (they eat meat). Some species eat decaying meat and dung, but most carnivorous insects hunt for their food.

KILLER BEETLE
Some insects are easily recognized as predators. The large jaws of this African ground beetle indicate that it is a hunter and its long legs show that it can run fast after its insect prey.

KILLER WASPS
There are many types of hunting wasp. Most adult hunting wasps are vegetarians – they hunt prey only as food for their larvae. Each hunting wasp species hunt a particular type of prey. The weevil-hunting wasp hunts only a type of beetle called a weevil.

ESSENTIAL INSECTS
Ants are the most important carnivores on Earth. They eat huge numbers of other insects, which helps keep the insect population from becoming too plentiful. Ants in turn are eaten by other animals, such as birds and lizards.

Wasp cocoons

PARASITES
The larvae of many species of wasp are parasites, which means they feed and grow inside another insect's body. This caterpillar has had about 50 wasp larvae feeding inside it. The larvae are pupating in the caterpillar's back. Soon they will hatch as adult wasps.

Wasp uses its antennae and sight to find cockroaches

SPECIALIST HUNTER
Many predatory insects specialize on one particular type of prey. This jewel wasp hunts only cockroaches, which it uses as food for its larvae. The adult wasp is not carnivorous – it feeds on the nectar in flowers.

ROVE BEETLE
Some rove beetles specialize in feeding on springtails. To catch such elusive prey the beetle can flick out a long, sticky "tongue" to pull an unwary springtail into its mouth.

Beetle raises tail before attacking prey

73

Camouflage

Insects whose body colouring matches their background are almost impossible to see. This method of hiding is known as camouflage. One of the first rules of successful camouflage is to keep still, as any movement can betray an insect to a sharp-eyed predator. Some insects use another type of camouflage called disruptive coloration. They disguise their body by breaking up its shape with stripes and blocks of colour.

GRASSY DISGUISE
The stripe-winged grasshopper can be heard singing in meadow grasses, but its camouflaged body is very hard to spot.

Grasshopper kicks any attackers with its back legs

DISRUPTIVE COLORATION
This tropical moth has disruptive coloration. The patterns on the wings break up their shape. A predator might notice the patterns, but not the whole moth.

LOOKING DISTASTEFUL
This treehopper has twig-like extensions on its thorax and abdomen. It looks like an inedible piece of wood, so hunters are likely to overlook it.

Extension on thorax

Eye

Wing

STILL HUNTER

Insect predators use camouflage so their prey cannot see them. The brown colouring of this mantid perfectly matches the brown leaf on which it sits. It completely surprises any prey which comes within striking distance.

Because of its brown colouring, the Indian leaf butterfly can only rest beside decaying, dried-out leaves.

Mid-vein on real leaf

Mantis is hard to spot

Butterfly's head

Wing of butterfly

LEAF MIMIC

It is almost impossible to distinguish the Indian leaf butterfly from the other leaves where it rests. It looks just like a decaying leaf, complete with leaf-like veins and mock fungus spots.

Bottom of wings are narrow to look like stalk of real leaf

Marking like mid-vein of real leaf

75

Warning coloration

Birds, mammals, and other intelligent predators learn through experience that some insects are poisonous or harmful. Such insects do not camouflage themselves. Instead they have brightly coloured bodies which warn predators that they have an unpleasant taste or a nasty sting. The most common warning colours are red, yellow, and black. Any insect with those colours is probably poisonous.

BASKER MOTH
Moths that fly by day are often brightly coloured, particularly when they taste unpleasant. The red, yellow, and black colouring of this basker moth tells birds that it is not a tasty meal.

PAINFUL REMINDER
The saddle-back caterpillar is eye-catching with its vivid colouring and grotesque appearance. No young bird would ever forget the caterpillar if it tried a mouthful of the poisonous, stinging spines.

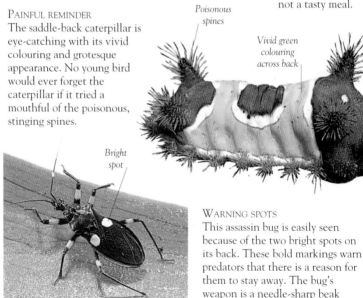

Poisonous spines

Vivid green colouring across back

Bright spot

WARNING SPOTS
This assassin bug is easily seen because of the two bright spots on its back. These bold markings warn predators that there is a reason for them to stay away. The bug's weapon is a needle-sharp beak which can give a very painful bite.

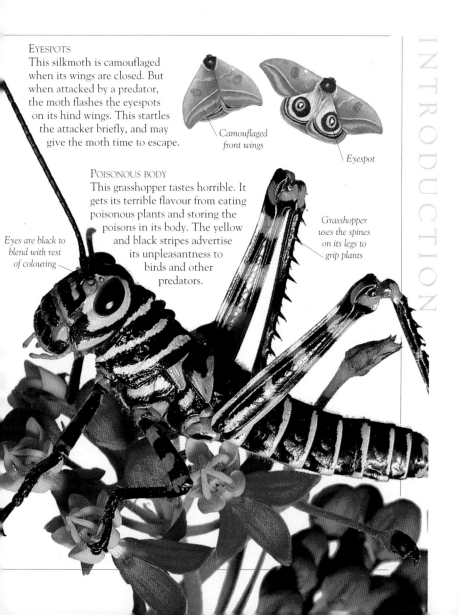

EYESPOTS
This silkmoth is camouflaged
when its wings are closed. But
when attacked by a predator,
the moth flashes the eyespots
on its hind wings. This startles
the attacker briefly, and may
give the moth time to escape.

*Camouflaged
front wings*

Eyespot

POISONOUS BODY
This grasshopper tastes horrible. It
gets its terrible flavour from eating
poisonous plants and storing the
poisons in its body. The yellow
and black stripes advertise
its unpleasantness to
birds and other
predators.

*Grasshopper
uses the spines
on its legs to
grip plants*

*Eyes are black to
blend with rest
of colouring*

Mimicry

Predators usually avoid preying on dangerous animals. Many harmless insects take advantage of this by mimicking harmful creatures. Mimicking insects copy a dangerous animal's body shape and colouring. They also behave like the animal they are copying to make the disguise more convincing. Inedible objects, such as twigs and thorns, are also mimicked by insects.

The treehoppers only move when they need a fresh source of food.

Markings make head resemble alligator's head

Real eye of bug

ALLIGATOR MIMIC
Scientists can often only guess at the reasons for the strange look and behaviour of some animals. It is not known why this tree-living bug looks like a tiny alligator. Perhaps its appearance briefly startles monkey predators, giving the bug time to fly off to safety.

HORNET MIMIC
The hornet moth looks very like a large wasp called a hornet. When flying, the moth even behaves like a hornet. Many insects find protection by mimicking wasps – birds avoid them because they might sting.

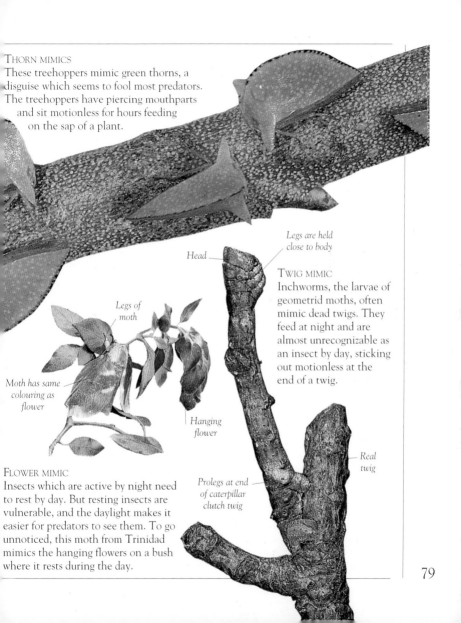

THORN MIMICS
These treehoppers mimic green thorns, a disguise which seems to fool most predators. The treehoppers have piercing mouthparts and sit motionless for hours feeding on the sap of a plant.

Legs are held close to body

Head

TWIG MIMIC
Inchworms, the larvae of geometrid moths, often mimic dead twigs. They feed at night and are almost unrecognizable as an insect by day, sticking out motionless at the end of a twig.

Legs of moth

Moth has same colouring as flower

Hanging flower

Real twig

FLOWER MIMIC
Insects which are active by night need to rest by day. But resting insects are vulnerable, and the daylight makes it easier for predators to see them. To go unnoticed, this moth from Trinidad mimics the hanging flowers on a bush where it rests during the day.

Prolegs at end of caterpillar clutch twig

79

WHERE INSECTS LIVE

INSECTS LIVE everywhere there is warmth and moisture. Many of the five million or more species have specialized habitat requirements. They can live only in particular places, and easily become extinct when humans change or destroy their surroundings. Other species are able to adapt to changing conditions; these adaptable insects often become pests.

TEMPERATE WOODLAND
The varied plant life and complex structure of temperate woodland provides insects with many different habitats. Trees, shrubs, and herbs all have flowers, fruits, and buds for insects to feed on, as well as stems and roots for insects to bore into.

GRASSLAND AND HEATHLAND
These habitats offer little shelter from bad weather. But they warm up quickly in the sun, and have a rich variety of flowering plants.

TOWNS AND GARDENS
Hundreds of insect species take advantage of human habitats. Insects find food and shelter in our roofs, cellars, food stores, kitchens, rubbish bins, farms, and in our flower-filled gardens.

RCTIC

UROPE

ASIA

FRICA

AUSTRALASIA

NTARCTIC

DESERTS, CAVES, AND SOILS
These are inhospitable habitats. Food and water are scarce in deserts. Caves are dark and cold. And it is hard for insects to move and communicate in dense soil.

TROPICAL FOREST
This is the richest habitat for insect species. Thousands of species of plants provide countless niches for insects to live in, from treetop fruits, to dead leaves and twigs on the ground.

LAKES AND RIVERS
Freshwater insects are highly specialized. They have had to modify their bodies to be able to swim and breathe underwater.

INSECTS

TEMPERATE WOODLAND

FIELD SCABIO
FLOWER

TEMPERATE WOODLANDS are often dominated by one tree species, such as oak, which is deciduous (the trees lose their leaves in winter). The types of insect found, and their numbers, will vary with the seasons, and also with the types of tree species in the woodlands.

DRAINING
Forests in wetlands have many different plant species. But people often drain this habitat because it is good for farming. Draining kills plants such as milk-parsley, the only plant the English swallowtail butterfly will breed on. This beautiful insect is now rarely seen.

+1.75

Although the English swallowtail will only lay eggs on milk-parsley, adults feed on a variety of flowers.

82

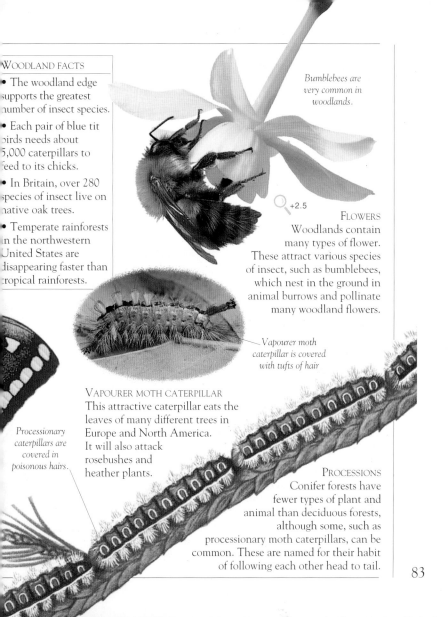

- The woodland edge supports the greatest number of insect species.

- Each pair of blue tit birds needs about 5,000 caterpillars to feed to its chicks.

- In Britain, over 280 species of insect live on native oak trees.

- Temperate rainforests in the northwestern United States are disappearing faster than tropical rainforests.

Bumblebees are very common in woodlands.

+2.5

FLOWERS
Woodlands contain many types of flower. These attract various species of insect, such as bumblebees, which nest in the ground in animal burrows and pollinate many woodland flowers.

Vapourer moth caterpillar is covered with tufts of hair

VAPOURER MOTH CATERPILLAR
This attractive caterpillar eats the leaves of many different trees in Europe and North America. It will also attack rosebushes and heather plants.

Processionary caterpillars are covered in poisonous hairs.

PROCESSIONS
Conifer forests have fewer types of plant and animal than deciduous forests, although some, such as processionary moth caterpillars, can be common. These are named for their habit of following each other head to tail.

83

OAK TREE

IN EUROPE AND North America, oak trees support a rich variety of insects. There are insects living on every part of the oak tree – the leaves, buds, flowers, fruits, wood, bark, and on decaying leaves and branches. All these insects provide food for the many birds and other animals found in oak woodland.

OAK TREE

GREEN OAK TORTRIX MOTH ON LEAF

GREEN OAK TORTRIX CATERPILLAR

GREEN OAK TORTRIX MOTH

The green wings of the green oak tortrix moth camouflage it on leaves. Green oak tortrix caterpillars are extremely common on oak trees. The caterpillars hide from predators by rolling themselves up in a leaf.

+1.5

+2.5

Leaf rolled around green oak tortrix caterpillar

Mine

MAKING A TUNNEL

The caterpillars of some small moths tunnel between the upper and lower surfaces of a leaf. They eat the green tissue between these surfaces as they tunnel, and leave a see-through trail called a mine.

84

+15

Chalcid wasp larvae have eaten the gall wasp larvae

GALLS

Oak trees have many tiny growths called galls. Galls are grown by the tree around eggs laid by gall wasps. When the eggs hatch, each gall provides food and shelter for up to 30 wasp larvae. Parasitic wasps called chalcid wasps sometimes burrow inside galls and lay their eggs beside the gall wasp eggs. When the chalcid larvae hatch they eat the gall wasp larvae.

CHALCID WASP ON GALL

NUT WEEVILS

Acorns are used as food by nut weevils. They drill a hole in an acorn with their long, thin snout, and then lay their eggs inside. The larvae feed inside the acorn, and this turns the acorn black.

Black acorn

ACORNS

Antenna

Long, thin snout

+5

NUT WEEVIL

85

TREE CANOPY

THE UPPER BRANCHES and leaves
of a tree are called the canopy.
Like a living green umbrella, the
canopy forms a protective
covering over the lower plants.
Countless insects find their food
in the canopy and they, in turn,
are food for many different birds.

*Inchworm
on leaf*

*Silken thread
suspends
inchworm*

INCHWORMS
Some young birds like
to feed on inchworms,
the caterpillars of
geometrid moths.
When in danger, inchworms
can drop from a leaf and hang
below by a silken thread.

*Very long antennae help
cricket find its way in the
dark and alert it to the
approach of enemies*

*Compound
eye*

OAK BUSH CRICKETS
At night, male oak bush crickets drum
on leaves with their feet so that a
female oak bush cricket, like this one,
knows where to find a mate. The
cricket's green body blends in well
with its leafy surroundings.

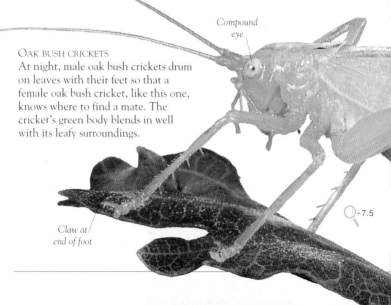

*Claw at
end of foot*

◯+7.5

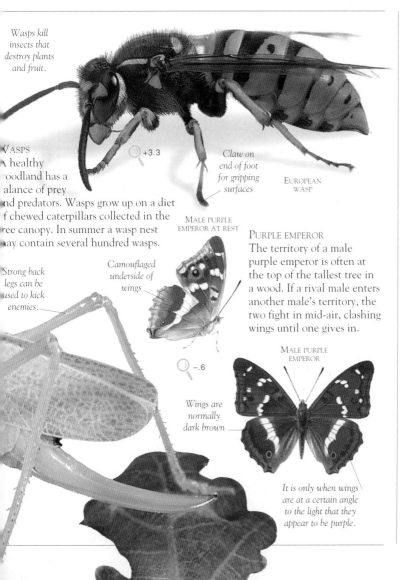

Wasps kill insects that destroy plants and fruit.

WASPS
A healthy woodland has a balance of prey and predators. Wasps grow up on a diet of chewed caterpillars collected in the tree canopy. In summer a wasp nest may contain several hundred wasps.

+3.3

Claw on end of foot for gripping surfaces

EUROPEAN WASP

MALE PURPLE EMPEROR AT REST

Strong back legs can be used to kick enemies.

Camouflaged underside of wings

−.6

PURPLE EMPEROR
The territory of a male purple emperor is often at the top of the tallest tree in a wood. If a rival male enters another male's territory, the two fight in mid-air, clashing wings until one gives in.

MALE PURPLE EMPEROR

Wings are normally dark brown

It is only when wings are at a certain angle to the light that they appear to be purple.

87

WOODLAND BUTTERFLIES

THE RICH VARIETY of habitats in woodland
supports many butterfly species.
Some live in the canopy, others
feed on low shrubs. But most
butterflies need sunshine and can be
found on flowers in sunny clearings.

Q .6

SILVER-WASHED FRITILLARY

This butterfly lays its eggs
in cracks in the bark of
mossy tree trunks, close to
where violets are growing.
The caterpillars feed on
the leaves of these plants.

*Brown
upperside*

Q .8

*Green
underside*

GREEN HAIRSTREAK

Whether it is
sitting on a
branch or resting
on a leaf, the
green hairstreak butterfly is well
camouflaged. Its upperside is a woody
brown while its underside is a leafy green.

PURPLE
HAIRSTREAK
BUTTERFLY

Female

Male

PURPLE HAIRSTREAK

High in the canopy
of oak trees the
caterpillars of the
purple hairstreak
butterfly feed on flowers
and young leaves.
Adult purple hairstreaks
spend most of their
lives in the treetops
feeding and sunbathing
with their wings open

*Eyespots on
underwings*

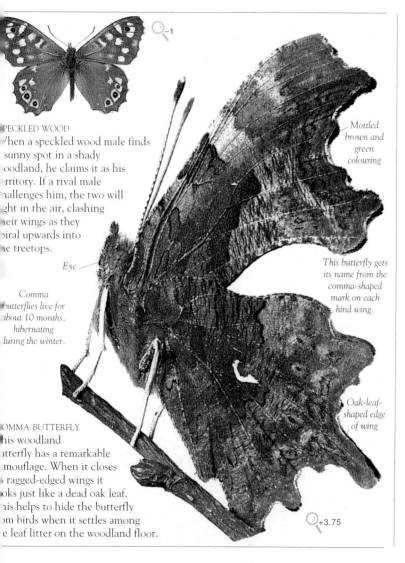

Q−1

SPECKLED WOOD
When a speckled wood male finds
a sunny spot in a shady
woodland, he claims it as his
territory. If a rival male
challenges him, the two will
fight in the air, clashing
their wings as they
spiral upwards into
the treetops.

Eye

*Comma
butterflies live for
about 10 months,
hibernating
during the winter.*

COMMA BUTTERFLY
This woodland
butterfly has a remarkable
camouflage. When it closes
its ragged-edged wings it
looks just like a dead oak leaf.
This helps to hide the butterfly
from birds when it settles among
the leaf litter on the woodland floor.

*Mottled
brown and
green
colouring*

*This butterfly gets
its name from the
comma-shaped
mark on each
hind wing.*

*Oak-leaf-
shaped edge
of wing*

Q+3.75

89

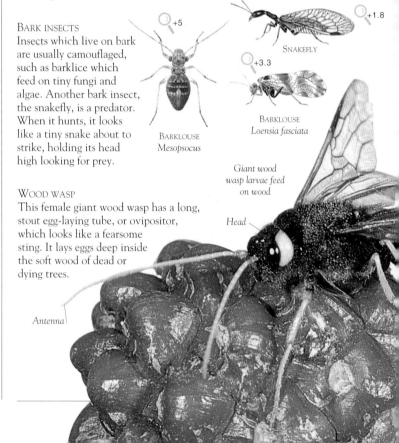

TREE TRUNKS AND BRANCHES

CRACKS IN THE bark of trees provide a hiding place fo[r]
many species of insect. Some burrow into the wood
and live completely concealed from predators. Many
insects also live and feed among the different plant lif[e]
that grows on tree trunks and branches.

BARK INSECTS

Insects which live on bark
are usually camouflaged,
such as barklice which
feed on tiny fungi and
algae. Another bark insect,
the snakefly, is a predator.
When it hunts, it looks
like a tiny snake about to
strike, holding its head
high looking for prey.

+5

SNAKEFLY

+1.8

+3.3

BARKLOUSE
Mesopsocus

BARKLOUSE
Loensia fasciata

WOOD WASP

This female giant wood wasp has a long,
stout egg-laying tube, or ovipositor,
which looks like a fearsome
sting. It lays eggs deep inside
the soft wood of dead or
dying trees.

Giant wood
wasp larvae feed
on wood

Head

Antenna

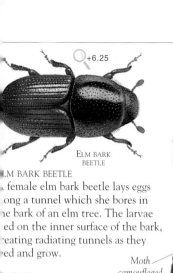

+6.25

ELM BARK
BEETLE

[E]LM BARK BEETLE

[A] female elm bark beetle lays eggs
[al]ong a tunnel which she bores in
[t]he bark of an elm tree. The larvae
[fe]ed on the inner surface of the bark,
[cr]eating radiating tunnels as they
[fe]ed and grow.

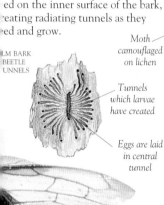

[E]LM BARK
BEETLE
[T]UNNELS

Moth
camouflaged
on lichen

Tunnels
which larvae
have created

Eggs are laid
in central
tunnel

+3.75

The merveille
du jour moth is
easy to see when
not on lichen.

Ovipositor bores
into wood where
it deposits eggs

MERVEILLE MOTH

The patterns on the front wings of
the merveille du jour moth help to
camouflage it when it rests on lichens
growing on a tree trunk. The moth is
active at night and rests during the
day. Its camouflage has to be good
to hide it in bright daylight from
predators such as birds and lizards.

91

GROUND LEVEL

THE WOODLAND floor does not get much sunlight, so few plants grow there. Most insects at ground level feed on plant and animal debris falling from the canopy, or, if they are carnivorous, eat other insects.

ANT NEST
The wood ant is a voracious predator. Colonies build huge nests of plant debris, with a network of tunnels below ground providing a home for thousands of ants.

WOOD CRICKET
Most crickets are nocturnal (active at night). But the wood cricket is active on sunny days when it can be heard chirping loudly. It is unable to fly because of its short wings.

Strong jaws bite into prey

WOOD ANT
Wood ants forage out from their nest for hundreds of metres, making distinct paths on the woodland floor. They catch huge numbers of insects and bring them to the nest in pieces as food for their young.

Ant can squirt poison from abdomen

+10

–1.25

IOLET GROUND BEETLE
his beetle can run fast
n its long legs, catching
·her insects among the
·af litter. It grips its prey
ith powerful jaws, and
ints mainly at night.

TAG BEETLE
he larvae of stag beetles spend about
aree years feeding on rotting wood
nside a dead tree. These handsome
eetles are now becoming rare
ecause dead wood is often
eared away and burnt.

WHITE ADMIRALS
On sunny days, white
admiral butterflies can
be spotted near the
ground feeding on the
nectar of bramble
flowers. They can often
be seen in the morning
sipping water from
puddles. They spend
much of their time in
the tree canopy, basking
in the sunshine.

+3

UPPERSIDE OF
WHITE ADMIRAL

UNDERSIDE OF
WHITE ADMIRAL

Antenna

*Only male
stag beetles
have enlarged
jaws.*

+3.75

TEMPERATE WOODLAND

This grass is called cocks-foot.

FIELD CHAFER

+1.5

GRASSLAND AND HEATHLAND

HERE, THE LACK OF PROTECTIVE tree canopy results in quick changes in the weather – from hot and dry, to windy, cold, or wet. Grassland and heathland habitats provide fewer dwelling places for insects than forest or woodland as there is little wood for them to burrow into, and hardly any leaf litter to live underneath.

FOOD SOURCE
Plant roots are an important food for insects in these habitats. Field chafer larvae eat roots, while the adults fly from plant to plant seeking a mate.

SPRINGTAILS
Cultivated grass fields, such as sports pitches, support few insect species. But they do contain vast numbers of tiny insects called springtails. An area the size of a tennis court might be home to up to three hundred million springtails.

94

OXFORD RAGWORT
A weed called the
Oxford ragwort is a
common invader of
neglected pasture in
Europe. The cinnabar
moth lays its eggs on
this weed, and its
caterpillars eat
the leaves.

CINNABAR
MOTH

The moth has
warning coloration
because it tastes
unpleasant.

An Oxford
ragwort is often
stripped of its leaves
by feeding caterpillars

GRASSLAND AND
HEATHLAND FACTS

• The grassland of
Argentina are called
Pampas, or "plains" in
the language of the
native people.

• Prairies of the U.S.A.
have long grasses.

• Steppes (prairie-like
land) of Siberia have
short grasses.

RICH IN PLANT LIFE
Natural grassland and
heathland have a huge
variety of grasses
and flowering
plants. These rich
habitats buzz with
insect life
in the
summer
months.

CRANESBILL

RARE BUTTERFLY
The English large copper
butterfly was once common
in fenland but is now
extinct. This is a result of
intensive land development
for agriculture, which
destroyed the butterfly's
special food plant.

GRASSLAND INSECTS

MOST INSECT species cannot survive in cultivated grass
land, such as garden lawns, since they usually contain
only one type of grass. Also, fertilizers and other
chemicals harm many insects. But natural grassland,
with their variety of plants, support thousands of insect
species which have adapted to this open, windy habitat

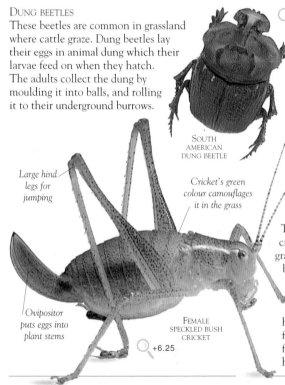

DUNG BEETLES
These beetles are common in grassland
where cattle graze. Dung beetles lay
their eggs in animal dung which their
larvae feed on when they hatch.
The adults collect the dung by
moulding it into balls, and rolling
it to their underground burrows.

+3.75

Antenna

SOUTH
AMERICAN
DUNG BEETLE

*Cricket's green
colour camouflages
it in the grass*

*Large hind
legs for
jumping*

BUSH CRICKET
The speckled bush
cricket is common in
grassland across Europe,
but is easily overlooked
due to its grass-
green colouring.
The male's song is too
high for us to hear, apart
from a sharp "tick". The
female's reply is even
harder for us to hear.

*Ovipositor
puts eggs into
plant stems*

FEMALE
SPECKLED BUSH
CRICKET

+6.25

NTEATER
here are so many ants in
e grassland of South
merica and Africa
at specialized
t-eating
ammals have
olved. They have
owerful claws to break open ant
sts, and long sticky tongues to
llect the ants.

ANTEATER

−1

+1.6

LARGE BLUE BUTTERFLY
This butterfly lays its eggs
on the wild thyme plant,
and the newly hatched
caterpillars feed on thyme
flowers. The caterpillars
attract red ants with a
special milk. The ants are
deceived into carrying the
caterpillars into their nest,
where the caterpillars eat
the ant eggs and larva.

*Ragwort
plant*

*Mating
soldier beetles*

ARBLED WHITE BUTTERFLY
his butterfly can be found in a
riety of grassland habitats, including
assy areas inside a wood. Marbled
hites often gather in groups to
sk in the early morning and
rly evening sunshine.

−.4

OLDIER BEETLES
me insects feed on one particular
wer, while others, such as
ldier beetles, eat pollen from
rious flowers. These feeding
es are also good places for
sects to find a mate.

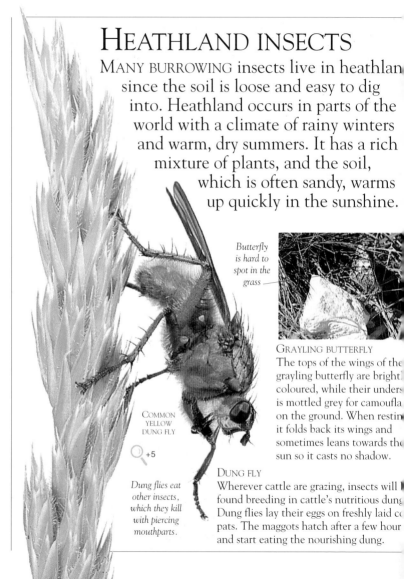

HEATHLAND INSECTS

MANY BURROWING insects live in heathland since the soil is loose and easy to dig into. Heathland occurs in parts of the world with a climate of rainy winters and warm, dry summers. It has a rich mixture of plants, and the soil, which is often sandy, warms up quickly in the sunshine.

Butterfly is hard to spot in the grass

GRAYLING BUTTERFLY
The tops of the wings of the grayling butterfly are bright coloured, while their unders is mottled grey for camoufla on the ground. When restin it folds back its wings and sometimes leans towards the sun so it casts no shadow.

COMMON
YELLOW
DUNG FLY

+5

Dung flies eat other insects, which they kill with piercing mouthparts.

DUNG FLY
Wherever cattle are grazing, insects will found breeding in cattle's nutritious dung Dung flies lay their eggs on freshly laid c pats. The maggots hatch after a few hour and start eating the nourishing dung.

rrow

FIELD CRICKET

This sturdy cricket is a sun-loving insect, although it nests in a burrow underground. Males sit at the mouth of their burrow in summer chirping hour after hour to attract a mate, although this male has attracted a second male.

~~TI~~GER BEETLE

~~T~~his brightly coloured beetle has large eyes ~~an~~d long legs. When it is warmed by the ~~su~~n it can run and fly very quickly. It ~~is~~ a fierce predator that lives in a ~~bu~~rrow in sandy soil, from which it dashes out to seize its insect prey.

Antenna

~~Ti~~ger beetles have ~~sha~~rp, cutting jaws ~~f~~or killing and eating prey.

Eye

Long legs for chasing prey

The prey of the ~~ti~~ger beetle includes ~~o~~ther beetles and grasshoppers.

+4.1

Ant-lion larva seizing ant

ANT-LION LARVA

The larva of the ant-lion fly often digs conical pits in sandy soils. Lying in wait at the bottom of its pit, the larva uses its long jaws to catch any small insect that falls in.

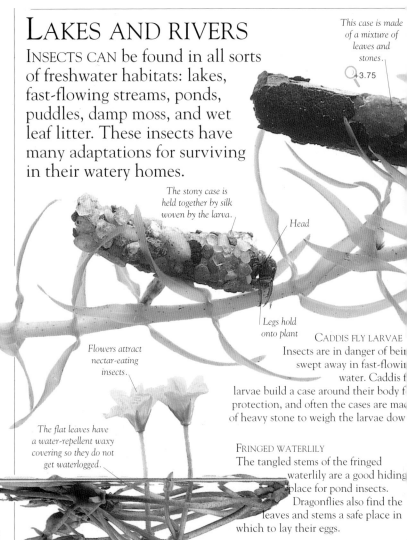

LAKES AND RIVERS

INSECTS CAN be found in all sorts of freshwater habitats: lakes, fast-flowing streams, ponds, puddles, damp moss, and wet leaf litter. These insects have many adaptations for surviving in their watery homes.

This case is made of a mixture of leaves and stones.

+3.75

The stony case is held together by silk woven by the larva.

Head

Legs hold onto plant

Flowers attract nectar-eating insects.

CADDIS FLY LARVAE
Insects are in danger of being swept away in fast-flowing water. Caddis fly larvae build a case around their body for protection, and often the cases are made of heavy stone to weigh the larvae down.

The flat leaves have a water-repellent waxy covering so they do not get waterlogged.

FRINGED WATERLILY
The tangled stems of the fringed waterlily are a good hiding place for pond insects. Dragonflies also find the leaves and stems a safe place in which to lay their eggs.

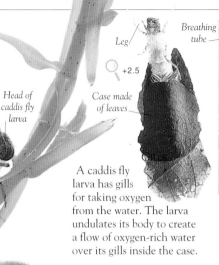

Leg

Breathing tube

🔍 +2.5

Head of caddis fly larva

Case made of leaves

A caddis fly larva has gills for taking oxygen from the water. The larva undulates its body to create a flow of oxygen-rich water over its gills inside the case.

SPRINGTAILS
In corners of ponds sheltered from the wind, swarms of springtails sometimes gather on the surface of the water. They feed on organic debris that has blown into the pond.

FAST STREAMS
Insects that live in fast-flowing streams have streamlined bodies and strong claws to help them cling to stones. The water that passes over their gills is always rich in oxygen, but cool temperatures mean that larvae develop more slowly than they would in a shallow, sun-warmed pond.

WATER SCORPION
The water scorpion has a breathing tube on its rear end so it can breathe the outside air while it is underwater. Insects with breathing tubes can survive in warm ponds or polluted waters which are low in oxygen.

LAKE AND RIVER FACTS

• Fish populations depend on plenty of insects as food.

• Dragonfly larvae are considered a delicacy in New Guinea.

• Swarms of non-biting midges are sometimes so dense in African lakes that fishermen have been suffocated.

101

eleven# WATER SURFACE INSECTS

A WATER SURFACE behaves like a skin due to a force called surface tension. This force enables certain insects to walk on the "skin" and others to hang beneath it. Many of these insects are predators, and much of their food comes from the constant supply of flying insects which have fallen into the water.

○ +7.5

WHIRLIGIG

The whirligig beetle swims round and round very fast on the water surface. It hunts insects trapped on the surface tension. The whirligig's eyes are divided into two halves, allowing it to see both above and below the water surface at the same time.

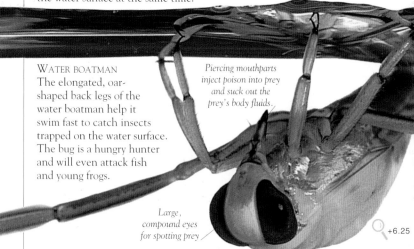

WATER BOATMAN

The elongated, oar-shaped back legs of the water boatman help it swim fast to catch insects trapped on the water surface. The bug is a hungry hunter and will even attack fish and young frogs.

Piercing mouthparts inject poison into prey and suck out the prey's body fluids.

Large, compound eyes for spotting prey

○ +6.25

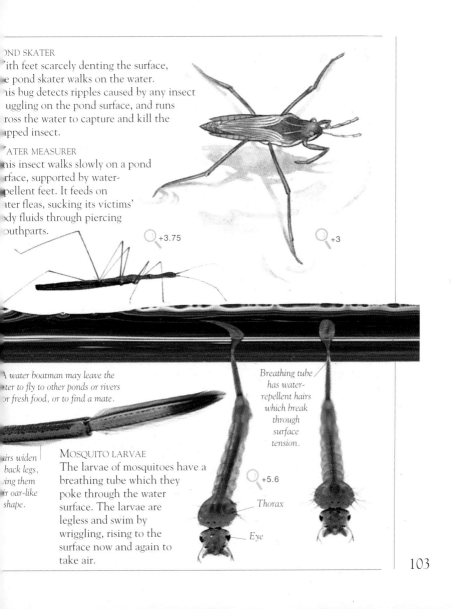

POND SKATER

With feet scarcely denting the surface, the pond skater walks on the water. This bug detects ripples caused by any insect struggling on the pond surface, and runs across the water to capture and kill the trapped insect.

WATER MEASURER

This insect walks slowly on a pond surface, supported by water-repellent feet. It feeds on water fleas, sucking its victims' body fluids through piercing mouthparts.

+3.75

+3

A water boatman may leave the water to fly to other ponds or rivers for fresh food, or to find a mate.

Hairs widen the back legs, giving them their oar-like shape.

MOSQUITO LARVAE

The larvae of mosquitoes have a breathing tube which they poke through the water surface. The larvae are legless and swim by wriggling, rising to the surface now and again to take air.

Breathing tube has water-repellent hairs which break through surface tension.

+5.6

Thorax

Eye

103

UNDERWATER INSECTS

MANY OF THE insects that live underwater are carnivorous, either hunting their prey or scavenging. Some of these insects are fierce, sometimes killing prey larger than themselves.

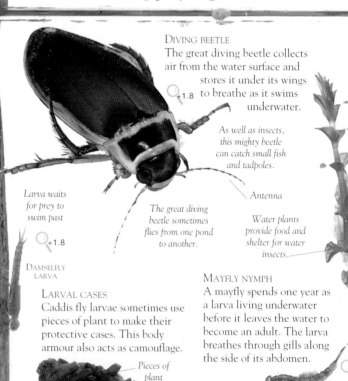

DIVING BEETLE
The great diving beetle collects air from the water surface and stores it under its wings to breathe as it swims underwater.

$Q_{+1.8}$

As well as insects, this mighty beetle can catch small fish and tadpoles.

Larva waits for prey to swim past

$Q_{+1.8}$

The great diving beetle sometimes flies from one pond to another.

Antenna

Water plants provide food and shelter for water insects.

DAMSELFLY LARVA

LARVAL CASES
Caddis fly larvae sometimes use pieces of plant to make their protective cases. This body armour also acts as camouflage.

Pieces of plant

MAYFLY NYMPH
A mayfly spends one year as a larva living underwater before it leaves the water to become an adult. The larva breathes through gills along the side of its abdomen.

Q_{+0}

ADULT DRAGONFLY
Male darter dragonflies perch
on plants that emerge from the
water. They fiercely attack and
drive away any rival males of
the same species, but attempt
to mate with any female darter
dragonfly that flies past.

×.8

DRAGONFLY EGGS
Darter dragonflies scatter their
eggs in the water. The eggs are
surrounded by a sticky, jelly-
like substance, and hatch
after a few days.

*Jelly holds
eggs in place*

×.8

BEETLE LARVA
The larva of the great diving beetle
injects juices into prey with its jaws.
The juices turn the prey's insides
into liquid for the larva to suck out.

DRAGONFLY NYMPH
Dragonfly larvae breathe by
pumping water in and out of their
rear end, where they have
complex gills.

+1.8

ORCHID

TROPICAL FOREST

INSECTS THRIVE in the humid heat and flourishing plant life of tropical forests. These forests have a complex structure which provides many habitats for insects. Trees vary in shape and size; vines and dead branches are everywhere, and thick leaf litter covers the ground.

ORCHIDS
Tropical forests contain a spectacular variety of plants – there are about 25,000 species of orchid alone. It is quite dark near the forest floor, and orchids are strongly scented to help insects find them.

EPIPHYTES
Many plants grow on the trunks and branches of trees where birds have wiped seeds from their beaks. These tree-dwelling plants, called epiphytes, provide extra habitats for insects.

INSECT PREDATORS
A tropical forest is a rich habitat for birds as well as insects. Tropical birds feed on countless insects each day. This high rate of predation is a major reason for the evolution of camouflage and mimicry in tropical insects.

FRUITY NOURISHMENT
Some tropical butterflies live for several months. An important source of fuel for their continued activity is rotting fruit and dung on the forest floor. This gives them not only sugars for energy, but also amino acids and vitamins to stay healthy.

Blue face

Red eye

TROPICAL FORESTS
Bright colours are typical of
tropical forests, and they can
be seen in both the plant and
animal life. This Central
American cricket looks as if
it would be easy to spot with
its multi-coloured body, but
it is camouflaged among
the shining leaves of the
forest trees.

*The bright colours of
this cricket surprised even
entomologists.*

Bright
green
abdomen

+2.5

*The cricket's
colours fade
when it dies.*

TROPICAL FOREST FACTS

• Tropical forests cover
about five per cent of
the Earth's land surface.

• They contain over
half of all living species.

• Around 1,200 species
of butterfly have been
recorded in one forest
in southern Peru.

• Over half the world's
rainforest has been
destroyed since 1945.

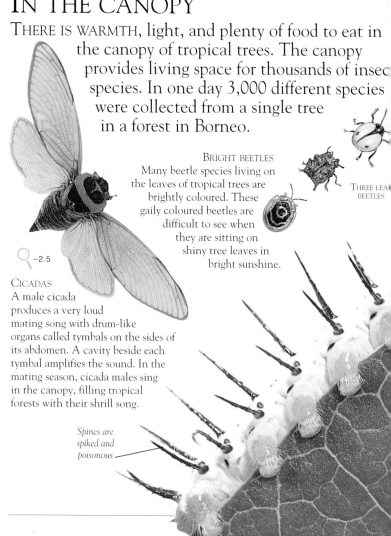

IN THE CANOPY

THERE IS WARMTH, light, and plenty of food to eat in the canopy of tropical trees. The canopy provides living space for thousands of insect species. In one day 3,000 different species were collected from a single tree in a forest in Borneo.

BRIGHT BEETLES
Many beetle species living on the leaves of tropical trees are brightly coloured. These gaily coloured beetles are difficult to see when they are sitting on shiny tree leaves in bright sunshine.

THREE LEAF BEETLES

–2.5

CICADAS
A male cicada produces a very loud mating song with drum-like organs called tymbals on the sides of its abdomen. A cavity beside each tymbal amplifies the sound. In the mating season, cicada males sing in the canopy, filling tropical forests with their shrill song.

Spines are spiked and poisonous

FROG BEETLE
This vividly coloured
jewelled frog beetle is
probably less noticeable
in the bright sunshine
of its leafy habitat.
Despite its name,
the frog-like hind
legs are not used for
jumping, but for
holding on to a
female while mating.

+0

−3.1

*Frog-like
hind leg*

VIOLIN BEETLE
Little is known about the curious
violin beetle, which got its name
because of its violin-like shape.
It is very flat, and has been seen
living between layers of bracket
fungi on tree-trunks in
Indonesian forests.

*Six simple eyes on either
side of the head can sense
whether it is light or dark.*

+5

PASSIONFLOWER

POISON SPINES
The body of the
postman butterfly
caterpillar contains
poisons. It gets the
poisons from chemicals
in the leaves of the
passionflower vines
which it eats. The
prickly spines remind
birds to avoid it.

NESTS IN THE CANOPY

WITH SO MANY insects feeding in the forest canopy, it is not surprising that the insect-eating ants and wasps build their nests there. But these ants and wasps are in turn hunted by mammals and lizards, so their nests must give protection.

Nest is made of paper-like material

GREEN WEAVER ANTS

Each green weaver ant colony has several nests made of leaves. To make a nest, the ants join forces to pull leaves together and sew the edges. They sew using silk which the larvae produce when they are squeezed by the adult ants. These carnivorous ants hunt through the tree canopy, catching other insects and carrying the prey in pieces back to the ants' nests.

Ants' pulling leaves together

WASP NESTS

Each wasp species makes a different type of nest. This nest from South America has been cut in half to reveal the "floors" which house the larvae. There is one small opening at the bottom where the wasps defend the nest from invading ants.

This nest hangs from a branch of a tree.

There may be half a million ants in one weaver ant colony.

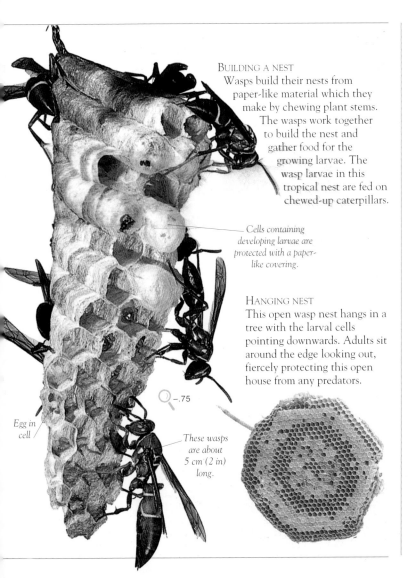

BUILDING A NEST

Wasps build their nests from paper-like material which they make by chewing plant stems. The wasps work together to build the nest and gather food for the growing larvae. The wasp larvae in this tropical nest are fed on chewed-up caterpillars.

Cells containing developing larvae are protected with a paper-like covering.

HANGING NEST

This open wasp nest hangs in a tree with the larval cells pointing downwards. Adults sit around the edge looking out, fiercely protecting this open house from any predators.

Egg in cell

These wasps are about 5 cm (2 in) long.

–.75

BRILLIANT BUTTERFLIES

MANY TROPICAL butterflies are large and brilliantly coloured, which ought to make it easy for predators to catch them. But they fly rapidly and erratically, flash their bright colours in the sun, and then seem to disappear, darting into the deep shade of the forest.

BLUE MORPHO
The iridescent blue of South American morpho butterflies is so vivid it can be seen from a great distance. But its underwings are a muddy brown for camouflage when feeding on the ground.

SOUTHEAST ASIAN MOTH
The vivid colours of this Southeast Asian moth shows that some day-flying moths can be as colourful as butterflies. The bright colours warn predators that this moth is poisonous.

NERO BUTTERFLY
The bright yellow Nero butterfly drinks from streams and puddles near mammal dung. This habit is common in butterflies of tropical forests. It supplies them with nutrients which are not available in flowers.

+2.5

Tops of
wings are
bright and
colourful

POSTMAN
BUTTERFLY
Brightly coloured
and slow-flying, the
postman butterfly is
poisonous. Birds quickly
learn to avoid it. At night,
groups of postman butterflies
often sleep together on branches.

−4

BIRDWING
BUTTERFLIES
The males of
Southeast Asian
birdwing butterflies
differ in size, colour, and   FEMALE BIRDWING
behaviour from the females. The brightly coloured
males sometimes fly near the ground, but the
larger brownish females remain in the treetops.

−3.5

MALE BIRDWING

113

INSECTS

TROPICAL BUTTERFLIES

THOUSANDS OF butterfly species live in tropical forests. Each butterfly has to recognize members of its own species among all the others in order to mate. They find each other by sight – butterflies can see more colours than any other animal – and by smell.

−.75

Tail brush

USING SCENTS
Striped blue crow butterfly males have a yellow brush at the end of their abdomen. When a male has found a female, he uses his brush to dust scented scales on her. The arousing scent encourages the female to mate with him.

DETECTING SCENTS
The complex nature of a silk-worm moth antenna can be seen when viewed at high magnification. It is divided into segments, and each bears two branches. The branches increase the antenna's surface area making it more sensitive.

Branches on each segment

Scent chemicals stimulate nerves in the silk-worm moth's antennae.

−3

SITTING TOGETHER
At sunny spots in the forest, butterflies gather at muddy puddles to drink water and salts. Butterflies of the same species usually sit together, so that white-coloured species form one group, blue another, and so on.

114

Postman butterflies and small postman butterflies are two different species. But they share the same wing patterns in different parts of South America.

POSTMAN BUTTERFLY
FROM SOUTHERN ECUADOR

SMALL POSTMAN BUTTERFLY
FROM SOUTHERN ECUADOR

POSTMAN BUTTERFLY
FROM SOUTHERN BRAZIL

SMALL POSTMAN BUTTERFLY
FROM SOUTHERN BRAZIL

SMALL POSTMAN BUTTERFLY
FROM WESTERN BRAZIL

POSTMAN BUTTERFLY
FROM WESTERN BRAZIL

COPYING PATTERNS

Sometimes two or more different species of poisonous butterfly share the same wing pattern. This kind of mimicry means that the different species protect each other. Birds only need to learn that one species is poisonous to avoid the other.

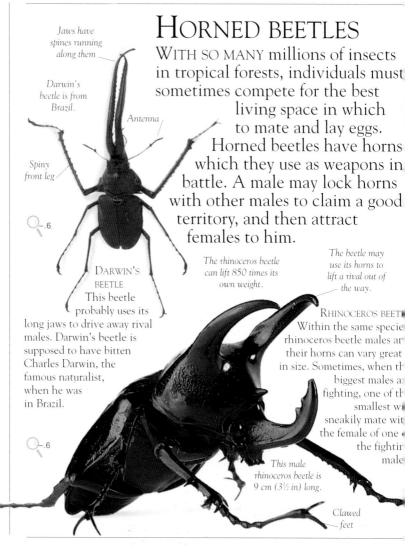

HORNED BEETLES

WITH SO MANY millions of insects in tropical forests, individuals must sometimes compete for the best living space in which to mate and lay eggs. Horned beetles have horns which they use as weapons in battle. A male may lock horns with other males to claim a good territory, and then attract females to him.

Jaws have spines running along them

Darwin's beetle is from Brazil.

Antenna

Spiny front leg

.6

DARWIN'S BEETLE

This beetle probably uses its long jaws to drive away rival males. Darwin's beetle is supposed to have bitten Charles Darwin, the famous naturalist, when he was in Brazil.

.6

The rhinoceros beetle can lift 850 times its own weight.

The beetle may use its horns to lift a rival out of the way.

RHINOCEROS BEETLE

Within the same species, rhinoceros beetle males and their horns can vary greatly in size. Sometimes, when the biggest males are fighting, one of the smallest will sneakily mate with the female of one of the fighting males.

This male rhinoceros beetle is 9 cm (3½ in) long.

Clawed feet

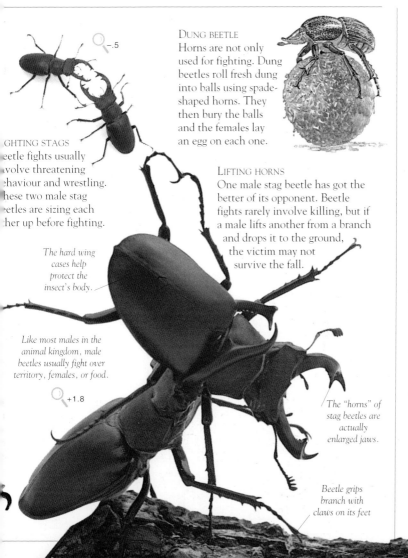

DUNG BEETLE
Horns are not only used for fighting. Dung beetles roll fresh dung into balls using spade-shaped horns. They then bury the balls and the females lay an egg on each one.

-.5

FIGHTING STAGS
Beetle fights usually involve threatening behaviour and wrestling. These two male stag beetles are sizing each other up before fighting.

The hard wing cases help protect the insect's body.

Like most males in the animal kingdom, male beetles usually fight over territory, females, or food.

+1.8

LIFTING HORNS
One male stag beetle has got the better of its opponent. Beetle fights rarely involve killing, but if a male lifts another from a branch and drops it to the ground, the victim may not survive the fall.

The "horns" of stag beetles are actually enlarged jaws.

Beetle grips branch with claws on its feet

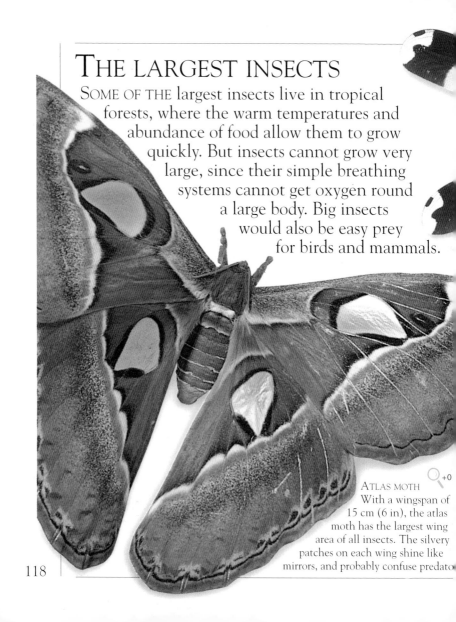

THE LARGEST INSECTS

SOME OF THE largest insects live in tropical forests, where the warm temperatures and abundance of food allow them to grow quickly. But insects cannot grow very large, since their simple breathing systems cannot get oxygen round a large body. Big insects would also be easy prey for birds and mammals.

ATLAS MOTH
With a wingspan of 15 cm (6 in), the atlas moth has the largest wing area of all insects. The silvery patches on each wing shine like mirrors, and probably confuse predato

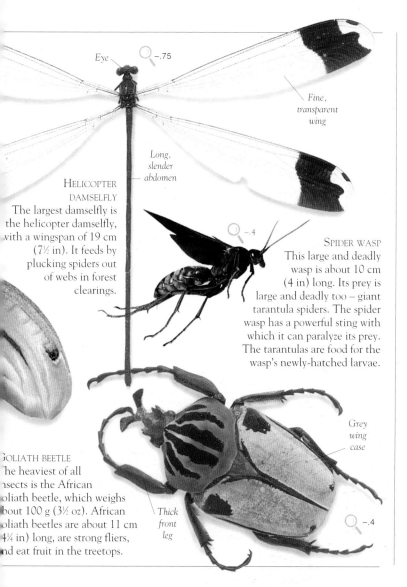

Eye ○ –.75

Fine, transparent wing

Long, slender abdomen

HELICOPTER DAMSELFLY
The largest damselfly is the helicopter damselfly, with a wingspan of 19 cm (7½ in). It feeds by plucking spiders out of webs in forest clearings.

○ –.4

SPIDER WASP
This large and deadly wasp is about 10 cm (4 in) long. Its prey is large and deadly too – giant tarantula spiders. The spider wasp has a powerful sting with which it can paralyze its prey. The tarantulas are food for the wasp's newly-hatched larvae.

Grey wing case

GOLIATH BEETLE
The heaviest of all insects is the African Goliath beetle, which weighs about 100 g (3½ oz). African Goliath beetles are about 11 cm (4¼ in) long, are strong fliers, and eat fruit in the treetops.

Thick front leg

○ –.4

119

STICK AND LEAF INSECTS

A TROPICAL FOREST is alive with animals, most of which eat insects. To survive, insects adopt many strategies. Stick and leaf insects hide from predators by keeping still and resembling their background of leaves and sticks.

STICK INSECTS

Some stick insects are slender, brown, or green, just like the twigs and leaf stalks they sit on. Other species are shorter and fatter, with spines and other projections. These often look like curled dead leaves.

Winged male of Macleay's spectre

Wingless female of Macleay's spectre

Indian stick insect

Spiny green nymph

120

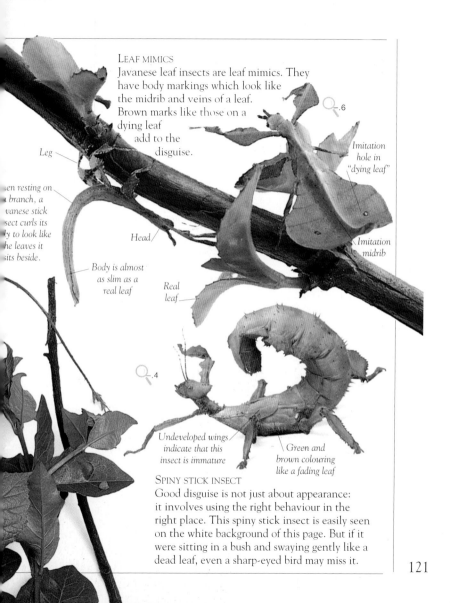

LEAF MIMICS

Javanese leaf insects are leaf mimics. They have body markings which look like the midrib and veins of a leaf. Brown marks like those on a dying leaf add to the disguise.

Q.6

Imitation hole in "dying leaf"

Leg

...en resting on a branch, a ...vanese stick ...sect curls its ...y to look like ...he leaves it ...its beside.

Head

Imitation midrib

Body is almost as slim as a real leaf

Real leaf

Q.4

Undeveloped wings indicate that this insect is immature

Green and brown colouring like a fading leaf

SPINY STICK INSECT

Good disguise is not just about appearance: it involves using the right behaviour in the right place. This spiny stick insect is easily seen on the white background of this page. But if it were sitting in a bush and swaying gently like a dead leaf, even a sharp-eyed bird may miss it.

121

ARMIES ON THE GROUND

ANTS ARE THE dominant creatures of tropical forests. They live in colonies made up of any number from 20 individuals to many thousands. Ants are mostly carnivorous. Some species make slaves of other ant species by invading their nest and killing their queen

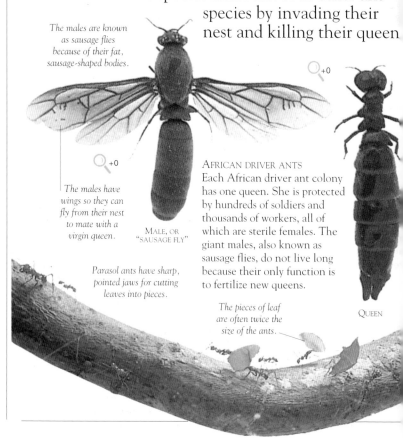

The males are known as sausage flies because of their fat, sausage-shaped bodies.

+0

The males have wings so they can fly from their nest to mate with a virgin queen.

MALE, OR "SAUSAGE FLY"

Parasol ants have sharp, pointed jaws for cutting leaves into pieces.

AFRICAN DRIVER ANTS
Each African driver ant colony has one queen. She is protected by hundreds of soldiers and thousands of workers, all of which are sterile females. The giant males, also known as sausage flies, do not live long because their only function is to fertilize new queens.

The pieces of leaf are often twice the size of the ants.

QUEEN

DRIVER ANTS MARCHING

These ants get their name from the way a colony creeps through an area catching all the insects it can find. They move their nests from place to place regularly, unlike most ants which have a permanent nest and territory.

+3.75

Beetle pupae are among the prey of driver ants.

CARRYING PREY

Ants in a column collaborate to cut large insects they have caught into smaller pieces. This is so they can carry their food back to the nest. Smaller prey can be carried whole.

ATTENTIVE SOLDIER
Driver ant soldiers have very large jaws. Often they can be seen standing beside a marching column of ants with their jaws wide open, waiting to attack intruders, such as parasitic flies.

Ant returning for more leaves

PARASOL ANTS
These South American ants are not carnivorous. They feed on fungus which they cultivate in huge underground nests. The fungus is grown on pieces of leaf which the ants bring to the nest.

DESERTS, CAVES, AND SOILS

SOME INSECTS flourish in habitats where it is difficult for living things to survive. Desert habitats, for example, lack water and have very high temperatures. Caves are dark and lack plant life for food. Life in the soil makes communication, both by scent and sight, difficult for insects.

Tiger beetle larva has hooks on body to help it climb upwards

+4

HIDING IN SOIL

Life in the soil is only a passing phase for some insect species. This tiger beetle larva hides underground by day. At night waits in its vertical tunnel with its jaws projecting at the ground surface, and snatches passing insects to devour in its burrow.

CAVE DWELLER

This cockroach lives all its life in the dark. Like other cave creatures, it feeds on debris from the outside world. Bat dung, dead animals, and pieces of plants washed into the cave provide the cockroach with its nourishment.

DESERT BEETLE
The lack of water in deserts means that insects have to find devious ways to obtain moisture. This darkling beetle lives in the Namib Desert where sea winds bring mists each night. The beetle holds its abdomen high to catch the moisture, which then runs down into its mouth.

DESERT HEAT
The hot and dry days in deserts can lead to rapid water loss and death for animals. Most living creatures hide under stones or in the sand to avoid drying out. These animals are active at night when it is much cooler.

DESERT FACTS

• The Sahara Desert is spreading at a rate of 5 km (3 miles) per year.

• In deserts the temperature may range from 30°C (90°F) in the day to below 0°C (32°F) at night.

• Caves have a nearly constant temperature throughout the year.

• 20% of the Earth's land surface is desert.

CACTUS FLOWER

DESERT PLANTS
Rain may not fall in a desert for months, or even years. Most desert plants store water so they can survive, and some desert animals rely on these plants for food. But many animals, including some insects, migrate in search of rain and the plant growth it produces.

125

DESERT INSECTS

HOT, DRY DESERTS are dangerous places in which to live. Animals often die from sunstroke and dehydrati (drying out). To prevent this, insects avoid the sun b staying in the shade or burrowing in the sand. Some insects have special methods of collecting water. Mar feed only at night because the surface of the sand is to hot for them to walk on during the day.

–.7

NAMIB DESERT BEETLE
Long legs keep the body of the Namib desert beetle off the hot sand. The larvae live in the sand, scavenging on detritus (organic debris), and complete development in about six months. The adults live for several years.

DESERT LOCUSTS
Adult desert locusts fly in swarms to find fresh food. When there is enough food they breed rapidly, and huge groups of wingless nymphs hop across the desert sand.

Grasses and other plants form the diet of desert locusts.

Desert locusts get water from plant food.

Antenna

+2

TWO DESER LOCUST NYM

ESERT CRICKET

ne large feet of
is desert cricket
ow it to dig speedily
the sand. It can
ry itself in a few
conds, either to hide
om predators or to
cape from the
tense heat
the midday sun. Its
ngtips are coiled to
otect them when
derground.

Large feet

*trong back
gs for long
leaps*

*Wing
buds*

*End of
wings
coiled up*

–.5

*Long
antenna*

*This hard
collar protects
the thorax.*

HONEYPOT ANTS

Honeypot ants are living water
stores. During the rainy season,
certain worker ants in a colony
are fed with water and nectar
until their abdomens are full
and swollen. In the dry season
the other ants feed from them
until the rainy season returns.

JEWEL WASP

These shiny green wasps
catch other insects, such as
cockroaches, for their young
to eat. Adult jewel wasps are
vegetarians, drinking nectar
from desert flowers. +1.2

Long antenna

−4.3

AFRICAN CAVE CRICKET
Some insects have developed very long antennae to make up for lack of vision in the dark of caves. This African cricket has the longest antennae for its body size of any insect.

CAVE INSECTS

ALL LIFE DEPENDS on the sun's energy. Plants change sunlight into food by a process called photosynthesis. In dark, sunless caves, nothing grows, and cave-dwelling insects must find food from outside. This food is sometimes washed in by floods, or dropped by bats and birds.

Long back legs for jumping out of danger

FEMALE AFRICAN CAVE CRICKET

Two sensitive spines, called cerci, can detect enemies approaching from behind.

Cricket uses its ovipositor (egg-laying tube) to lay eggs in soil.

 +3

ACOCK
TTERFLY

r some insects,
ves provide shelter
m the uncomfortable
ather conditions. During
ld northern winters a
ve is an ideal place
peacock butterflies
hibernate.

*Dark underside of
ings camouflages the
eacock butterfly as it
hibernates.*

AVE CRICKET

ickets living in caves have
aller eyes and paler bodies
an crickets living in
nlight. Cave crickets breed
year round because the
nperature and the amount
food in the cave
y constant.

*Very long,
sensitive
antennae*

*Top of wings
are brightly
coloured.*

−1

PEACOCK BUTTERFLY

COCKROACH

Cave-dwelling cockroaches eat bat droppings
and bat carcasses, as well as mites and fungi.
Cockroaches often eat each other, too. Caves
make an ideal home for cockroaches since
they love dark, damp places.

+3.75

SURINAM
COCKROACH

SOIL INSECTS

WHEN PLANTS and animals die, their remains usually get absorbed into the soil. Insects which live in soil are among the most important creatures on Earth because they help to recycle these remains, releasing their nutrients and so helping new crops and forests to grow. Soil insects are also an important food for many mammals and birds.

BEETLE LARVA
Roots and decaying tree trunks provide food for many types of insect larva, such as this lamellicorn beetle grub. The grub breathes through holes called spiracles, which are along the side of its body. Although there is not very much air underground, there is enough for insects.

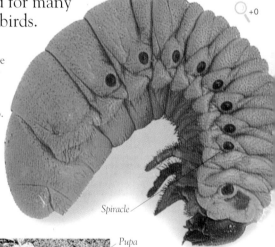

Spiracle

Pupa

GOOD HABITAT
Living in soil has advantages. Insec[ts] are unlikely to dehydrate, and ther[e] is plenty of food in plant roots and decaying plants. This spurge hawk moth pupa has sharp plates on its abdomen which help it climb to th[e] surface just before the adult emerg[es.]

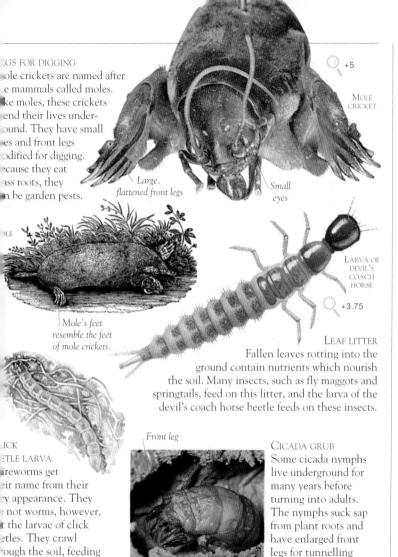

LEGS FOR DIGGING

Mole crickets are named after the mammals called moles. Like moles, these crickets spend their lives underground. They have small eyes and front legs modified for digging. Because they eat grass roots, they can be garden pests.

+5

MOLE
CRICKET

Large,
flattened front legs

Small
eyes

MOLE

Mole's feet
resemble the feet
of mole crickets.

LARVA OF
DEVIL'S
COACH
HORSE

+3.75

LEAF LITTER

Fallen leaves rotting into the ground contain nutrients which nourish the soil. Many insects, such as fly maggots and springtails, feed on this litter, and the larva of the devil's coach horse beetle feeds on these insects.

CLICK
BEETLE LARVA

Wireworms get their name from their wiry appearance. They are not worms, however, but the larvae of click beetles. They crawl through the soil, feeding on the roots of plants.

Front leg

CICADA GRUB

Some cicada nymphs live underground for many years before turning into adults. The nymphs suck sap from plant roots and have enlarged front legs for tunnelling through the soil.

131

INSECTS

TOWNS AND GARDENS

SINCE INSECTS HAVE managed to make homes for themselves in practically every natural habitat, it is n surprising that they have turned human habitats into their homes, too. Insects live in our houses, feeding c our furniture, clothes, food-stores, and rubbish dump: Our gardens and farms are also teeming with insect life nourished by the abundance of flowers and vegetables.

Colorado beetle

—1.75

POTATO PESTS
When potatoes were brought to Europe from South America, the Colorado beetle came with them. This insect eats potato plant leaves, and can cause great damage to crops.

CABBAGE EATERS
Cabbage white butterflies lay eggs on cabbage plants so the larvae can eat the leaves. Farm provide acres of cabbage and the butterflies become pests since they breed at an unnaturally high rate because of the abundance of food.

Leaves of potato plant

Potato

132

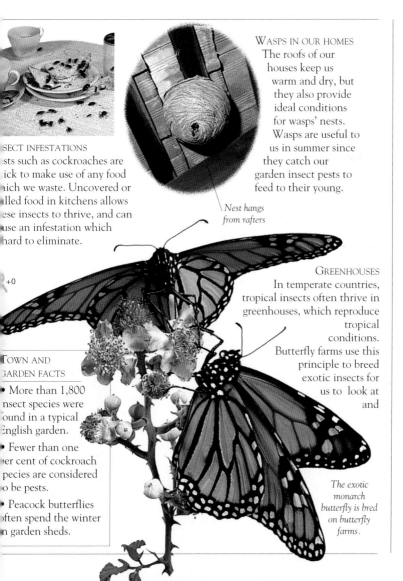

WASPS IN OUR HOMES
The roofs of our houses keep us warm and dry, but they also provide ideal conditions for wasps' nests. Wasps are useful to us in summer since they catch our garden insect pests to feed to their young.

Nest hangs from rafters

...SECT INFESTATIONS
...sts such as cockroaches are ...ick to make use of any food ...hich we waste. Uncovered or ...illed food in kitchens allows ...ese insects to thrive, and can ...use an infestation which ...hard to eliminate.

+0

GREENHOUSES
In temperate countries, tropical insects often thrive in greenhouses, which reproduce tropical conditions. Butterfly farms use this principle to breed exotic insects for us to look at and

TOWN AND GARDEN FACTS

• More than 1,800 insect species were found in a typical English garden.

• Fewer than one per cent of cockroach species are considered to be pests.

• Peacock butterflies often spend the winter in garden sheds.

The exotic monarch butterfly is bred on butterfly farms.

133

HOUSEHOLD INSECTS

SINCE PREHISTORIC times, insects have lived in huma
homes, attracted by warmth, shelter, and food. These
insects eat our food, our furniture, and some even ea
our carpets. Parasitic insects also live in our homes,
feeding on the human inhabitants.

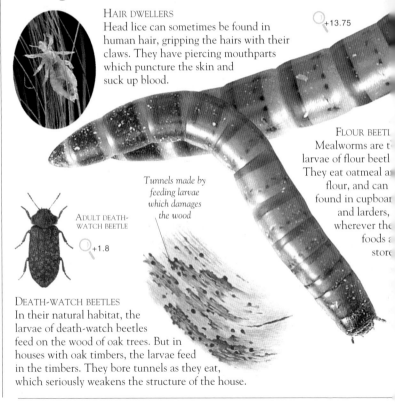

HAIR DWELLERS
Head lice can sometimes be found in
human hair, gripping the hairs with their
claws. They have piercing mouthparts
which puncture the skin and
suck up blood.

+13.75

FLOUR BEETL
Mealworms are t
larvae of flour beetl
They eat oatmeal a
flour, and can
found in cupboar
and larders,
wherever th
foods a
stor

*Tunnels made by
feeding larvae
which damages
the wood*

ADULT DEATH-
WATCH BEETLE

+1.8

DEATH-WATCH BEETLES
In their natural habitat, the
larvae of death-watch beetles
feed on the wood of oak trees. But in
houses with oak timbers, the larvae feed
in the timbers. They bore tunnels as they eat,
which seriously weakens the structure of the house.

e mealworm has
a segmented
oskeleton which
es it flexibility.

CARPET
EATERS
The larvae of
carpet beetles, called
woolly bears, eat wool.
They can be pests since
they chew holes in
costly woollen carpets.

BED
BUGS

BED BUGS
Prehistoric humans shared their
caves with bats and birds, in whose
nests were blood-sucking bugs.
Some of these, including bed bugs,
developed a taste for human blood,
and have been with us ever since.

IES IN OUR HOME
ouseflies can be found
most households
roughout the world.
he larvae, called
aggots, feed on our
bbish and food.
dult houseflies
ed on food we
ave uncovered.
his can be harmful
ecause houseflies
rry diseases on
eir feet.

*Houseflies
taste food with
their feet.*

+5

*Sponge-like
mouthparts
soak up food*

135

GARDEN INSECTS

A GARDEN IS a good place to watch and study insects. Many different insects are attracted into gardens to feed on the flowers, vegetables, and other plants. Some predatory insects come to eat the plant-eating insects. But most garden insects are just tourists, feeding on flower nectar as they pass through.

DEVIL BEETLES
Devil's coach horse beetles hunt at night, scouring the garden for insects to eat. These large beetles are common in compost heaps, scurrying away from the daylight when the compost is turned.

+3.1

GARDENER'S FRIENDS
Hoverflies hover in front of flowers on hot, sunny days as they feed on nectar. They are particularly attracted to thistle flowers. Hoverfly larvae are the gardener's friends, feeding voraciously on plant-damaging aphids.

+3.75

Eye

Antenna

WK-MOTH

e caterpillars of
wk-moths can be
ognized by their
ort, erect "tail". Most
ilt hawk-moths fly at
ht, hovering in front of
wers to gather nectar with
eir long tongues.

SILVER-STRIPED HAWK-
MOTH CATERPILLAR

"Tail"

+0

Eyespot

*Caterpillar has
eyespots to frighten
off predators*

*Fuchsia
flower*

ARDEN GRASSHOPPER

ie common field grasshopper is widespread in
rope on short grass in sunny places, and often
ds a home in gardens. Like tropical locusts,
mmon field grasshoppers sometimes develop
arms, but on a much smaller scale.

RED
ADMIRAL

−.4

*Butterflies
often stop to
sunbathe for
a while.*

OD FOR BUTTERFLIES

e flower border of a garden is like a filling
tion for passing butterflies. They feed on
ctar to give them energy as they search for
table plants on which to lay eggs.

PEACOCK

SILVER-SPOTTED
SKIPPER

−.4

−.75

FRIENDS AND FOES

THE RELATIONSHIP between insects and humans is not always a good one. Many insects are useful to us, although others are pests. We enjoy seeing wild animals but we destroy their habitats. This kills insects that other animals need as food. Ecology is about understanding the balance between our needs and the needs of other animals and plants.

Aphids drink the rose's sap. This eventually kills the rose, because the sap is like the plant's blood.

APHIDS
Aphids are major pests of our food plants and flowers. Some aphid species are common on roses, while others carry diseases which ruin potatoes and strawberries, as well as many other food crops.

Intricate pattern of veins in wings

138

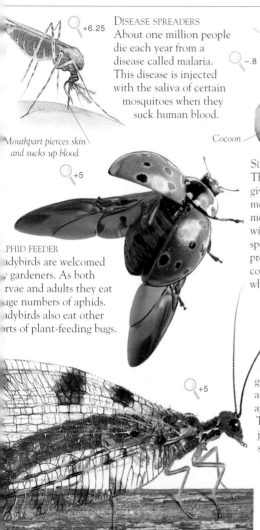

DISEASE SPREADERS
About one million people die each year from a disease called malaria. This disease is injected with the saliva of certain mosquitoes when they suck human blood.

Moth

Mouthpart pierces skin and sucks up blood

+6.25

−.8

Cocoon

+5

SILK PROVIDERS
The silk we use in clothes is given to us by silk-worm moth caterpillars. Silk-worm moths no longer occur in the wild. Instead, they are bred in special farms. The caterpillars produce the silk to form cocoons which protect them when they pupate.

APHID FEEDER
Ladybirds are welcomed by gardeners. As both larvae and adults they eat huge numbers of aphids. Ladybirds also eat other sorts of plant-feeding bugs.

PEST EATERS
Lacewings are delicate insects, often with shining golden eyes. Their larvae are voracious predators of aphids and other plant lice. They have long, tubular jaws through which they suck the body contents of their prey. Lacewing larvae hide themselves from predators by sticking the remains of their prey onto small hairs on their backs.

+5

139

BEES AND POLLINATION

BEES AND PLANTS depend on each other.
Plants need bees to carry pollen
between flowers to produce seeds.
Bees collect pollen and nectar
from flowers to feed their larva
Nectar in a hive is made into
honey for winter food.

BEE-KEEPING
For thousands of years people have
kept bees for their honey. Modern hives
have racks of frames, each with a ready-made
comb of cells. Individual frames can be
removed and the honey drained.

POLLINATION
Other insects, such as butterflies, also
pollinate flowers. Many flowers are a
special colour or shape to attract
particular insects. These insects
receive pollen and nectar in
exchange for their work in
carrying pollen to
another flower.

+2.5

+7.5

POLLEN BASKETS
Bees carry pollen back to their hive in special pollen baskets on their back legs. The baskets are made from curved bristles. A bee uses its front legs to comb pollen dust from its furry body and put it in the baskets.

Shape of dance shows bees direction of flowers

BEE COMMUNICATION
When a bee finds flowers with nectar it tells other bees in the hive by dancing. The bee conveys the distance of the flowers by how fast it shakes its abdomen, and the direction by the angle of its dance.

Pollen basket

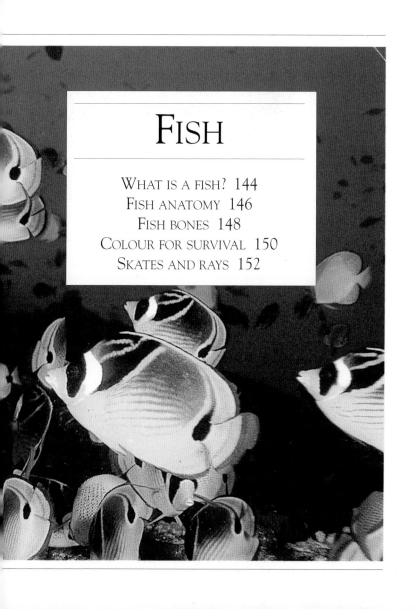

FISH

FISH

WHAT IS A FISH?

THE FIRST FISH appeared in the seas 470 million years ago. Today, more than 20,000 species have been discovered. Fish live in water, breathe through gills, have a scaly body, and manoeuvre themselves using fins. All fish are vertebrates, which means that they have a backbone or similar structure, and an internal skeleton. The three main fish groups are bony fish, cartilaginous fish, and jawless fish.

Caudal fin or tail for stabilizing fish

Lateral line helps fish feel vibrations

BONY FISH FINS
Most bony fish have a dorsal fin, paired pectoral and pelvic fins, and a tail for movement. In some fish, fins have become specialized as lifting foils, walking legs, suckers for holding on, or poisoned spines for protection.

Anal fin

Pelvic fin for manoeuvring

WHALE SHARK

CARTILAGINOUS FISH
Sharks are cartilaginous fish, which means that they have skeletons made of extremely hard cartilage, not bone. The world's biggest fish is the whale shark, which grows to 15 m (49 ft) in length.

144

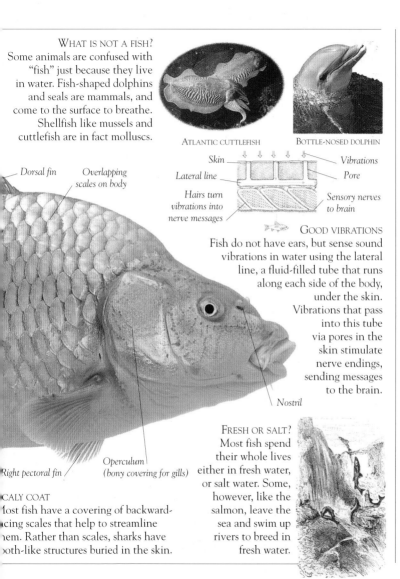

WHAT IS NOT A FISH?
Some animals are confused with "fish" just because they live in water. Fish-shaped dolphins and seals are mammals, and come to the surface to breathe. Shellfish like mussels and cuttlefish are in fact molluscs.

ATLANTIC CUTTLEFISH

BOTTLE-NOSED DOLPHIN

Skin — Vibrations
Lateral line — Pore
Hairs turn vibrations into nerve messages — Sensory nerves to brain

GOOD VIBRATIONS
Fish do not have ears, but sense sound vibrations in water using the lateral line, a fluid-filled tube that runs along each side of the body, under the skin. Vibrations that pass into this tube via pores in the skin stimulate nerve endings, sending messages to the brain.

Dorsal fin

Overlapping scales on body

Nostril

Right pectoral fin

Operculum
(bony covering for gills)

CALY COAT
Most fish have a covering of backward-facing scales that help to streamline them. Rather than scales, sharks have tooth-like structures buried in the skin.

FRESH OR SALT?
Most fish spend their whole lives either in fresh water, or salt water. Some, however, like the salmon, leave the sea and swim up rivers to breed in fresh water.

145

FISH ANATOMY

FISH HAVE MANY of the same internal organs found in reptiles, birds, and mammals, such as a heart, brain, lungs, and liver. However, in order to live and "breathe" underwater, a fish also needs some unique body parts.

BREATHING AND GILLS
Fish "breathe" in water using their gills. Oxygen passes from the water through the thin gill membranes into the fish's blood, and is then distributed around the body, to power the muscles.

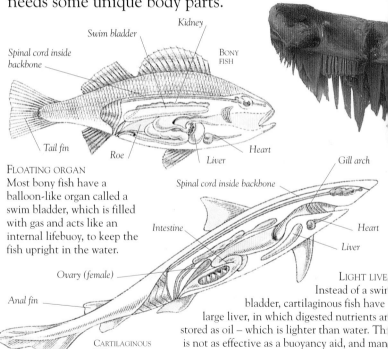

Swim bladder

Kidney

Spinal cord inside backbone

BONY FISH

Tail fin

Roe

Liver

Heart

Gill arch

FLOATING ORGAN
Most bony fish have a balloon-like organ called a swim bladder, which is filled with gas and acts like an internal lifebuoy, to keep the fish upright in the water.

Spinal cord inside backbone

Intestine

Heart

Liver

Ovary (female)

Anal fin

CARTILAGINOUS FISH

LIGHT LIVE
Instead of a swir bladder, cartilaginous fish have large liver, in which digested nutrients ar stored as oil – which is lighter than water. Th is not as effective as a buoyancy aid, and man sharks need to keep moving, or they will sink

Stiff gill rakers sieve
clean water
passing over gills

Gill filaments, through
which oxygen in the water
passes into the
fish's blood

Bony support
of gill arch

TUNA FISH GILL

WATER FLOW
To obtain oxygen, the fish takes
in a mouthful of water, while
the gill cover shuts flat to stop
water escaping. The fish then
closes its mouth, forcing the water
inside to flow past the gills. On
its way out, the water pushes
open the flap-like gill cover.

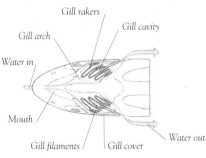

Gill rakers

Gill cavity

Gill arch

Water in

Mouth

Gill filaments

Gill cover

Water out

147

FISH BONES

ALL FISH HAVE internal skeletons.
Sharks and rays have skeletons
made of cartilage, but most
fish have skeletons
made of bone (bony
fish or teleosts).

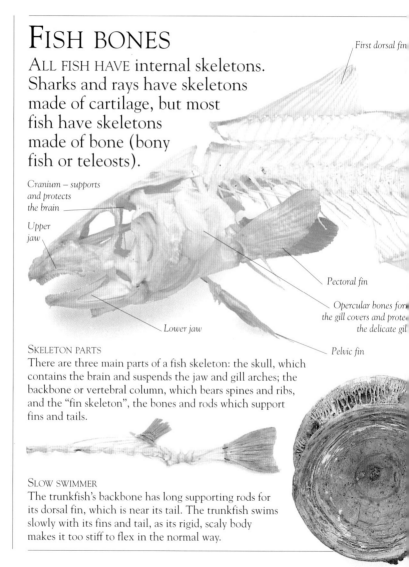

First dorsal fin

*Cranium – supports
and protects
the brain*

*Upper
jaw*

Pectoral fin

*Opercular bones form
the gill covers and protect
the delicate gill*

Lower jaw

Pelvic fin

SKELETON PARTS

There are three main parts of a fish skeleton: the skull, which
contains the brain and suspends the jaw and gill arches; the
backbone or vertebral column, which bears spines and ribs,
and the "fin skeleton", the bones and rods which support
fins and tails.

SLOW SWIMMER

The trunkfish's backbone has long supporting rods for
its dorsal fin, which is near its tail. The trunkfish swims
slowly with its fins and tail, as its rigid, scaly body
makes it too stiff to flex in the normal way.

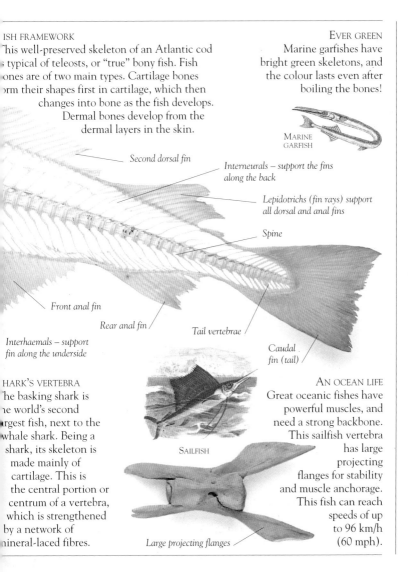

FISH FRAMEWORK

This well-preserved skeleton of an Atlantic cod is typical of teleosts, or "true" bony fish. Fish bones are of two main types. Cartilage bones form their shapes first in cartilage, which then changes into bone as the fish develops. Dermal bones develop from the dermal layers in the skin.

EVER GREEN
Marine garfishes have bright green skeletons, and the colour lasts even after boiling the bones!

MARINE GARFISH

Second dorsal fin

Interneurals – support the fins along the back

Lepidotrichs (fin rays) support all dorsal and anal fins

Spine

Front anal fin

Rear anal fin

Tail vertebrae

Caudal fin (tail)

Interhaemals – support fin along the underside

SHARK'S VERTEBRA
The basking shark is the world's second largest fish, next to the whale shark. Being a shark, its skeleton is made mainly of cartilage. This is the central portion or centrum of a vertebra, which is strengthened by a network of mineral-laced fibres.

SAILFISH

AN OCEAN LIFE
Great oceanic fishes have powerful muscles, and need a strong backbone. This sailfish vertebra has large projecting flanges for stability and muscle anchorage. This fish can reach speeds of up to 96 km/h (60 mph).

Large projecting flanges

149

COLOUR FOR SURVIVAL

MANY FISH USE colour for survival tactics, and have evolved almost every imaginable hue and pattern, for various reasons. Colour is an excellent means of camouflage or defence, or of advertising a territory, whether it be in the open sea, in rivers or lakes, or on a coral reef.

Barbels for finding way in muddy water

CLOWN LOACH

HIDING IN SHADOWS
The clown loach's dark stripes camouflage it in plants at the bottom of lakes.

Long, thin mouth for nibbling in crevices

False eyespot

FORCEPS FISH

NOW YOU SEE IT...
The forceps fish has a false eyespot near its tail base, so that when a predator tries to attack its "head", it is able to swim away.

FRENCH ANGELFISH

Eye hidden in a stripe

ZEBRA PIPEFISH

A COLOURFUL ANGEL
As this young French angelfish grows older, the four vertical bars on its body will deepen to a bright yellow, and the rest of its body colour will deepen.

Eye hidden by head stripe

Eyespot

LOTS TO LOOK AT
The threadfin butterfly fish, which lives in warm Australian seas, is a highly patterned and coloured fish. It has a white mustard-lined forehead, zig-zags on the front half of the body, and a false eyespot on the rear of the dorsal fin.

THREADFIN
BUTTERFLY FISH

DIRTY DEALER
Scattered darker scales on the Cuban hock's body and fins give it a slightly "dirty" appearance, aiding camouflage.

CUBAN
HOCK

CLOWN
TRIGGERFISH

REGAL
TANG

CONFUSING CLOWN
The contrasting patterns of the clown triggerfish confuse predators, making it less likely to be attacked.

INTO THE BLUE
The regal tang starts life mostly yellow, but turns blue gradually.

BLUE-RINGED
ANGELFISH

STRIPY CAMOUFLAGE
The zebra pipefish hides horizontally in the stems of waterweed. Its stripes blend in with the weed, disguising it from predators.

LOOK AT ME!
The electric-blue bands of this blue-ringed angelfish give a strong visual signal to members of the same species.

SKATES AND RAYS

IT IS HARD TO BELIEVE that flat, slow-moving skates and rays, which live on the bed of the sea, are related to fast, streamlined sharks. However, the anatomy of rays and sharks is very similar: for example, both have cartilaginous skeletons, and up to seven gill slits.

Underside is pale in colour, while upper surface is camouflaged

SEABED FEEDER
Rays feed mainly on sand-living creatures, so their mouths are on the underside of their bodies. There is a hole called a spiracle on the upper side through which clean water for breathing is taken in and passed over the gills.

MOLLUSCS
Rays feed on hard-shelled animals, such as sea snails, that live in the sand.

Grinding teeth crush the armour of prey

POISON GLAND
Some rays have sharp, saw-like stings on their tails. These are good protection against their enemies.

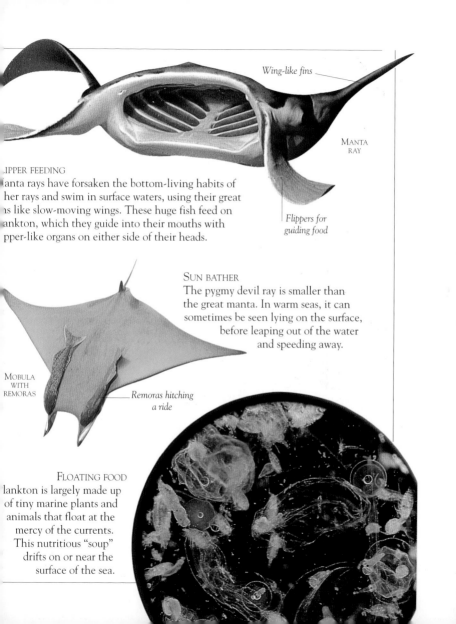

Wing-like fins

MANTA RAY

Flippers for guiding food

ƖIPPER FEEDING
Ɩanta rays have forsaken the bottom-living habits of
ƀher rays and swim in surface waters, using their great
ɲs like slow-moving wings. These huge fish feed on
ƀankton, which they guide into their mouths with
ƀpper-like organs on either side of their heads.

SUN BATHER
The pygmy devil ray is smaller than
the great manta. In warm seas, it can
sometimes be seen lying on the surface,
before leaping out of the water
and speeding away.

MOBULA
WITH
REMORAS

Remoras hitching a ride

FLOATING FOOD
Ɩlankton is largely made up
of tiny marine plants and
animals that float at the
mercy of the currents.
This nutritious "soup"
drifts on or near the
surface of the sea.

AMBHIBIANS

AMPHIBIANS

WHAT IS AN AMPHIBIAN?

AMPHIBIANS ARE DIVIDED into frogs and toads, salamanders, sirens, and the worm-like caecilians. They are vertebrates, and are cold-blooded, which means that their body temperature varies with their surroundings. Amphibians have no hair, feathers, or surface scales on their skin, and can breathe through their skin, as well as their lungs.

Smooth, slimy skin of a frog is typical

EUROPEAN
COMMON FROG

FIRE SALAMANDER

FROG FEATURES
Frogs and toads have a distinctive body shape – a large head and wide mouth, prominent eyes, no tail, and back legs longer than the front ones.

OT AMPHIBIANS
izards and snakes are
ptiles, although
ey look similar to
ome amphibians.
eptiles can be easily
istinguished by their dry, scaly skin.
ome tadpoles may look like small fish,
ut the lack of scales and body fins
hows that they are quite different.

TEGU LIZARD

Typical dry, scaly
skin of a reptile

AMPHIBIAN ODDITY
The body rings on a caecilian
make it look like a worm, but
the shark-like head and
needle-sharp teeth
show it is not!

The smooth,
damp skin of a
salamander is
typical of many
amphibians

A SPECIFIC SHAPE
Newts and salamanders have
narrower heads with smaller eyes and
mouths than frogs and toads. The body is
also longer and more lizard-shaped,
and there is always a well-developed tail.

157

EARLY AMPHIBIANS

THE FIRST AMPHIBIANS appeared some 360 million years ago. They evolved from fishes with fleshy fins that looked like legs, and had fish-like features. These amphibians may have been attracted onto land by a good food supply, and relatively few enemies to prey on them. Most amphibians had become extinct by the Triassic period, leaving only a few to evolve into modern amphibians.

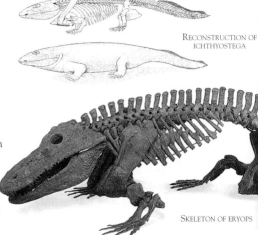

SKELETON OF ICHTHYOSTEGA

RECONSTRUCTION OF ICHTHYOSTEGA

FISH-LIKE AMPHIBIAN
Ichthyostega was an early amphibian from the Devonian period in Greenland. It had some fish-like features, but also had legs suitable for walking.

SWAMP DWELLER
This skeleton is of *Eryops*, a crocodile-like amphibian that lived in swamps in Texas, USA, about 270 million years ago. These terrestrial creatures used their strong limbs to move around.

SKELETON OF ERYOPS

Wide, flat skull, like modern frogs

FOSSIL SANDWICH
This fossil is the only known specimen of *Triadobatrachus*, which was found in France, dating from the Triassic period about 210 million years ago. It has a wide, flat, frog-like skull, but contains more vertebrae than modern frogs do, and also has a bony tail and short hind legs.

Short tail

KEEPING WELL
Well-preserved fossil frog skeletons like *Rana pueyoi* show how little some groups have changed in the last 25 million years.

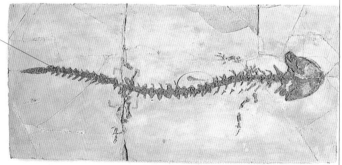

Body shape of fossil salamander is like that of modern hellbender

Short, stout legs supporting heavy body

LONG LOST RELATIVE
This fossil salamander was found in Switzerland and is about eight million years old. It is a close relative of the hellbender salamander, the only living member now found in the southeastern USA.

159

SKELETONS AND BONES

AMPHIBIANS HAVE SIMPLE SKELETONS with fewer bones than other modern vertebrates and many fewer than their fishy ancestors. This shows an evolutionary trend in amphibians – towards reducing the number of bones in the skull and vertebra (spine).

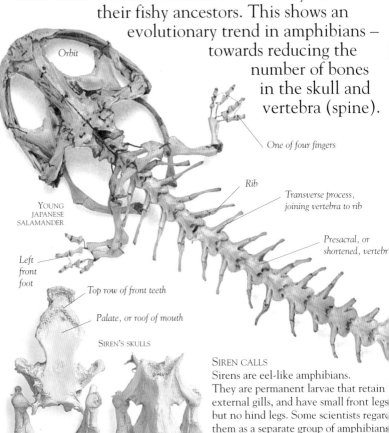

Orbit

One of four fingers

Rib

Transverse process, joining vertebra to rib

YOUNG
JAPANESE
SALAMANDER

Presacral, or shortened, vertebra

Left front foot

Top row of front teeth

Palate, or roof of mouth

SIREN'S SKULLS

SIREN CALLS
Sirens are eel-like amphibians. They are permanent larvae that retain external gills, and have small front legs but no hind legs. Some scientists regard them as a separate group of amphibians due to this combination of features.

160

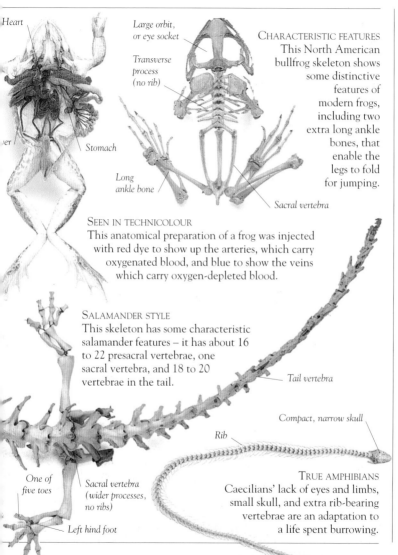

Heart

Large orbit, or eye socket

Transverse process (no rib)

er

Stomach

Long ankle bone

Sacral vertebra

CHARACTERISTIC FEATURES
This North American bullfrog skeleton shows some distinctive features of modern frogs, including two extra long ankle bones, that enable the legs to fold for jumping.

SEEN IN TECHNICOLOUR
This anatomical preparation of a frog was injected with red dye to show up the arteries, which carry oxygenated blood, and blue to show the veins which carry oxygen-depleted blood.

SALAMANDER STYLE
This skeleton has some characteristic salamander features – it has about 16 to 22 presacral vertebrae, one sacral vertebra, and 18 to 20 vertebrae in the tail.

Tail vertebra

Compact, narrow skull

Rib

One of five toes

Sacral vertebra (wider processes, no ribs)

Left hind foot

TRUE AMPHIBIANS
Caecilians' lack of eyes and limbs, small skull, and extra rib-bearing vertebrae are an adaptation to a life spent burrowing.

161

AMPHIBIAN SENSES

AMPHIBIANS HAVE THE FIVE basic senses of touch, taste, sight, hearing, and smell. But they can also detect ultraviolet and infrared light, and the Earth's magnetic field. Through touch, amphibians can feel temperature and pain, and respond to irritants, such as acids in the environment. As cold-blooded animal with porous skin, amphibians need to respond quickly to external changes.

AFRICAN
CLAWED TOAD

Lateral line, or plaque

Lateral line

THE PRESSURE'S ON
Aquatic frogs, newts, salamanders, sirens, and amphibian larvae have a lateral line sense system for detecting pressure changes from moving or stationary objects in the water.

PAINTED REED
FROG

RED-EYED
TREEFROG

ORIENTAL FIRE-
BELLIED TOAD

EELING HOT?

n hot or drying conditions, amphibians
ose body water by evaporation. They
ontrol their body temperature by
asking in the sun if too cold, or going
nto the shade if too hot. By tucking in
s legs, the painted reed frog reduces the
mount of body area exposed to the sun.

EYE SEE

Eye colour and pupil shape are
variable in frogs. The red-eyed treefrog
has vertical, cat-like pupils for night
vision or quick response to rapidly
changing light conditions. The fire-
bellied toad has heart-shaped pupils.

*Ear of American
bullfrog*

AMERICAN
BULLFROG
TADPOLE

LISTEN UP

Hearing is one of
the most important
senses in frogs. The size
of, and distance between,
a frog's ears are related
to the wavelength and
frequency of the sound
of the male's call.

TAILED AMPHIBIANS

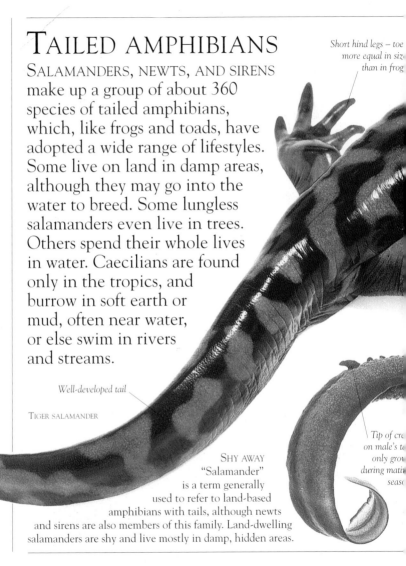

*Short hind legs – toe
more equal in size
than in frog*

SALAMANDERS, NEWTS, AND SIRENS make up a group of about 360 species of tailed amphibians, which, like frogs and toads, have adopted a wide range of lifestyles. Some live on land in damp areas, although they may go into the water to breed. Some lungless salamanders even live in trees. Others spend their whole lives in water. Caecilians are found only in the tropics, and burrow in soft earth or mud, often near water, or else swim in rivers and streams.

Well-developed tail

TIGER SALAMANDER

*Tip of cre
on male's t
only grow
during mati
seas*

SHY AWAY
"Salamander"
is a term generally
used to refer to land-based
amphibians with tails, although newts
and sirens are also members of this family. Land-dwelling
salamanders are shy and live mostly in damp, hidden areas.

longer body than
frogs and toads

One of four toes
on hind foot

One of five
toes on
hind foot

Newts are
semi-aquatic
salamanders,
that return to
the water to breed

A LIFE IN THE WATER
Sirens are distinct from
salamanders – they have
lungs as well as gills and are
permanent aquatic larvae
(they never leave the water).

LESSER SIREN

Gills

MALE GREAT
CRESTED NEWT

165

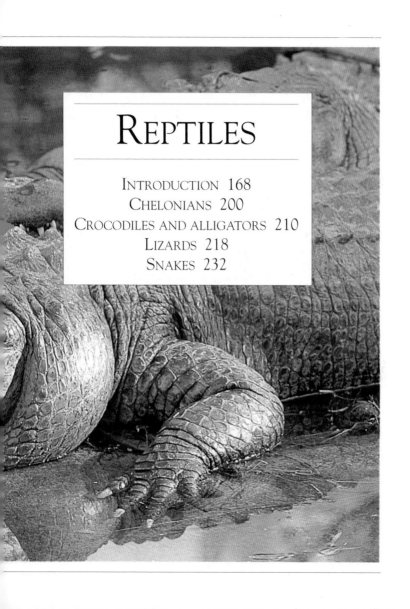

REPTILES

WHAT IS A REPTILE?

PAINTING OF MEDUSA

LIKE FISH, amphibians, birds, and mammals, reptiles are vertebrates (have backbones). But what makes them different from fish and amphibians is that they are basically land animals – they do not have to live in or keep returning to water. And unlike birds and mammals, they are cold-blooded. That is, their bodies remain at the same temperature as their surroundings.

MEDUSA
Throughout history, reptiles have been feared. Medusa, a monster from Greek mythology, had snakes for hair.

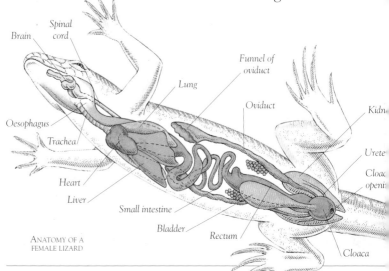

Brain

Spinal cord

Funnel of oviduct

Lung

Oviduct

Kidn

Oesophagus

Trachea

Urete

Heart

Cloac openi

Liver

Small intestine

Bladder

Rectum

Cloaca

ANATOMY OF A
FEMALE LIZARD

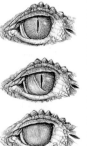

SEEN FROM THE OUTSIDE
Lizards are typical reptiles. The crested water dragon, shown below, is found in Asia. It has scaly skin that is waterproof – thus retaining moisture inside the reptile's body.

Eye

GLASSY STARE
Snakes and some lizards do not have movable eyelids. Instead the eye is covered with a transparent membrane, called the spectacle, that protects the eye from damage.

ong tail for balance

ong toes for support

Scaly skin

CRESTED WATER DRAGON

EGG LAYERS
Some reptiles produce active young, but most species lay eggs. Here a young rat-snake is hatching.

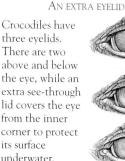

RATSNAKE

..SIDE A REPTILE
..reptile has a small ..in and a heart with three ..ambers (a human heart has ..r). The cloaca, a chamber at ..e rear of the gut, is used by ..e bladder when excreting and ..the reproductive system ..ring sexual reproduction.

AN EXTRA EYELID

Crocodiles have three eyelids. There are two above and below the eye, while an extra see-through lid covers the eye from the inner corner to protect its surface underwater.

REPTILES

REPTILE GROUPS

REPTILES FIRST APPEARED about 340 million years ago,
during the Carboniferous period (see diagram). Their
ancestors were amphibians, but the first reptiles could
breed without having to return to water. Today, four
main groups remain: turtles and tortoises (chelonians),
snakes and lizards, crocodilians,
and the tuatara.

GIANT SEA SNAKE

PALAEOPHIS
Snakes first appeared
in the late Jurassic
period. *Palaeophis* was
an ancient sea snake.

MODERN PYTHON
These vertebrae are
from a python that is
four times smaller
than *Palaeophis*.

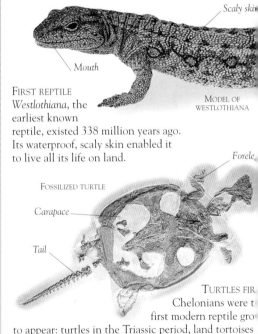

Scaly skin

Mouth

FIRST REPTILE
Westlothiana, the
earliest known
reptile, existed 338 million years ago.
Its waterproof, scaly skin enabled it
to live all its life on land.

MODEL OF
WESTLOTHIANA

FOSSILIZED TURTLE

Forele

Carapace

Tail

TURTLES FIR
Chelonians were t
first modern reptile gro
to appear: turtles in the Triassic period, land tortoises
the Cenozoic period. This fossil is 200 million years ol

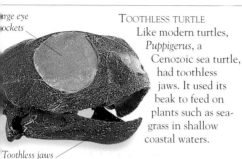

large eye sockets

Toothless jaws

Toothless turtle

Like modern turtles, *Puppigerus*, a Cenozoic sea turtle, had toothless jaws. It used its beak to feed on plants such as sea-grass in shallow coastal waters.

Semi-sprawling stance

Five-toed feet

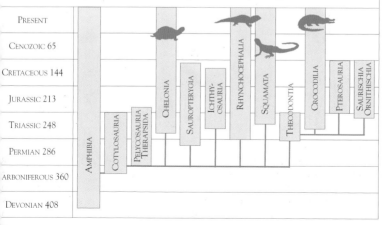

Reptile group facts

• Rhynchocephalians were common in the Triassic period. The only one left is the tuatara.

• Mammal-like reptiles appeared in the Permian period, giving rise to the first mammals in the Triassic period.

Reptile evolution

This diagram shows the evolution of reptiles. The column on the left shows when they existed and how many millions of years ago that was.

	AMPHIBIA	COTYLOSAURIA	PELYCOSAURIA THERAPSIDA	CHELONIA	SAUROPTERYGIA	ICHTHY-OSAURIA	RHYNCHOCEPHALIA	SQUAMATA	THECODONTIA	CROCODILIA	PTEROSAURIA	SAURISCHIA ORNITHISCHIA
PRESENT												
CENOZOIC 65												
CRETACEOUS 144												
JURASSIC 213												
TRIASSIC 248												
PERMIAN 286												
CARBONIFEROUS 360												
DEVONIAN 408												

PREHISTORIC REPTILES

THE FIRST REPTILES encountered no competition for the wide range of land habitats available. Over millions of years they adapted to every possible type of lifestyle and diet. Some of them even learned to fly. Others returned to living in the sea.

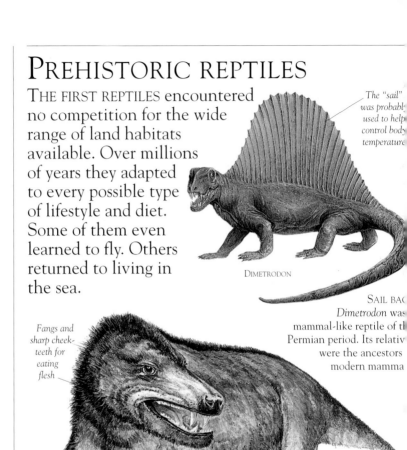

The "sail" was probabl⟨ used to help⟩ control body temperature

DIMETRODON

SAIL BAC⟨
Dimetrodon was mammal-like reptile of tl⟨ Permian period. Its relativ⟨ were the ancestors ⟨ modern mamma⟨

Fangs and sharp cheek-teeth for eating flesh

CYNOGNATHUS

Sharp claws

REPTILE DC⟨
Cynognathus liv⟨ in the early Triass⟨ period. It was abo⟨ 2 m (7 ft) long ar⟨ looked like a lar⟨ dog. Scientists ha⟨ discovered that it probably had ha⟨

BACK TO THE SEA
In the Jurassic and Cretaceous periods, some reptiles returned to living in water, but this time they chose the sea; there were invertebrates and fish to eat. Plesiosaurs had long necks and their limbs had become paddles.

REPTILE DOLPHINS
Ichthyosaurs were the most fish-like of reptiles. They were the same size – and ate the same food – as modern dolphins. Like many of today's fish, they used their tails to propel themselves and steered with their fins.

GIANT SEA LIZARDS
Mosasaurs were huge, measuring about 15 m (49 ft) in length. They preyed on fish and ammonites (a type of shellfish), crushing the shells in their powerful jaws.

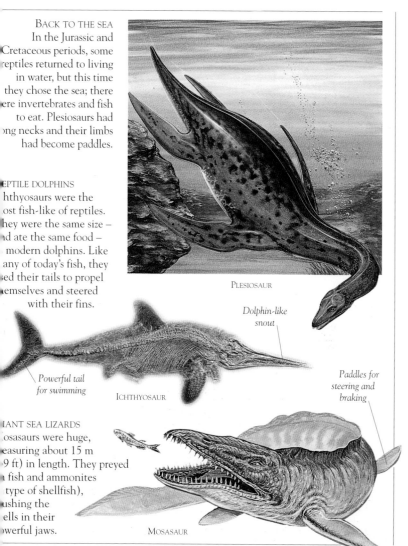

PLESIOSAUR

Dolphin-like snout

Powerful tail for swimming

ICHTHYOSAUR

Paddles for steering and braking

MOSASAUR

173

More prehistoric reptiles

During the Jurassic and Cretaceous periods reptiles ruled the land. Among these reptiles were the dinosaurs ("terrible lizards"). Some dinosaurs were gentle herbivores, others were ferocious carnivores. At the same time a number of reptiles adapted to life in the air, 100 million years before flying birds appeared.

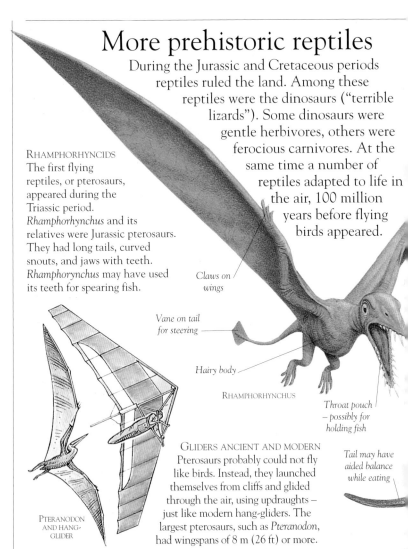

RHAMPHORHYNCIDS
The first flying reptiles, or pterosaurs, appeared during the Triassic period. *Rhamphorhynchus* and its relatives were Jurassic pterosaurs. They had long tails, curved snouts, and jaws with teeth. *Rhamphorynchus* may have used its teeth for spearing fish.

Claws on wings

Vane on tail for steering

Hairy body

RHAMPHORHYNCHUS

Throat pouch – possibly for holding fish

Tail may have aided balance while eating

PTERANODON AND HANG-GLIDER

GLIDERS ANCIENT AND MODERN
Pterosaurs probably could not fly like birds. Instead, they launched themselves from cliffs and glided through the air, using updraughts – just like modern hang-gliders. The largest pterosaurs, such as *Pteranodon*, had wingspans of 8 m (26 ft) or more.

174

Strong neck to support
the huge head

Skin stretched
between elongated
fingers and the body,
forming wings

Tyrannosaurus
moved around on its
massive hind legs

TYRANNOSAURUS

LIZARD TYRANT
Standing taller than a
giraffe and weighing about
100 tonnes (98 tons),
Tyrannosaurus was a two-
legged carnivore with teeth up
to 18 cm (7 in) long.

Tough hide
helped protect
against predators

Bony club to
deter predators

EUOPLOCEPHALUS

EUOPLOCEPHALUS
Ankylosaurs, such as *Euoplocephalus*, needed
protection from their carnivorous relatives. The
tanklike ankylosaurs developed an armoured
covering of bony plates and knobs. Some
of them had clublike tails.

GENTLE GIANTS
Brachiosaurus
and its relatives
were huge, but only
ate vegetation. Its long
neck, balanced by a
long tail, enabled it to
reach into high branches
inaccessible to other creatures.

Massive legs to
support the body's
great weight

BRACHIOSAURUS

PREHISTORIC FACTS

• *Brachiosaurus* would
have eaten 400 kg
(882 lb) of food a day.

• Large carnivorous
dinosaurs may have
been warm-blooded.

• The fastest dinosaurs
could run at up to
80 km/h (50 mph).

175

SCALY SKIN

REPTILES TYPICALLY have skins covered by overlapping, horny scales. These act as a waterproof covering and help to retain precious body moisture. In some reptiles, the scales form an armoured protection. As a reptile grows, its old skin becomes too small and starts to wear out. A new skin replaces it.

ARMOURED ALLIGATOR
Like all crocodilians, this Chinese alligator is covered in large, tough, partly ossified (turned into bone) scales. As it grows, the scales flake off and are replaced by new ones.

SECTION THROUGH SKIN

Scales

Upper layer of skin (epidermis)

Lower layer of skin (dermis)

Scales form in the epidermis. They are made mostly of keratin – the same substance found in hair and nails.

Each time a new piece is added, the oldest one falls off the end

WARNING RATTL
A rattlesnake's ratt
is made up of hollo
pieces of kerati
formed at the end
the tail. A ne
segment is adde
when the snak
sheds its skir

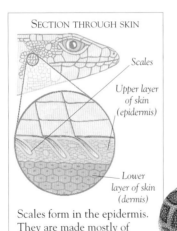
The ratt
warns o
attacker

176

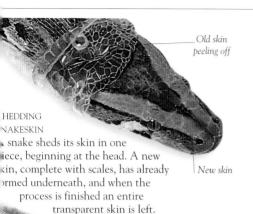

Old skin
peeling off

New skin

SHEDDING
SNAKESKIN
A snake sheds its skin in one
piece, beginning at the head. A new
skin, complete with scales, has already
formed underneath, and when the
process is finished an entire
transparent skin is left.

A SHED SNAKESKIN

SCALY SKIN FACTS

• A reptile grows
throughout its life.

• The crests and spines
sported by some lizards
are formed from scales.

• Turtle shells are
made of bony plates
covered by horny
material.

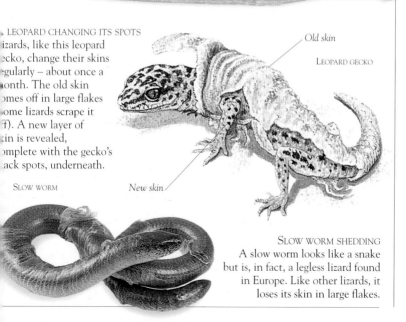

A LEOPARD CHANGING ITS SPOTS
Lizards, like this leopard
gecko, change their skins
regularly – about once a
month. The old skin
comes off in large flakes
(some lizards scrape it
off). A new layer of
skin is revealed,
complete with the gecko's
black spots, underneath.

Old skin

LEOPARD GECKO

SLOW WORM

New skin

SLOW WORM SHEDDING
A slow worm looks like a snake
but is, in fact, a legless lizard found
in Europe. Like other lizards, it
loses its skin in large flakes.

INTRODUCTION

177

COLD-BLOODED CREATURES

REPTILES ARE DESCRIBED as cold-blooded. This does not mean that their blood is always cold. But, unlike birds and mammals, they do not make their own heat by using the chemical reactions in their bodies. Instead, a reptile relies on heat from the outside, and its body temperature goes up or down according to the external temperature.

CHILLING OUT
To cool, a reptile finds shade, or angles its body to expose the smallest possible area to the sun.

Reptiles warm up by basking in the sun

COLD-BLOODED FACTS

• Scientists call "cold-blooded" animals poikilotherms or ectotherms.

• For digestion to take place, a high body temperature is needed. A snake that has just eaten may die if it is not warm enough.

AGAMA LIZARD

WARMING UP
When a reptile starts to get too cold, it warms itself by basking in the sun, presenting as much of its body as possible to the sun's rays. By moving regularly between sun and shade, a reptile is able to maintain an almost constant body temperature.

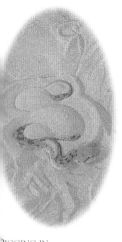

REPTILE CIRCULATION

LIZARD HEART
Most reptiles have three-chambered hearts. When blood-pressure increases, as when turtles dive, this arrangement allows oxygen-poor blood to mix with oxygen-rich blood from the lungs.

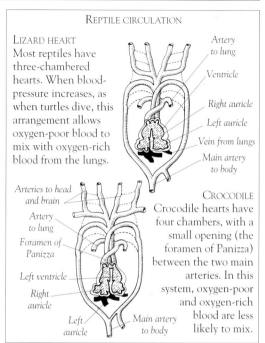

Artery to lung

Ventricle

Right auricle

Left auricle

Vein from lungs

Main artery to body

Arteries to head and brain

Artery to lung

Foramen of Panizza

Left ventricle

Right auricle

Left auricle

Main artery to body

CROCODILE
Crocodile hearts have four chambers, with a small opening (the foramen of Panizza) between the two main arteries. In this system, oxygen-poor and oxygen-rich blood are less likely to mix.

DIGGING IN
Shade is difficult to find in the desert. A sand viper solves this problem by wriggling its body down into the sand. If it did not do this it would literally fry in the heat.

Water evaporates from mouth

Like all reptiles, the crocodile cannot sweat to lose heat

OPEN-MOUTHED COOLING
One way of cooling is to let water evaporate from the body. A crocodile lies with its mouth open to let water evaporate from its mouth. American crocodiles lie in burrows when they get too hot. Other species cool down in water.

179

SENSES

MOST REPTILES have eyes
and ears. Snakes and
lizards also "taste"
their surroundings
using their tongues.
The tuatara, and
many lizards, also have a
light-sensitive organ on
their heads, which may be
important to temperature
regulation and to reproduction.

Scaly skin contai
sensors that detec
touch, pain, heat
and cold

Notched iris
with vertical slit

Heat-sensitive
pit

SLIT EYES

A gecko is mostly
active at night and its
eyes are very sensitive.
In daylight, the iris of
each eye closes to a slit,
stopping too much light
reaching the retina.
Notches in the iris
allow the animal to see.

HEAT SENSITIV

A pit viper has
heat-sensitive pit o
either side of its head
Using these it ca
follow the he
trail of a warm
blooded animal b
day or night. A p
viper can detec
temperature changes o
0.002°C (0.002°F

TEGU SENSES

A tegu lizard's well-developed eyes are designed for use in daylight and are protected by movable eyelids. Its eardrums are visible as small patches on the sides of its head, behind the jaws. Its flicking, forked tongue is used, in conjunction with its Jacobson's organ, to "taste" the air.

SWIVELLING EYES

To see without being seen, a chameleon remains perfectly still, while swivelling its eyes to see in almost any direction. The eyes swivel independently of each other.

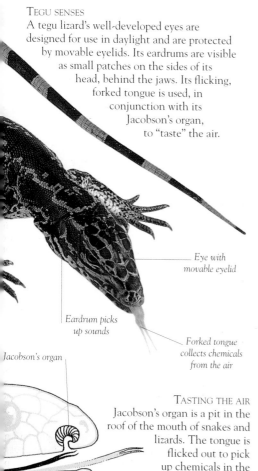

Eye with movable eyelid

Eardrum picks up sounds

Jacobson's organ

Forked tongue collects chemicals from the air

TASTING THE AIR

Jacobson's organ is a pit in the roof of the mouth of snakes and lizards. The tongue is flicked out to pick up chemicals in the air and is then inserted into the pit, where sense cells detect the nature of the chemicals.

SENSES FACTS

• A chameleon can use one eye to hunt and the other to watch out for predators.

• Most snakes "hear" by feeling vibrations through the ground; however, most lizards hear airborne sounds.

MOVEMENT

THE LEGS OF A typical reptile, such as a lizard, protrude sideways from its body. Heavier reptiles may require considerable physical effort to lift their bodies off the ground. Larger, land-based reptiles tend to move slowly, but smaller, lighter ones can be fast-moving and agile. Some reptiles, notably snakes, have dispensed with legs altogether.

GECKO

STICKY FEET
Geckos are small and light, and able to move rapidly. Pads on their feet have millions of tiny hooks that enable them to cling to smooth surfaces, even glass.

Fringe-like scales on feet

SANDFISH

SWIMMING IN SAND
A sandfish (a type of skink) has fringe-like scales on its feet to help it move on sand. It can also dive into the sand, wriggling like a snake.

SIDEWINDING
Some desert snakes move over the sand by looping their bodies sideways and moving in a series of sideways steps, known as sidewinding.

SIDEWINDER

182

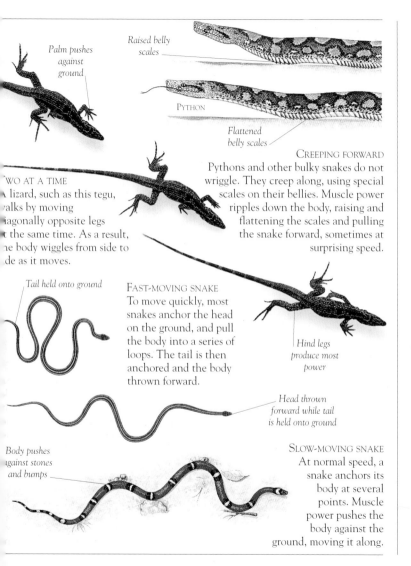

Palm pushes against ground

Raised belly scales

PYTHON

Flattened belly scales

CREEPING FORWARD
Pythons and other bulky snakes do not wriggle. They creep along, using special scales on their bellies. Muscle power ripples down the body, raising and flattening the scales and pulling the snake forward, sometimes at surprising speed.

TWO AT A TIME
A lizard, such as this tegu, walks by moving diagonally opposite legs at the same time. As a result, the body wiggles from side to side as it moves.

Tail held onto ground

FAST-MOVING SNAKE
To move quickly, most snakes anchor the head on the ground, and pull the body into a series of loops. The tail is then anchored and the body thrown forward.

Hind legs produce most power

Head thrown forward while tail is held onto ground

Body pushes against stones and bumps

SLOW-MOVING SNAKE
At normal speed, a snake anchors its body at several points. Muscle power pushes the body against the ground, moving it along.

183

Flying reptiles

Reptiles have never learned to fly like
bats or birds. The first "flying" reptiles, the
pterosaurs of the Triassic period, were gliding
animals rather
than fliers, and
the same is true of the
modern species that
have taken to the air.
Nevertheless, the ability to
glide can be very useful in
escaping quickly from predator
or simply moving swiftly from
one tree branch to the next in
the search for food.

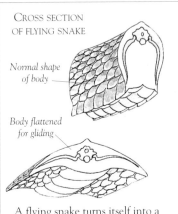

CROSS SECTION
OF FLYING SNAKE

*Normal shape
of body*

*Body flattened
for gliding*

A flying snake turns itself into a
wing by pushing out its ribs and
holding in its belly, so that the
body becomes flattened.

FLYING DRAGON
The "wings" of the flying dragon
of Southeast Asia are flaps of skin
supported by
elongated ribs.
They normally lie
folded against the
body, but can be
spread out wide
for gliding
flights.

*Six or seven pairs of
ribs support skin flaps*

*Limbs spread
out to help
steering*

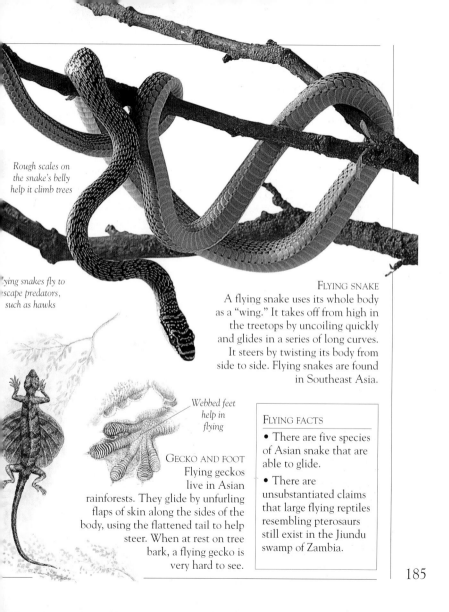

Rough scales on the snake's belly help it climb trees

Flying snakes fly to escape predators, such as hawks

FLYING SNAKE

A flying snake uses its whole body as a "wing." It takes off from high in the treetops by uncoiling quickly and glides in a series of long curves. It steers by twisting its body from side to side. Flying snakes are found in Southeast Asia.

Webbed feet help in flying

GECKO AND FOOT

Flying geckos live in Asian rainforests. They glide by unfurling flaps of skin along the sides of the body, using the flattened tail to help steer. When at rest on tree bark, a flying gecko is very hard to see.

FLYING FACTS

• There are five species of Asian snake that are able to glide.

• There are unsubstantiated claims that large flying reptiles resembling pterosaurs still exist in the Jiundu swamp of Zambia.

COURTSHIP

LIKE ALL ANIMALS, reptiles need to attract members of the opposite sex in order to reproduce. They do this in various ways: by signals, colourful displays, or eye-catching ornaments, such as frills or crests.

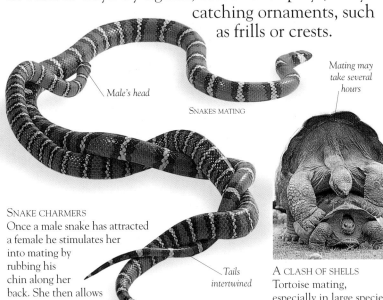

Male's head

SNAKES MATING

Mating may take several hours

SNAKE CHARMERS
Once a male snake has attracted a female he stimulates her into mating by rubbing his chin along her back. She then allows him to intertwine her body with his. Their cloacal openings meet, allowing sperm to pass from male to female.

Tails intertwined

A CLASH OF SHELLS
Tortoise mating, especially in large species such as these Galápagos tortoises, is a laborious affair. The males roar during mating.

All anoles have very long tails

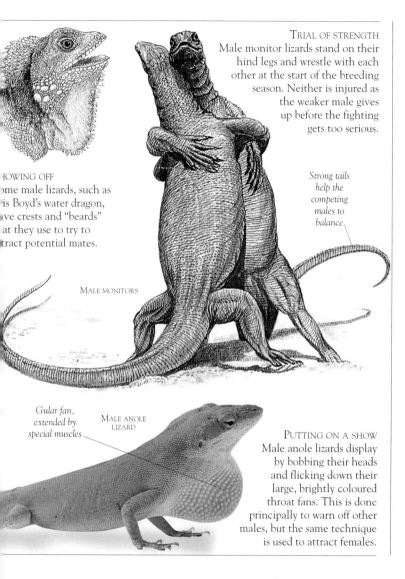

TRIAL OF STRENGTH
Male monitor lizards stand on their
hind legs and wrestle with each
other at the start of the breeding
season. Neither is injured as
the weaker male gives
up before the fighting
gets too serious.

SHOWING OFF
Some male lizards, such as
this Boyd's water dragon,
have crests and "beards"
that they use to try to
attract potential mates.

*Strong tails
help the
competing
males to
balance*

MALE MONITORS

*Gular fan,
extended by
special muscles*

MALE ANOLE
LIZARD

PUTTING ON A SHOW
Male anole lizards display
by bobbing their heads
and flicking down their
large, brightly coloured
throat fans. This is done
principally to warn off other
males, but the same technique
is used to attract females.

187

NESTS AND EGGS

ANIMALS THAT TAKE CARE of their young generally have fewer offspring than those that leave their young to fend for themselves. Some reptiles, such as the marine turtles, lay thousands of eggs, but because they abandon them only a few hatchlings reach maturity. A crocodile, on the other hand, guards not only her eggs but also her young for some time after they hatch. So a higher percentage of eggs and young survive.

ALLIGATOR NEST

ROTTEN NEST

A female American alligator builds a mound of mud and decaying vegetation, in which she lays 15 to 80 eggs. The heat produced by the rotting material incubates the eggs for two to three months.

ON GUARD

The estuarine, or saltwater crocodile of Southeast Asia and northern Australia builds a mound of leaves for her eggs. She builds her nest near water and shade so she can keep cool as she guards her offspring against predators, including lizards, herons, mongooses, turtles, and other crocodiles.

The mother uncovers the eggs when they hatch

The female covers the nest with her body

SAFE IN MOTHER'S MOUTH
After baby Nile
crocodiles have
hatched, their mother
gathers as many as she
can in her mouth and
carries them to the
safety of a pool,
making several trips
to complete the task.
She remains to
defend her offspring.

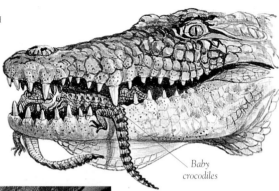

Baby
crocodiles

NO SAFETY IN NUMBERS
A marine turtle lays up to 200
eggs, burying them in a nest in
the sand. If the nest remains
undiscovered, the eggs hatch
6 to 10 weeks later, but the
hatchlings fall prey to crabs,
seabirds, and other predators
on the way to the sea.

GREEN TURTLE LAYING EGGS

LIVE BIRTH
A rattlesnake keeps her
eggs inside her body
until they hatch, which
greatly improves their
chances of survival.
Approximately 10 to 20
young are born, measuring
about 35 cm (13½ in) in
length. The mother abandons
them soon after birth.

RATTLESNAKE AND YOUNG

189

More nests and eggs

Reptile eggs have shells that retain moisture, so they can be laid on land. Most reptile eggs have soft, leathery shells, but some, such as a crocodile's, have hard shells. In most cases the eggs hatch outside the mother's body, although a few reptiles produce live young. In some cases the eggs hatch just before laying, in others the embryos obtain nourishment from their mother through a placenta.

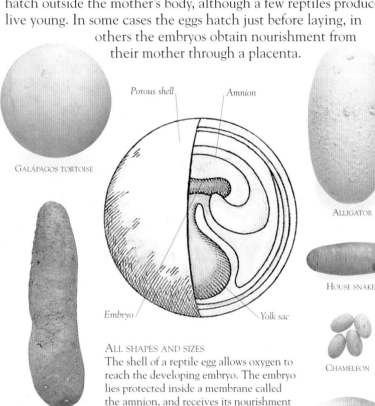

GALÁPAGOS TORTOISE

Porous shell

Amnion

ALLIGATOR

Embryo

Yolk sac

HOUSE SNAKE

CHAMELEON

PYTHON

BLOODSUCKER

ALL SHAPES AND SIZES
The shell of a reptile egg allows oxygen to reach the developing embryo. The embryo lies protected inside a membrane called the amnion, and receives its nourishment from the yolk sac. Reptile eggs vary widely in size, shape, and texture.

G TOOTH

it grows inside the egg, a young lizard
snake develops a sharp "egg tooth" on
e tip of its upper jaw. When the time
hatching arrives, the animal escapes
m the shell by using the egg tooth to
t its way out.

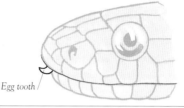

Egg tooth

HOW A SNAKE HATCHES

Just before a snake hatches, the yolk sac is drawn into the snake's body and the
remaining yolk is absorbed into its intestine. Then, using its egg tooth, the snake
cuts a slit large enough to push its head through. It may remain like this for up to
two days before finally emerging from the egg. When it is fully hatched, the
snake may be up to seven times longer
than the egg from which it came.

*The young snake checks
its surroundings.*

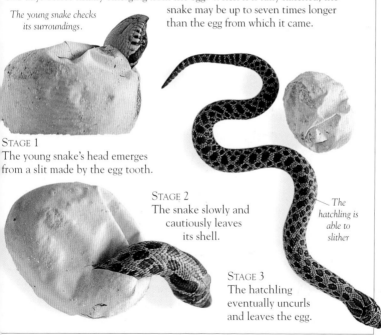

STAGE 1
The young snake's head emerges
from a slit made by the egg tooth.

STAGE 2
The snake slowly and
cautiously leaves
its shell.

*The
hatchling is
able to
slither*

STAGE 3
The hatchling
eventually uncurls
and leaves the egg.

DEADLY ENEMIES

MOST REPTILES are predators, but they are also preyed upon by other animals. Sometimes reptiles eat other reptiles. Eggs and young are especially vulnerable and in many cases adults, too, have their enemies. Even the largest and most dangerous reptiles may fall victim to human hunters.

A secretary bird either bites or tramples its reptile prey

SECRETARY BIRD
This African bird hunts tortoises, snakes, and lizards, flushing them from grass by stamping its feet. It uses its wings as a shield against venomous snakes.

The mongoose has lightning reactions

ENEMY FACTS

• When they are away from water, Nile crocodiles are vulnerable to attack by lions.

• The giant tortoises of Mauritius and Reunion Island were wiped out by hunters in the late 1700s.

Faced with a mongoose, a cobra looks fierce but its chances are slim

LEGENDARY ENEMIES
The mongoose is the only mammal that includes poisonous snakes in its diet. Although smaller than some of its prey, it is very courageous and is immune snake venom. When tackling a snake, such as a spitti cobra, it bites the head of its prey with lightning spee

SNAKE EATS SNAKE

Kingsnakes, some of which are also known as milk snakes, feed on small mammals, lizards, frogs, and other snakes. Kingsnakes, which squeeze their prey, are not afraid to tackle venomous snakes, such as copperheads.

Kingsnake

A kingsnake swallows a copperhead

Copperhead

A gull has easy pickings when a turtle nest hatches

GULL GAUNTLET

Young turtles hatch out from eggs buried high on the beach. They immediately head for the sea, but in doing so run the gauntlet of a number of predators. Seabirds, such as gulls, gather in large numbers to feast on the hatchlings, and many of them never reach the safety of the water.

HATCHLINGS AND GULL

HUMAN HUNTERS

Humans hunt reptiles for various reasons – for food, for their skins, or simply because they are poisonous. Humans have also reduced the natural habitat of many species. A combination of these factors has brought some species to extinction and made others very rare.

The cobra was pulled out of a hole

SOUTH INDIAN VILLAGERS DISPLAY A LIVE COBRA

193

BATTLE FOR SURVIVAL

SURVIVAL IN THE ANIMAL WORLD means not only being able to find something to eat, but also avoiding being eaten by other animals. Large reptiles deter predators by their sheer size, but smaller species have to use a range of strategies, including camouflage, warning colours, mimicry, and bluff.

Skin cells draw pigments from below to change skin colour

PARSON'S CHAMELEON

SLOW BUT SURE
In the branches of trees, a chameleon hides from prey and predators alike. Its movements are very slow, so as not to attract attention, and it adjusts its colouring to blend in with its surroundings.

CHANGING COLO
A chameleon does not only change colo to camouflage itself. It may also darken heat or sunlight, or to indicate a change mood – an angry chameleon turns blac

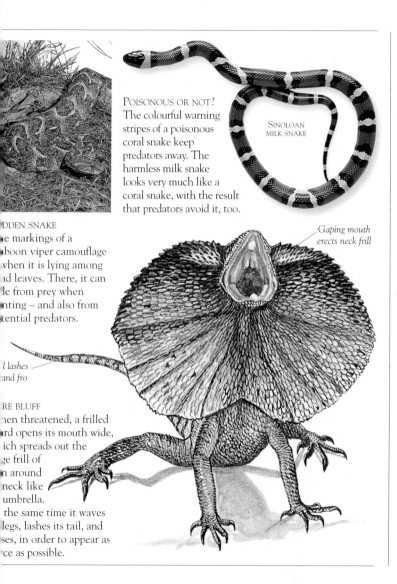

POISONOUS OR NOT?
The colourful warning stripes of a poisonous coral snake keep predators away. The harmless milk snake looks very much like a coral snake, with the result that predators avoid it, too.

SINOLOAN MILK SNAKE

DDEN SNAKE
e markings of a
boon viper camouflage
when it is lying among
d leaves. There, it can
le from prey when
nting – and also from
ential predators.

*Gaping mouth
erects neck frill*

*l lashes
and fro*

RE BLUFF
en threatened, a frilled
rd opens its mouth wide,
ich spreads out the
ge frill of
around
neck like
umbrella.
the same time it waves
legs, lashes its tail, and
ses, in order to appear as
ce as possible.

195

Defence strategies

Reptiles have evolved many ways to avoid being eaten. Small lizards often use speed to escape, and many species retreat into underground burrows or rock crevices. Some use water as a means of escape. When cornered, many lizards, particularly large ones like monitors, will turn to face their attackers. Two lizards, the Gila monster and the beaded lizard, are venomous.

*The snake l[...]
absolutely s[...]*

*The stinkpot is
very aggressive*

STINKING STINKPOT

The stinkpot turtle is the reptile equivalent of the skunk. It produces such an unpleasant smell that predators avoid it.

PLAYING DE[...]
When it cannot escape, a grass snake tu[...]
over, curls up, then lies still. It is play[...]
dead, hoping its attacker will go aw[...]

*As it loses spee[...]
basilisk drops in[...]
water and must [...]*

BASILISK

SURVIVAL FACTS

• Horned lizards squirt blood at their attackers from their eyes.

• Some skinks have a bright blue tail that attracts predators away from vital body parts.

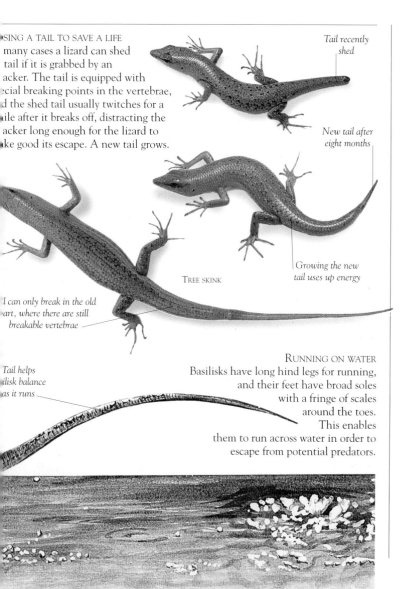

USING A TAIL TO SAVE A LIFE
In many cases a lizard can shed its tail if it is grabbed by an attacker. The tail is equipped with special breaking points in the vertebrae, and the shed tail usually twitches for a while after it breaks off, distracting the attacker long enough for the lizard to make good its escape. A new tail grows.

Tail recently shed

New tail after eight months

Growing the new tail uses up energy

TREE SKINK

Tail can only break in the old part, where there are still breakable vertebrae

Tail helps basilisk balance as it runs

RUNNING ON WATER
Basilisks have long hind legs for running, and their feet have broad soles with a fringe of scales around the toes. This enables them to run across water in order to escape from potential predators.

197

LIVING IN WATER

ALTHOUGH REPTILES EVOLVED as land animals, many species have become adapted to living in water, where food is often plentiful. For these species, swimming is more important than walking and many are equipped with paddles instead of feet. But they are still air-breathing animals and so have special adaptations enabling them to cope with a watery environment.

GOGGLE EYES
Crocodilians, like this caiman, lie submerged in the water, waiting for prey. The eyes and nostrils are placed high on the head, so that only these parts show above the water.

The spectacled caiman has a bony ridge between its eyes, resembling the frame of a pair of glasses

SNORKELLING TURTLE
The matamata turtle of Brazil waits for its prey on the river bed. It pokes its nostrils out of the water to breathe, without moving – and so avoids disturbing the fish.

Sea snakes are very poisonous

Powerful tail moves the snake forward

PADDLE TAIL
A sea snake is virtually helpless on land but is an excellent swimmer. Its tail is flattened vertically to form a powerful, oar-like paddle.

The four paddles propel the turtle

WEB-FOOTED SLIDER
Freshwater chelonians, such as terrapins, have webbed feet for swimming. The red-eared slider has a habit of sliding back into the water if disturbed.

~DDLE FEET
~marine turtle can ~erate high levels of ~bon dioxide in its blood ~d so can swim under ~ter for long periods.

199

CHELONIAN ANATOMY

CHELONIANS are reptiles whose bodies are protected by shells. The shells are made up of the plastron which protects the belly, and the carapace, which covers the back. There are between 250 and 300 species of chelonian. Some live in salt water, others in fresh water, and yet others on land. Water dwellers are usually called turtles or terrapins, while land dwellers are known as tortoises.

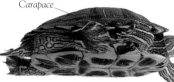

FROM THE OUTSIDE
The red-eared terrapin is a typical chelonian. It has a carapace made up of several layers. The outer layer consists of horny shields, known as scutes.

INSIDE A CHELONIAN
The internal anatomy of a chelonian is similar to that of other vertebrates. A three-chambered heart lies between a pair of lungs. The gut, bladder, and oviduct all lead to a chamber known as the cloaca (meaning "sewer").

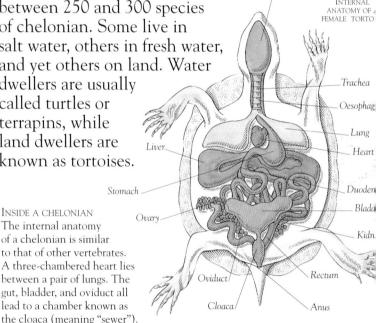

INTERNAL ANATOMY OF A FEMALE TORTOISE

Carapace

Mouth cavity

Trachea

Oesophagus

Lung

Heart

Liver

Stomach

Ovary

Duodenum

Bladder

Kidney

Oviduct

Cloaca

Rectum

Anus

USED VERTEBRAE
he carapace is made up of
out 50 bony plates formed
the skin. The shell has
outer layer of horny
ields and an inner
e of bone. The
rtebrae, with the ribs and
e two limb girdles, are fused
the carapace. This has
sulted in the limb girdles
ing inside the ribs.

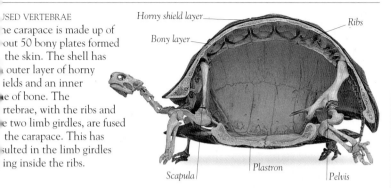

Horny shield layer

Bony layer

Ribs

Scapula

Plastron

Pelvis

SKELETON OF A TURTLE

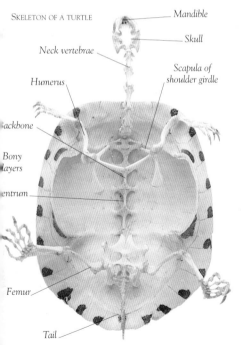

Mandible

Skull

Neck vertebrae

Scapula of
shoulder girdle

Humerus

ackbone

Bony
layers

entrum

Femur

Tail

FLEXIBLE NECK
Inside the horny outer
layer, the carapace is made
of several layers of bone.
The eight neck vertebrae
are very flexible. The
upper limb bones are
short, with enlarged ends
to take the weight of the
animal's body and shell.

CHELONIAN FACTS

• Some female turtles
produce eggs four years
after mating.

• All chelonians lay
eggs on land, even the
marine turtles.

• Some turtles can live
for more than a year
without food.

201

MARINE TURTLES

TURTLES INVADED the world's seas and oceans during the Triassic period, some 200 million years ago. Today there are seven species, six of which are grouped together in the one family, the Chelonidae. The leatherback turtle is classified by itself in another family, called the Dermochelidae.

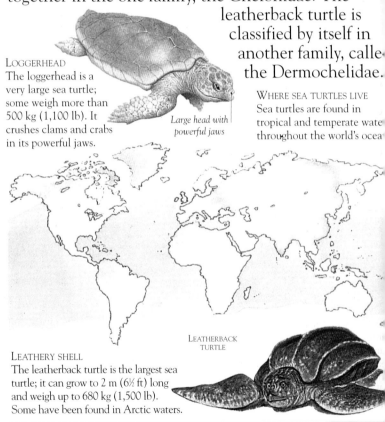

LOGGERHEAD
The loggerhead is a very large sea turtle; some weigh more than 500 kg (1,100 lb). It crushes clams and crabs in its powerful jaws.

Large head with powerful jaws

WHERE SEA TURTLES LIVE
Sea turtles are found in tropical and temperate waters throughout the world's oceans

LEATHERBACK TURTLE

LEATHERY SHELL
The leatherback turtle is the largest sea turtle; it can grow to 2 m (6½ ft) long and weigh up to 680 kg (1,500 lb). Some have been found in Arctic waters.

IMMUNE TO POISON
Hawksbill turtles are found near coral
reefs. They feed on invertebrates, such
as sponges, many of which contain
poisons. These do not affect the turtles
but may kill anyone who eats them.

NESTING TOGETHER
Ridley turtles come ashore in large
numbers to nest together on certain
beaches. Each female digs a hole in
which she lays about 100 eggs. Olive
ridleys live in the Atlantic, Indian,
and parts of the Pacific Oceans.

CHELONIAN FEET

The limbs of marine turtles are
very different to those of land and
freshwater chelonians. Land
tortoises have large, clawed feet.
Freshwater turtles have webbing
between the toes. Marine turtles
have no claws; instead, their
limbs have evolved into flippers.

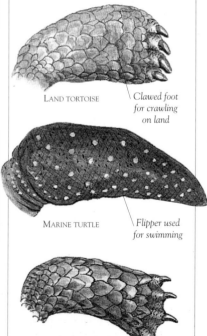

LAND TORTOISE   *Clawed foot
for crawling
on land*

MARINE TURTLE   *Flipper used
for swimming*

FRESHWATER TURTLE

203

Turtles in danger

Sea turtles are among the world's most vulnerable animals. They are relatively slow moving and easy to catch, and their nest sites are mostly well known – for example, Kemp's ridley turtles only nest on one beach in Mexico. Turtle products are much in demand, and large numbers of turtles are killed. In addition, their overall rate of reproduction is slow; although a green turtle may lay 1,000 eggs in one season, only a few survive into adulthood.

TURTLE EXPLOITATION

Turtles are large, meaty animals and in many places are hunted for food; green turtles are especially prized, particularly for turtle soup. When polished, the shell of a green turtle is a popular tourist souvenir. Pieces of turtle shell are also used in furniture-making.

END OF THE LINE
Green turtle eggs are popular as food. The nests are easy to find as the females leave an obvious trail to the nest.

GREEN TURTLE EGGS

STUFFED TURTLES

TURTLES FOR SALE
Rows of stuffed turtles provide an income for a local trader. Trade in wild turtles is banned under the provisions of international agreements on trade in endangered animal products. Some trade in specially bred animals is allowed.

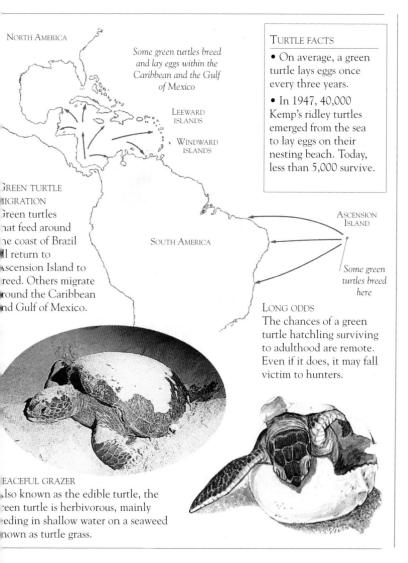

NORTH AMERICA

Some green turtles breed and lay eggs within the Caribbean and the Gulf of Mexico

LEEWARD ISLANDS

WINDWARD ISLANDS

GREEN TURTLE MIGRATION
Green turtles that feed around the coast of Brazil will return to Ascension Island to breed. Others migrate round the Caribbean and Gulf of Mexico.

SOUTH AMERICA

TURTLE FACTS

• On average, a green turtle lays eggs once every three years.

• In 1947, 40,000 Kemp's ridley turtles emerged from the sea to lay eggs on their nesting beach. Today, less than 5,000 survive.

ASCENSION ISLAND

Some green turtles breed here

LONG ODDS
The chances of a green turtle hatchling surviving to adulthood are remote. Even if it does, it may fall victim to hunters.

PEACEFUL GRAZER
Also known as the edible turtle, the green turtle is herbivorous, mainly feeding in shallow water on a seaweed known as turtle grass.

TURTLES AND TORTOISES

THE ORIGINS of the first chelonians are obscure because there is very little fossil evidence. However, i seems likely that their ancestors belonged to an early group of reptiles known as diadectomorphs that lived in swamplands. As some of them moved further onto the land, they acquired protective shells. Some ancestors of modern chelonians remained on land; others returned to the water.

Soft shell

Snorkel-like nose for breathing when underwater

SOFT KILLER
The shell of a soft-shelled turtle is covered in leathery skin instead of horny plates. Soft-shelled turtles are found in southern Asia, Africa, and North America. They live in rivers where they feed on water creatures, striking with lightning speed.

Fish being sucked in

FISH SUCKER
Disguised as a rock, the matamata turtle of South America lurks on the river bed patientl waiting for a fish to swim close by. When its prey approaches, it expands its throat and sucks the fish into its gaping mouth.

TERRAPIN HEAPS
The red-eared slider lives in ponds and rivers in the US and Central America. These terrapins like to bask on logs in the sun and may pile up several terrapins deep. The name slider comes from its habit of sliding back into the water when disturbed.

Distinctive red markings on side of head

Sharp beak for grabbing fish

Mouth contains a worm-like appendage to attract fish

TURTLE SNAPPER
The alligator snapping turtle from the US is the largest freshwater turtle; some males have carapaces measuring more than 75 cm (2½ ft) long and weigh more than 90 kg (198 lb).

BONE HEAD
The head of the big-headed turtle is too large to be retracted into the shell, and so it has a bony roof with a tough outer scute. This turtle is a skilful climber and may feed away from water.

BIG-HEADED TURTLE

207

More chelonians

Tortoises are among the most popular reptiles, being slow-moving, peaceful herbivores. Species of tortoise that have evolved in isolated places, where predators are few and competition for food is slight, may live to great ages and grow to vast sizes. Freshwater turtles are carnivorous and tend to be much more active.

RED-LEGGED TORTOISE

RED FEET
The red-legged tortoise is common in South America where it lives in rainforests. Large specimens can reach 50 cm (19½ in) in length.

PANCAKE TORTOISES
An African pancake tortoise's shell is light and flattened in shape, enabling it to move quickly and climb over rocks. It can also squeeze into small spaces when danger threatens.

PANCAKE TORTOISE

HINGE-BACK
The hinge-back tortoises of southern Africa have a hinge of cartilaginous tissue that allows the back of the shell to drop and protect the animal's rear. Hinge-backs sometimes share their burrow with lizards.

TARRED CAMOUFLAGE
he starred tortoise is found in
ndia and Sri Lanka. It is well
amouflaged; its shell blends in
ith dry grassland. Less than
5 cm (9½ in) long, it crawls
owly, at little over
2 km/h (⅛ mph).

STARRED
TORTOISE

Sturdy legs

SNAKE-NECK
The snake-necked turtles of Australia live in rivers,
where they hunt freshwater animals. However, like all
chelonians, they leave the water to lay eggs in a nest on
dry land. When threatened, they fold the head back
into the shell.

*hell may be up to
0 cm (1 ft) long*

*Neck is nearly as
long as the shell*

SNAKE-NECKED TURTLE

GALÁPAGOS
TORTOISE

ALÁPAGOS GIANT
he lumbering giant tortoises of
e Galápagos Islands weigh up to
kg (198 lb). They were
iginally present in large
umbers, but predation by
umans, dogs, and pigs, plus
mpetition for food with
ats, have brought about a
vere decline in numbers.

209

CROCODILE ANATOMY

CROCODILES AND ALLIGATORS are the only remaining group of archosaurs, or "ruling reptiles" – the group to which the dinosaurs belonged. They are large animals with an armoured skin that covers the whole body. Apart from the estuarine crocodile, they are found near the shores of freshwater rivers and lakes in warm regions of the world.

CROCODILE-
BONE
FIGURINE

Powerful tail

CROCODILE BONE
Animal bones have often been used to make ornaments. This Egyptian figurine was carved from a crocodile bone.

NILE CROCODILE
The Nile crocodile is found in many parts of Africa, although its range has been much reduced due to hunting. It often swims out to sea, and so is also found in Madagascar.

ANATOMY FACTS

• A crocodile's skin is composed of partly ossified (converted into bone) horny plates.

• Crocodilians propel themselves through the water with their powerful tails.

SKELETON
Like all crocodilians, a caiman has a long skull, with nostrils and eyes set high. The body is long with two pairs of short legs held out sideways from the body.

Hind feet with four toes

Tail vertebrae

210

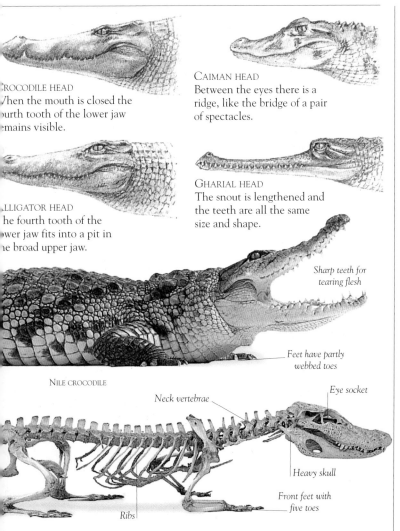

CROCODILE HEAD
When the mouth is closed the fourth tooth of the lower jaw remains visible.

ALLIGATOR HEAD
The fourth tooth of the lower jaw fits into a pit in the broad upper jaw.

CAIMAN HEAD
Between the eyes there is a ridge, like the bridge of a pair of spectacles.

GHARIAL HEAD
The snout is lengthened and the teeth are all the same size and shape.

Sharp teeth for tearing flesh

Feet have partly webbed toes

NILE CROCODILE

Neck vertebrae

Eye socket

Heavy skull

Front feet with five toes

Ribs

CROCODILES

CROCODILES ARE FOUND in many tropical parts of the world. Large species include the American crocodile, the Orinoco crocodile, the Nile crocodile, and the saltwater crocodile, all of which can grow to more than 23 ft (7 m) in length. Smaller species include the mugger of India and Sri Lanka, and the Australian crocodile.

Prominent tooth

SKULL
A crocodile's skull is almost solid bone. The jaws are long, for holding prey, but the teeth cannot slice or chew, only tear.

SALTWATER TRAVELER
Unlike other crocodiles, the estuarine, or saltwater, crocodile is never found in freshwater. It lives near coasts in the sea or in the brackish waters of estuaries. It can travel long distances.

Eye socket

CROCODILE SKULL
(TOP VIEW)

Female guards young in mouth

SHARING A MEAL

In Africa, crocodiles feed mostly on antelopes, which are seized as they come near the water to drink. However, other animals are also taken and crocodiles will feed on animals that have died, such as this zebra.

LYING IN WAIT

Even large animals, such as wildebeest, may fall victim to a crocodile attack. With a sudden rush the crocodile grabs the prey in its jaws and drags it into the water to drown.

UNLIKELY PARTNERS

As a crocodile lies with its mouth open, to keep cool, a spur-winged plover picks food from between its teeth. This looks dangerous for the bird, but the crocodile may benefit from having its teeth cleaned and the plover's cry warns the crocodile of danger.

ESTUARINE CROCODILE

CROCODILES & ALLIGATORS

213

Crocodiles

An adult crocodile swallows stones, which accumulate in its stomach. The stones do not break up food, but scientists believe that they may act as ballast, allowing the animal to remain submerged under the water.

CROCODILE SKIN

NILE CROCODILE

CRACKING EGGS
When her eggs are about to hatch, the female uncovers them. She may gently crack them to help the young emerge.

SHOES AND HANDBAGS
Formerly many wild crocodiles and alligators were hunted for their skins used for making shoes, handbags, and suitcases. Wild crocodiles are now protected, but are still illegally killed

CROCODILE FACTS

• A saltwater crocodile arrived at the Cocos Islands in the Indian Ocean, having swum 1,100 km (684 miles).

• The ancient Egyptians worshipped a crocodile-headed god named Sebek.

ESTUARINE CROCODILE

CROCODILE TEARS
The estuarine crocodile gets rid of the excess salt it swallows with its food by excreting it via the tear glands in its eyes.

THE GHARIAL

The family Gavialidae contains just one species, the gharial, or Indian gavial. The Gavialidae is thought to have arisen during the Cretaceous period, some 100 million years ago. The modern gharial has rather weak limbs and spends nearly all its life in water, using its oar-like tail for swimming. It lives in the deep waters of the Ganges, Mahanadi, and Brahmaputra Rivers of India, as well as the Koladan and Maingtha Rivers in Southeast Asia.

GHARIAL SKULL
(TOP VIEW)

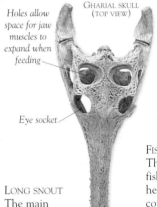

Holes allow space for jaw muscles to expand when feeding

Eye socket

Nasal opening

NO PROTECTION
For a long time, the gharial was protected from hunters because it was sacred to the Hindu god Vishnu. Today, however, it is illegally hunted for its skin.

FISH FEEDER
The gharial feeds entirely on fish. It lies in wait, moving its head from side to side to cover a large area, and catches its prey with a sudden jerk of its head.

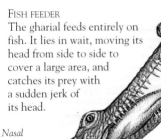

LONG SNOUT
The main characteristic of the gharial is its long snout. At the tip it widens into an oval area that bears the nostrils; in males this region is bulbous. Each jaw contains more than 50 sharp teeth.

ALLIGATORS AND CAIMANS

ALLIGATORS AND CAIMANS have shorter snouts than crocodiles, and they live solely in fresh water. There are two species of alligator, the American alligator and the rare Chinese alligator. The various species of caiman are all found in the Americas, ranging from Mexico to South America and the Caribbean.

SLOW DOWN, LIVE LONGER
Alligators are more sluggish than crocodiles. This may be why they live longer – there are records of alligators living for up to 50 years. Widespread hunting, however, severely threatens the animal's survival in the wild.

AMERICAN
ALLIGATOR

*Males roar
during breeding
season*

SKULL
An alligator's skull is shorter and broader than a crocodile's. The fearsome jaws can carry young with surprising delicacy.

HUNTED DOWN
American alligators can grow to 6 m (20 ft) in length, but because of hunting it is rare nowadays to find individuals longer than 3 m (10 ft).

216

CAIMAN

The skin on a caiman's belly is reinforced with bony plates, making it difficult for use as leather. Caimans are still hunted – to protect livestock.

Caimans can move surprisingly quickly on land

Hind foot is used to scratch body, rub eyes, and tear food

Caimans hiss when threatened

ALLIGATOR YOUNG

Alligators are 20 cm (8 in) long at hatching. They grow 30 cm (1 ft) each year, reaching maturity at six. The young are vulnerable to predators, including mammals, birds, and fish and, at any age, may be eaten by other alligators.

YOUNG ALLIGATORS

Adults feed on fish and small mammals

ALLIGATOR FACTS

• The English word "alligator" comes from the Spanish for lizard, "el largato".

• The Chinese alligator is nearly extinct. It is killed for food and to make charms and medicines.

LIZARD ANATOMY

THE FIRST LIZARDS appeared 220 million years ago, in the Triassic period. They fed on insects and looked similar to modern lizards. Typically, a lizard has a broad head, a long, slender body with limbs held out sideways, and a long tail. However, there are more specialized forms, such as chameleons and legless lizards.

ANATOMY OF A FEMALE LIZARD

Heart

Lungs

Ovary

Intestine

Opening of cloaca

INTERNAL ANATOMY
A lizard's body is symmetrically arranged both externally and internally. As in nearly all reptiles, the heart has three chambers and the gut, oviduct, and ureter empty into a common chamber, the cloaca.

UNUSUAL LIZARD
A chameleon does not have the flexible spine of most lizards. In addition, its legs are proportionately longer, and it can raise its body higher than other lizards.

Spine is less flexible than other lizards'

Prehensile tail for gripping onto branches

CHAMELEON SKELETON

Broad body with many ribs

Toes designed for grasping

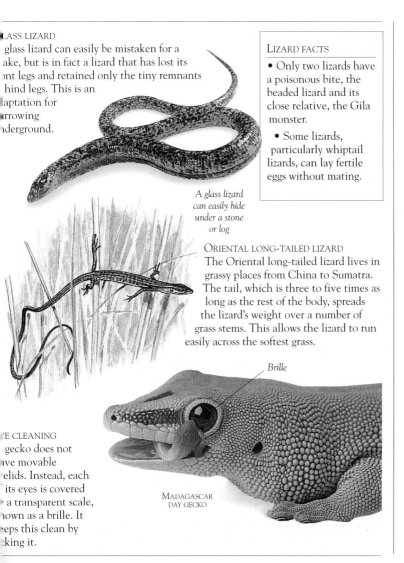

GLASS LIZARD

glass lizard can easily be mistaken for a
[sn]ake, but is in fact a lizard that has lost its
[fr]ont legs and retained only the tiny remnants
[of] hind legs. This is an
[ad]aptation for
[bu]rrowing
[un]derground.

*A glass lizard
can easily hide
under a stone
or log*

ORIENTAL LONG-TAILED LIZARD

The Oriental long-tailed lizard lives in
grassy places from China to Sumatra.
The tail, which is three to five times as
long as the rest of the body, spreads
the lizard's weight over a number of
grass stems. This allows the lizard to run
easily across the softest grass.

Brille

MADAGASCAR
DAY GECKO

[EY]E CLEANING

[A] gecko does not
[ha]ve movable
[ey]elids. Instead, each
[of] its eyes is covered
[by] a transparent scale,
[kn]own as a brille. It
[ke]eps this clean by
[li]cking it.

LIZARDS

219

HOW LIZARDS FEED

SOME LIZARDS eat almost anything; others, such as the plant-eating Galápagos iguanas, have a specialized diet. Many lizards prey on insects, and some of them also eat vegetable matter. Some species prey on other animals, such as birds, small mammals, and other lizards.

VEGETARIAN
The Galápagos land iguana feeds only on plants, particularly the fleshy leaves and fruits of the prickly pear cactus. It deals with the spines by working the food around in its mouth until they break off.

GALÁPAGOS LAND IGUANA

CHAMELEON

Insect trapped in sticky mucus

Muscular tongue is as long as the lizard's body

STICKY TONGUE
A chameleon moves very slowly and deliberately towards its potential prey. When within range, it shoots out its long, muscular tongue at incredible speed. The insect is trapped on the end of the lizard's sticky tongue and drawn into its mouth.

EYED LIZARD

CATCHING INSECTS

The eyed lizard feeds on insects, small birds, rodents, and some fruits. An insect, such as a cricket, is shaken rapidly to stun it and then passed to the back of the lizard's mouth. It is then crushed by the jaws in a series of rapid, powerful snaps.

The eyed or jewelled lizard is native to southern Europe and North Africa

NT EATER

espite its fierce appearance, the ustralian thorny devil, or moloch, ves solely on ants, which it eats in rge quantities. It obtains much of s water from dew, which condenses n its spines and runs into its mouth.

THORNY DEVIL

KOMODO DRAGON

REDATORY DRAGON

he huge Komodo dragon is a large monitor lizard und only on a few Indonesian islands, including omodo. It feeds mostly on carrion, but is capable catching and killing a small deer.

FEEDING FACTS

• The caiman lizards of South America feed almost exclusively on marsh snails.

• In crowded conditions, chameleons have been known to eat the young of their own species.

THE WORLD'S LIZARDS

BECAUSE THEY ARE COLD-BLOODED and use their
environment to maintain body temperature, lizards
prefer warm climates. Thus most species
are found in tropical and subtropical
regions. There are 14 families,
the largest of which are the skinks
(about 1000 species), the
geckos (830 species), the
iguanids (650 species), and
the agamids (300 species).

*Large toes with
hooked pads*

GECKO

MARINE IGUANA

BY THE SEA
The Galápagos
marine iguana can
often be seen sunning
itself on seashore
rocks. It feeds solely
on seaweed and is an
excellent swimmer.

HOUSE GUES
Pads on th
gecko's feet help
cling to any surfac
Geckos can often be see
hunting for insects o
walls in the tropic

MADAGASCAR
DAY GECKO

FORES
DWELL
This geck
bright green coloratic
is perfect camouflage for i
home – the forests o
Madagascar. Unlike mo
geckos, it hunts during the da

LIZARD FACTS

• Some lizards do
live in temperate
climates, for example
the common lizard and
slow worm of Britain.

• On West Indian
islands, numbers of
anoles (which belong
to the iguanids) exceed
20,000 per hectare.

THE JUNGLE
⟩me rainforest iguanas are
⟩nder animals with long toes.
⟩ales are often larger and
⟩ore brightly coloured than
⟩e females. In some cases,
the colours become
more apparent
during the
breeding season.

PLUMED BASILISK
The most spectacular
species of basilisk is the
⟩entral and South American
⟩umed basilisk, which has a
⟩il-like crest along its head and
⟩ick. The male displays its crest
⟩ring the breeding season.

PLUMED BASILISK

Long hind legs

ON WATER
Basilisks are found in
Central and South
America, near streams and
lakes. Their splayed feet and long
tails enable them to run across the
surface of the water.

⟩SERT ISLANDER
⟩e common, or
⟩en, iguana is
⟩nd in Central
⟩d South
⟩nerica and on many
⟩ribbean islands.
⟩ere are about
⟩ species of iguana.

COMMON IGUANA

223

The Agamid family

Agamids, of which there are about 300 species, are found in central, south, and Southeast Asia, Australia, and Africa. The only species found in Europe is the starred lizard, or hardun, which lives on some Greek islands, in North Africa, and in southwest Asia. Many species spend their lives in the branches of trees, but agamids have adapted to a wide range of habitats. Some species live at high altitudes; *Agama himalayama* is found on Himalayan slopes at 3,300 m (10,800 ft).

GARDEN LIZARD

BLOODSUCKER
Like a chameleon, the garden lizard, or blood-sucker, can change colour rapidly. It is found in India, Afghanistan, and China.

Large scales protect underside of jaw

BEARDED DRAGON
Some seven species of Australian lizard are known as bearded dragons because of the long, pointed scales on their throats.

BEARDED DRAGON

THORNY DEVIL

Spines provide excellent defence

HOT AND SPINY
The thorny devil, or moloch, is an Australian desert dweller. It allows its body to heat up to an almost lethal temperature so that can spend as much time as possible feeding in the open.

224

SPINY TAIL
Spring-tailed lizards tolerate very
high temperatures and are among
the hardiest lizards of the African
Sahara. They feed on plants
and insects and
survive on the
moisture they
obtain from their
food and from dew.

*Channels between
scales guide water
condensed from
the air towards
the mouth*

*"Eyebrows"
protect eyes
from twigs and
leaves*

*Spiny tail is
used for defence
and acts as a
fat store*

SPRING-TAILED
LIZARD

*Dorsal crest
of pointed
scales*

PRICKLY NECK
The pricklenape agama
lives high in the trees in
mountain forests from China
to Indonesia. Its name comes
from the long, sharp spines on
its neck. Its long toes have
fringed scales that help it
cling to branches.

PRICKLENAPE AGAMA

WATER DRAGON
The crested water dragon is an Asian
species. It lives mainly in trees that grow
near water. If disturbed on the ground,
it escapes by rearing up on its hind
legs and running off in a burst
of speed.

CRESTED
WATER
DRAGON

*Tail acts as
balance when
running*

225

REPTILES

More lizards of the world

Many lizards are specially adapted for particular environments. A chameleon's body, for example, is greatly modified for living in trees. The body is flattened from side to side, a shape that helps the reptile avoid the heat of the sun during the hottest part of the day, but absorb heat in the early morning and late evening. It also helps to camouflage the body and makes it easier to balance on the branches of trees.

CHAMELEON
Chameleons have pincer-like toes for gripping branches. The largest species, found in Madagascar, may be over 60 cm (2 ft) in length.

JEWEL OF THE TREES
The emerald tree skink of Indonesia is a typical member of the skink family. Its long slender body is designed for scuttling rapidly among tree branches.

Long tail helps balance

EMERALD TREE SKINK

Coloration makes skink hard to see among trees

THREE HORNS
Jackson's chameleon is found around Mt Kenya in Africa. Males have horns or crests on their heads and use them for combat and defence.

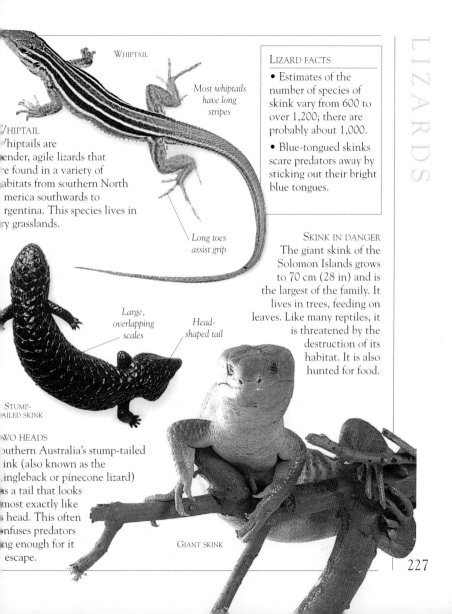

WHIPTAIL

Most whiptails have long stripes

WHIPTAIL
Whiptails are slender, agile lizards that are found in a variety of habitats from southern North America southwards to Argentina. This species lives in dry grasslands.

Long toes assist grip

LIZARD FACTS
• Estimates of the number of species of skink vary from 600 to over 1,200; there are probably about 1,000.

• Blue-tongued skinks scare predators away by sticking out their bright blue tongues.

SKINK IN DANGER
The giant skink of the Solomon Islands grows to 70 cm (28 in) and is the largest of the family. It lives in trees, feeding on leaves. Like many reptiles, it is threatened by the destruction of its habitat. It is also hunted for food.

Large, overlapping scales

Head-shaped tail

STUMP-TAILED SKINK

TWO HEADS
Southern Australia's stump-tailed skink (also known as the shingleback or pinecone lizard) has a tail that looks almost exactly like its head. This often confuses predators long enough for it to escape.

GIANT SKINK

227

Lizard protection

For a small animal that lives in the open, a scaly skin affords only limited protection, and so some lizards have additional protective features. Girdle-tailed lizards and their relatives are well armoured, and the armadillo lizard makes good defensive use of its spines. Beaded lizards, such as the Gila monster, defend themselves with poison, while monitor lizards are protected by their sheer size.

Hissing warns off an attacker

ON GUARD
Gould's monitor uses it tail as a third hind leg to threaten an attacker or simply raise itself up and survey its surroundings. Monitors include a number of large lizards, and 20 of the 30 known species are Australian.

GOULD'S MONITOR

Male is brigh coloured dur the breedin season

Thick scales protect body

Food consists mostly of insects, with some plant material

STUCK FAST
The flat lizards of southern Africa live in rock crevices. When threatened, a flat lizard inflates its body, jamming it into a crevice and making it impossible fo a predator to prise out.

Female lays a few eggs in a communal nesting site

FLAT LIZARD

RMOUR PLATING

he plated lizards of Africa
ave an armoured covering
f large rectangular scales
rranged in rows down
e body.
he body is
us fairly
gid, and to
low for
xpansion after a
eal, there is a deep
eat of skin that runs
om the angle of the
w to the hind limbs.

*Thick scales
protect body*

*Food consists
of both insects
and plants*

*Inward fold
of skin*

LIZARD FACTS

• The Gila monster
feeds on birds' eggs,
birds, and young
mammals. It can eat a
third of its body weight
at one time.

• The giant girdle-
tailed lizard plugs its
burrow with its tail.

*Belly protected
by spiky head
and tail*

BALL OF PRICKLES

The African armadillo lizard has
an unusual method of defence,
reminiscent of that of an
armadillo. It curls itself up and grasps
its tail in its mouth, presenting an
attacker with a prickly problem.

ody is about
0 cm (1 ft)
ng but only
n (½ in) thick

LA MONSTER

he Gila (pronounced "heela")
onster of the southwestern US is
e of only two poisonous
ards. Its venom glands
scharge into its mouth
ar large, grooved
gs. The venom is
t injected, but seeps in
en the lizard bites.

*Pink and black
coloration warns
reptile is poisonous*

THE TUATARA

THE TUATARA LOOKS LIKE A LIZARD, but it differs from true lizards in the structure of its skeleton and skull. In fact it is the sole survivor of the rhynchocephalians, a primitive reptile group that thrived between 150 and 240 million years ago, during the Jurassic and Triassic periods.

Tuatara is Maori for "peaks on the back"

LIVING FOSSIL
The tuatara is called a living fossil because it has changed little in 200 million years. All its closest relatives died out; no one knows why the tuatara alone survived.

LONG LIFE
Male tuataras grow to about 61 cm (2 ft) long, while females are slightly shorter. Both sexes reach sexual maturity at the age of 20, and may live for another 100 years.

LIZARD ANCESTORS
Homoeosaurus, a relative of the tuatara, lived about 140 million years ago. Its ancestors probably evolved from lizards 200 million years ago.

MALE
TUATARA

Short, powerful legs for burrowing

A third, or pineal, eye under the skin may act as a thermostat or help to regulate the tuatara's "biological clock"

Crest runs down the back and tail

FEMALE TUATARA

A LONG WAIT
After mating, a female tuatara stores the male's sperm for 10–12 months before fertilization occurs. She then lays 5–15 eggs in a shallow burrow.

Teeth are fused with the jaws

KULL STRUCTURE
he tuatara's skull is ifferent to that of lizards. t resembles a crocodile's n having two bony rches at the back. Most zards have just one arch, hile in burrowing lizards nd snakes the arches ave disappeared.

Two bony arches

Tuatara has large, wedge-shaped teeth at the front

TUATARA SKULL

.AND HOME
ataras are found on a w small islands off the ast of New Zealand. ey live in burrows hich they often share h seabirds) and are ive at night, when they ne out to search for ects and earthworms. ey grow very slowly.

TUATARA FACTS

• Eggs hatch 15 months after laying – the longest incubation period of any reptile.

• A tuatara breathes very slowly, about once every seven seconds, and can hold its breath for nearly an hour.

SNAKE ANATOMY

SNAKES ARE PROBABLY descended from burrowing lizards that gradually lost their legs as they adapted to an underground life. Today's snakes do not generally live underground, but the have retained their ancestral form and found new ways of getting around.

RHINOCEROS VIPER

VENOMOUS RHINO
Like all snakes, the deadly African rhinoceros viper has a long, legless body. Its name comes from the rhino-like "horns" (actually long scales) on its nose.

SNAKE FACTS

• The longest snakes have skeletons with some 400 vertebrae.

• Snakes can probably hear only a limited range of sounds.

• Some snakes use part of the windpipe as an extra lung.

INSIDE A SNAKE
A snake's body is long ar thin, so the stomach, liver, kidneys, and ovarie are greatly elongated, as the right lung; the left lung is very small. Th intestines form a lon tube straight dow the body.

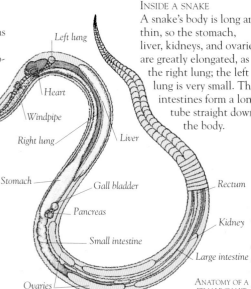

Left lung

Heart

Windpipe

Right lung

Liver

Stomach

Gall bladder

Rectum

Pancreas

Kidney

Small intestine

Large intestine

Ovaries

ANATOMY OF A
FEMALE SNAKE

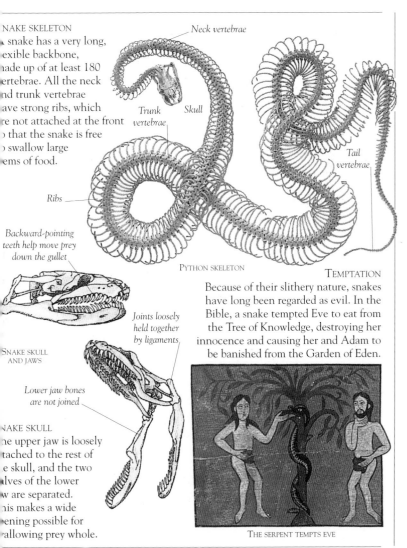

SNAKE SKELETON

A snake has a very long, flexible backbone, made up of at least 180 vertebrae. All the neck and trunk vertebrae have strong ribs, which are not attached at the front so that the snake is free to swallow large items of food.

Neck vertebrae

Trunk vertebrae

Skull

Tail vertebrae

Ribs

PYTHON SKELETON

Backward-pointing teeth help move prey down the gullet

SNAKE SKULL AND JAWS

Joints loosely held together by ligaments

Lower jaw bones are not joined

SNAKE SKULL

The upper jaw is loosely attached to the rest of the skull, and the two halves of the lower jaw are separated. This makes a wide opening possible for swallowing prey whole.

TEMPTATION

Because of their slithery nature, snakes have long been regarded as evil. In the Bible, a snake tempted Eve to eat from the Tree of Knowledge, destroying her innocence and causing her and Adam to be banished from the Garden of Eden.

THE SERPENT TEMPTS EVE

CONSTRICTORS

BOAS, PYTHONS, AND ANACONDAS are known as
constrictors – snakes that kill by wrapping prey in
their strong body coils until the animal suffocates.
Their victims are usually mammals, but
many constrictors kill birds
as well, and some are
known to prey
on other
reptiles.

*Coils tighten
each time the
rat breathes out*

BALL PYTHON

DEADLY SQUEE
This West African ba
python is killing its prey, a rat, by coilir
itself around the animal's chest ar
gradually tightening its grip. Soon, tl
rat will not be able to inhale, ar
it will die fro
suffocatio

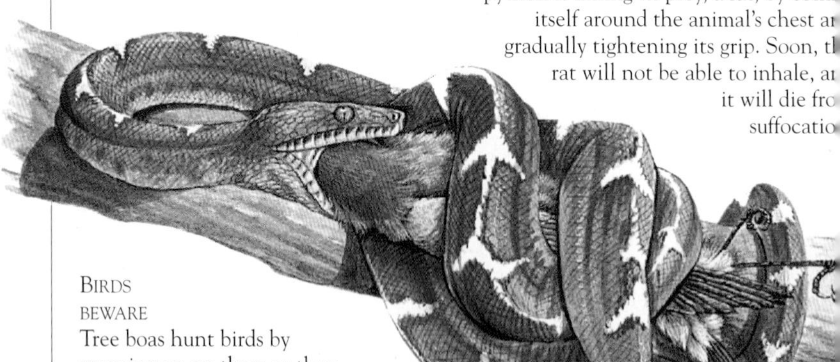

BIRDS
BEWARE
Tree boas hunt birds by
creeping up on them as they
roost in the branches of trees;
mammals are also eaten. The emerald
tree boa lives in the lush rainforests of
the Amazon basin.

EMERALD TREE BOA

234

PRIMITIVE SNAKES

Scientists call pythons, boas, and some other species "primitive" because these snakes have tiny claws where the hind legs and hips of their lizard ancestors once were. The claws lie on either side of the cloaca and are said to play a part in mating.

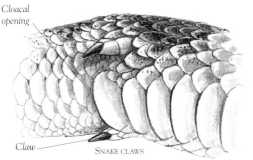

Cloacal opening

Claw

SNAKE CLAWS

HOW A CONSTRICTOR CONSUMES ITS PREY

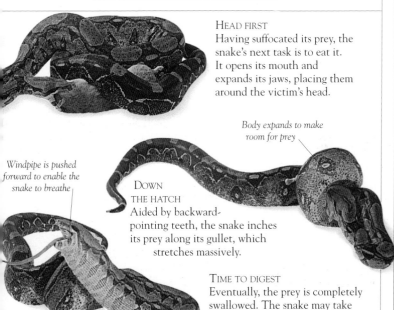

HEAD FIRST
Having suffocated its prey, the snake's next task is to eat it. It opens its mouth and expands its jaws, placing them around the victim's head.

Body expands to make room for prey

Windpipe is pushed forward to enable the snake to breathe

DOWN THE HATCH
Aided by backward-pointing teeth, the snake inches its prey along its gullet, which stretches massively.

TIME TO DIGEST
Eventually, the prey is completely swallowed. The snake may take several days to digest its meal.

Boas

All but three species of boa are found in the
tropical warmth of Central and South America.
These constrictors have adapted to a wide
variety of habitats, many spending their lives
in trees, while a number of others live on
the ground or burrow into it.

COOK'S TREE
BOA

RAINBOW COLOURS
The dazzlingly
iridescent rainbow
boa lives in the forests,
woodlands, and
grassy plains of
northwestern
South America.
It feeds on small
mammals and birds.

RAINBOW BOA

BOA CONSTRICTOR
The red-tailed boa
is one of 11
subspecies of boa
constrictor. It grows
to an average of 3 m
(10 ft) in length
(although snakes over
4 m [13 ft] have been
seen), and lives in the
semidesert plains of
northwestern Peru.

RED-TAILED BOA

COOK'S BO
Cook's tree boa is the large
of several subspecies of tre
or garden boa. It is foun
only on the Caribbea
islands of Trinida
Grenada, Carriaco
Union, and St Vincen

PACIFIC BOA

BOA FACTS

• When a rubber boa is threatened, it rolls itself into a ball, hides its head among its coils, and presents its tail towards the intruder.

• Boas do not hatch from eggs. Instead, females give birth to live young.

CUNNING IMPOSTER

The Pacific boa, native to the rainforests, marshes, and swamps of New Guinea and nearby islands, lives and hunts on the ground. To defend itself against attack, it mimics a venomous viper, hissing and striking at the intruder.

TREE OR GARDEN BOA

AGILE TREE DWELLER

The tree boa of northern South America and southern Central America, also known as the garden boa, uses its prehensile tail to cling to the branches of trees. Although not venomous, it can inflict a painful bite.

RUBBER ROBBER

The North American rubber boa lives in woodlands and meadows, where it hunts among fallen logs, in crevices, or down burrows. It also climbs trees to steal young birds from their nests. This snake looks and feels rubbery, hence its name.

RUBBER BOA

237

More constrictors

Pythons, from Australasia, Africa, and
Asia, and anacondas, from South
America, are some of the biggest
snakes in the world. But despite tales
of man-eating serpents, they are not
large enough to devour people or any
other large mammal. If a snake did eat such
a meal, it would be defenceless for at least
a week digesting it.

*Tail acts
as anchor*

D'ALBERT'S WATER PYTHON

WATER PYTHON
D'Albert's water python lives
in rainforests and swamps in
southern New Guinea and on
neighbouring islands. Its dark body
has no markings, except for some pale
areas around the mouth. It eats
mammals and birds.

LARGEST PYTHO
The reticulate
python o
Southeast Asia
well camouflage
for life on the fore
floor. It may grow t
10 m (33 ft) in length
making it the longe
snake in the world.
feeds on mammal
lizards and th
occasional snak

RETICULATED PYTHON

SHORT AND BLOODY
The blood python gets its name from its
colourful camouflage markings. It is also
known as the short python because its
tail is much shorter than those of other
species. It comes from wet places in the
central and southern Malay peninsula
and on neighbouring islands.

BLOOD PYTHON

238

HUNTED FOR ITS SKIN

The Indian python lives in a wide range of habitats, feeding on mammals, birds, and reptiles. It is now an endangered species because people have slaughtered it for its skin and destroyed much of its natural habitat.

Skin is used to make belts and shoes

INDIAN PYTHON

ANACONDAS

YELLOW ANACONDA

SWAMP SNAKE

The yellow anaconda lives in swamps and marshes and on the banks of rivers and streams in Brazil, Bolivia, Paraguay, and Argentina. At 3.5 m (11½ ft) in length, it is about half the size of the common anaconda.

RECORD HOLDER

The common anaconda is probably the world's largest snake, being heavier than its rival for the title, the reticulated python. The average adult length is about 6 m (20 ft), although individuals of over 8 m (26 ft) have been seen. It is found in Trinidad and many parts of tropical South America.

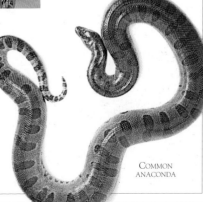

COMMON ANACONDA

REPTILES

COLUBRID SNAKES

ABOUT THREE-QUARTERS of the world's snakes – over 2,000 species – belong to the colubrid family. Some are venomous, but a large number are completely harmless. Among the harmless ones are kingsnakes, water snakes, ratsnakes, the egg-eating snake, and the grass snake.

CALIFORNI KINGSNAK

VARIABLE PATTERNS
The colours and pattern of California kingsnake vary greatly – individual may be cross-banded o have stripes runnin down the body Kingsnakes eat wide range o small animals includin venomou snake

Markings look similar to a coral snake's

CALIFORNIA MOUNTAIN KINGSNAKE

COLUBRID FACTS

• A Japanese albino form of the yellow ratsnake is considered to be an earthly form of a fertility goddess called Benzai-ten.

• Scientists call colubrids "typical" snakes.

MOUNTAIN KINGS
California mountain kingsnakes prey on small animals, including rodents, lizards, and nestling birds. When not hunting, they often hide under stones, logs, or piles of leaves. They come from the west coast of the US.

240

MILK DRINKER?

The milk snake is a species of kingsnake; there are over 17 subspecies. The name comes from the popular but totally incorrect belief that they take milk from cows. This subspecies occurs in Mexico, where it preys mostly on rodents, killing them by constriction.

Coloured bands mimic those of a poisonous coral snake

SINOLOAN MILK SNAKE

Markings resemble the patterns on an ear of corn (maize)

Iridescent colours give the sunbeam snake its name

SUNBEAM SNAKE

NIGHT HUNTER

Like boas and pythons, the Asian sunbeam snake still has the remnants of hind limbs. It lives in burrows in areas where the soil is damp and emerges at night to prey on frogs, small mammals, and other snakes.

URBAN MYTH?

The corn snake, also called the red ratsnake, is said to be common in the sewers of cities in the southeastern US. Its natural surroundings are, in fact, woodlands, where it preys on rodents, bats, birds, and lizards. A shy snake, it uses logs and tree stumps for cover.

CORN SNAKE

241

More colubrid snakes

Non-venomous colubrid snakes kill either by constriction or by overpowering and swallowing the victim. For defence, they usually rely on camouflage and the ability to escape quickly. Ratsnakes, however, defend themselves by throwing the front end of their bodies into an S-shape and vibrating their tails, while bullsnakes puff themselves up to appear more formidable.

EUROPEAN
WATER SNAKE

Markings look
like an adder's

HARMLESS VIPER
The European water snake, also called the viperine grass snake, has warning markings that resemble those of a venomous adder. It is actually completely harmless, like all other water snakes. A good swimmer, it feeds on fish and frogs.

Flower-like
patterns give
this snake its
Chinese name

MOELLENDORFF
RATSNAKE

HUNDRED FLOWER
Moellendorff's ratsnake, known poetically as the "hundred flower snake" in Chinese, comes from southeaster China, where it feeds on rodents and birds.

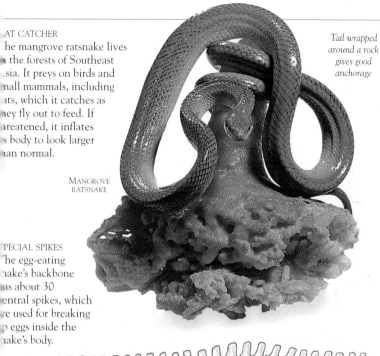

AT CATCHER

he mangrove ratsnake lives
n the forests of Southeast
sia. It preys on birds and
mall mammals, including
ats, which it catches as
hey fly out to feed. If
hreatened, it inflates
s body to look larger
han normal.

*Tail wrapped
around a rock
gives good
anchorage*

MANGROVE
RATSNAKE

PECIAL SPIKES

he egg-eating
nake's backbone
as about 30
entral spikes, which
re used for breaking
e eggs inside the
nake's body.

EGG-EATER'S SPINE   *Ventral spikes*

GG-EATER

gg-eating snakes are virtually
othless and have unusually
astic skins.
his enables
em to
allow a whole
g, which is crushed
side the body. About
minutes later, the
ake ejects the shell
mains from its mouth.

*Egg may be up to three
times the size of the
snake's mouth*

AFRICAN EGG-EATING SNAKE

243

VENOMOUS SNAKES

VENOM – a poisonous fluid produced by an animal – is widely used for killing or incapacitating prey. Snake venom, which is a very complex substance, serves two main purposes. First, the poison quickly subdues a prey animal, thus reducing the risk to the snake of injury from retaliation. At the same time, chemicals within the venom start to break down the prey's tissues, making digestion easier.

KING COBRA

FIXED FANGS
Cobras have fixed fangs at the front of the mouth, as do kraits, sea snakes, coral snakes, the taipan, and the tiger snake.

WARNING RATTLE
A rattlesnake is a typical front-fanged snake. As it opens its mouth the snake rotates its fangs forwards, ready to inject venom. This species is the most venomous snake in North America and feeds mainly on rats and rabbits.

Fangs are in forward position, ready to strike

Fangs normally lie flat inside the mouth

Rattle warns off predators

EASTERN DIAMONDBACK RATTLESNAKE

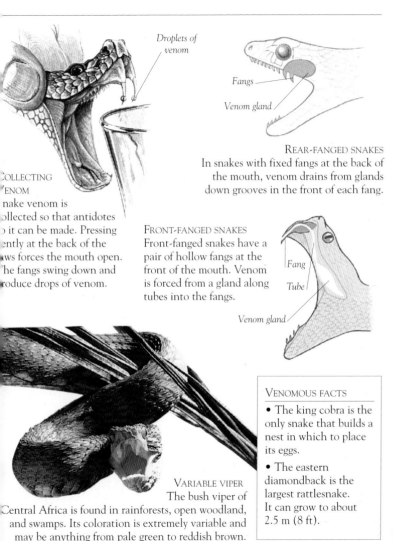

Droplets of venom

Fangs

Venom gland

REAR-FANGED SNAKES
In snakes with fixed fangs at the back of the mouth, venom drains from glands down grooves in the front of each fang.

COLLECTING VENOM
Snake venom is collected so that antidotes to it can be made. Pressing gently at the back of the jaws forces the mouth open. The fangs swing down and produce drops of venom.

FRONT-FANGED SNAKES
Front-fanged snakes have a pair of hollow fangs at the front of the mouth. Venom is forced from a gland along tubes into the fangs.

Fang

Tube

Venom gland

VARIABLE VIPER
The bush viper of Central Africa is found in rainforests, open woodland, and swamps. Its coloration is extremely variable and may be anything from pale green to reddish brown.

VENOMOUS FACTS

• The king cobra is the only snake that builds a nest in which to place its eggs.

• The eastern diamondback is the largest rattlesnake. It can grow to about 2.5 m (8 ft).

245

REAR-FANGED SNAKES

SNAKES WITH FANGS in the back of their mouth are found in both the Old and New Worlds and, as with other groups of snakes, they vary greatly in colour, size, and habitat. They are not as efficient as front-fanged snakes at injecting venom, and so most species are harmless to humans. Large rear-fanged snakes, however, can be dangerous.

CORAL MIMIC
The false coral snake preys on lizards, small mammals, and other small snakes. It is found in the forests of Central America, from Venezuela to Costa Rica.

FALSE CORAL SNAKE

Colours resemble those of a more dangerous snake

MANGROVE SNAKE
In the mangrove swamps of the Malay Peninsula this large snake – adults grow to over 2 m (6½ ft) – preys on a wide variety of small animals. The seven subspecies of mangrove snake each have a different number of yellow bands.

LIZARD HUNTER
The blunt-headed tree snake is found
in trees and shrubs from southern
Mexico to Bolivia and Paraguay. It is
active by night and feeds mostly on
lizards such as anoles and geckos.

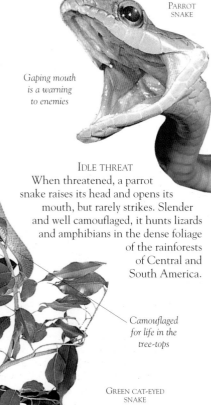

PARROT
SNAKE

*Gaping mouth
is a warning
to enemies*

BLUNT-HEADED TREE SNAKE

IDLE THREAT
When threatened, a parrot
snake raises its head and opens its
mouth, but rarely strikes. Slender
and well camouflaged, it hunts lizards
and amphibians in the dense foliage
of the rainforests
of Central and
South America.

*This snake often
feeds on eggs laid
on leaves by frogs*

AT EYES
The green cat-eyed
snake lives in the forests
of northeastern India,
where it hunts at
night for frogs,
lizards, and
small birds.

*Camouflaged
for life in the
tree-tops*

GREEN CAT-EYED
SNAKE

247

More rear-fanged snakes

The venom produced by rear-fanged snakes is just as lethal as that of front-fanged snakes, and in some cases is specific to a particular prey. For example, the venom of a snake that usually eats frogs may be more toxic to frogs than to other animals, such as mice. The venom of both the boomslang and the twigsnake has occasionally killed people.

HOG-NOSED BURROWER
The Madagascan giant hognose snake eats birds and small mammals. It shelters in rock crevices, beneath debris, or in burrows that it digs itself. It lives in grassland and grows to about 1.5 m (5 ft).

When threatened, this snake flattens its neck like a cobra and hisses loudly

MADAGASCAN GIANT HOGNOSE SNAKE

SONORAN LYRE SNAKE

REAR-FANGED FACTS

• The mussurana first constricts its prey, then injects venom into it.

• The Australasian brown tree snake, introduced into Guam, has caused the decline of many native birds.

LYRE HEAD
Lyre snakes get their name from the lyre-shaped marking on the head. They live in rocky places in California, Arizona, and Mexico, feeding on lizards, small birds, and mammals. They are nocturnal.

FROG-EATER
The night snake, also known locally as the cat-eyed snake, is found in Mexico and Central America. It spends much of its time in trees and hunts at night for frogs and lizards.

NIGHT SNAKE
EATING FROGS' EGGS

*Vine snake hangs
from a branch,
waiting for prey*

VINE CREEPER
The vine snake's camouflage allows it to creep unseen among bushes and vines. Native to bush-covered hillsides in Mexico and Arizona, it preys mainly on lizards, and occasionally on small birds and nestlings.

MEXICAN
VINE SNAKE

BOOMSLANG
The African boomslang moves with speed and grace through woodland, scrub, savannah, and swamp. It eats birds' eggs and also uses its quick-acting venom to kill small mammals, frogs, and birds. Its name is Afrikaans for "tree snake".

FRONT FANGS

FRONT-FANGED SNAKES, such as cobras, can inject venom into almost any animal, making them among the most dangerous of all reptiles. As with all venomous snakes, their venom is normally used for killing or disabling prey, but it is equally effective as a defence. However, most snakes usually prefer to escape rather than attack a predator.

HORUS
The Egyptian sky god, Horus, demonstrates his dominion over reptiles by grasping snakes and standing on a crocodile.

COBRA FACTS

• Every year, thousands of Asian cobras are killed for their skins.

• The king cobra is the world's largest venomous snake – individuals exceeding 5 m (16½ ft) in length have been recorded.

RED SPITTING COBRA

Cobra rears up
before spitting

VENOM SPITTER
A spitting cobra has a very effective method of defence. When threatened, and with no means of escape, it rears up and squirts a jet of poison into the attacker's eyes, causing severe pain and even permanent blindness.

MARK OF BUDDHA
The Asian cobra has a characteristic "eye" or "monocle" on its hood. This is said to be the fingerprint of Buddha, who blessed this snake after it had shaded him as he slept in the desert.

MONOCLED COBRA

"Eye" is meant to frighten aggressors

Cobras are active at dawn and dusk

Some snake charmers remove a cobra's fangs

Cobras follow the instrument's movements

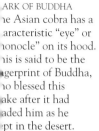

SNAKE CHARMER AND COBRAS

HOODED MENACE
Most cobras have a hood, created by spreading the neck ribs as the front of the body is raised off the ground. This characteristic is particularly well developed in Asian species, such as the Ceylonese cobra.

A cobra can move forward while keeping its front raised

CHARMED SNAKES
Snake charmers in Asia and North Africa have long induced cobras to "dance" to their tunes. The snakes, however, are deaf and are probably reacting to the swaying movements of the instrument, not to the music.

The hood is spread as the body is raised

CEYLONESE COBRA

Vipers

With their long, hollow fangs, vipers and their close relatives, the pit vipers and rattlesnakes, are among the most dangerous snakes in the world. When one of these snakes opens its mouth to bite, it swings its fangs downwards and forwards, ready to stab the victim. The snake has absolute control over the movement of its fangs – it can even choose to erect them one at a time.

RECORD RANGE
The adder has the greatest range of any living snake. I is found throughout Europe and Asia, as far north as th Arctic circle and eastwards through northern China to the Pacific coast.

This viper's venom is very toxic

Blunt nose gives the snake its alternative name

Depending on the climatic conditions, this viper lays eggs or gives birth to live young

LEVANT VIPER

BLUNT-NOSED VIP
Levant, or blunt-nose
vipers, of which the
are seven subspecies, a
found in dry, roc
places southwards fro
Georgia to northe
Israel, Iraq, Iran, anc
few of the Greek islan

SAND VIPER
The Avicenna viper is a sidewinder that occurs in sandy places from Lebanon, through Israel westwards to the northwestern coast of Africa. It is closely related to the horned viper.

AVICENNA VIPER

...LLOW PERIL

...e eyelash viper has
...ny scales above its eyes
...at resemble eyelashes.
...is tree-dwelling pit
...er is found in
...nforests from southern
...exico southwards to
...uador and western
...nezuela. It varies in
...lour from brown or
...en to lemon yellow.

EYELASH VIPER

LOOKS LIKE A VIPER...
The death, or deaf, adder
looks and behaves like
a viper, but is related
to the cobras, coral
snakes, and kraits.
It lives in dry, sandy
places in Australia,
New Guinea, and
nearby islands.

DEATH ADDER

...LL PUFFED UP

...good climber and swimmer, the puff
...der is found in all habitats except
...serts in Africa south of the
...hara. It preys on a wide
...riety of animals and, like
...vipers, it prefers to lie in
...it for its victims. The puff
...der's venom is highly toxic.

*Grey-and-brown
colouring for
camouflage in
dry grass*

PUFF ADDER

253

Rattlesnakes

The distinctive feature of these well-known, front-fanged snakes is the rattle at the end of the tail, which is made up of a series of special, ring-like scales. Rattlesnakes, all of which are found in the southern half of North America, are under threat, mainly from excessive slaughter by hunters, together with the continued spread agriculture and urban development. All rattlesnakes give birth to live young.

SOUTHERN PACIFIC
RATTLESNAKE

ADAPTABLE
The southern Pacific rattlesnake is found in rocky and sandy environments. An adaptable species, it can also survive in urban and agricultural areas. It preys mainly on rodents.

EASTERN
DIAMONDBACK
RATTLESNAKE

RATTLESNAKE FACTS

• Organized hunts called "rattlesnake roundups" in the US have wiped out many local populations.

• Western diamondbacks always return to the same den to hibernate.

LARGE – BUT SECRET
The eastern diamondback secretive reptile found in pine a oak woods and abandoned agricultural are It is a large, heavy-bodied snake that preys small mammals, particularly rabbits and ra

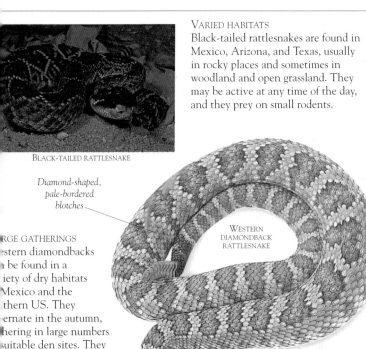

VARIED HABITATS

Black-tailed rattlesnakes are found in Mexico, Arizona, and Texas, usually in rocky places and sometimes in woodland and open grassland. They may be active at any time of the day, and they prey on small rodents.

BLACK-TAILED RATTLESNAKE

Diamond-shaped, pale-bordered blotches

WESTERN DIAMONDBACK RATTLESNAKE

[LA]RGE GATHERINGS

[We]stern diamondbacks [ca]n be found in a [var]iety of dry habitats [in M]exico and the [sou]thern US. They [hib]ernate in the autumn, [gat]hering in large numbers [at s]uitable den sites. They [fee]d on small mammals [and] birds.

A diamondback will defend itself vigorously if cornered

DUSKY PYGMY RATTLESNAKE

PYGMY RATTLER

The dusky pygmy rattlesnake lives in dry, sandy places near water. It is active at any time of the day or night, and it preys on small animals, including small snakes and large insects. It grows to only about 50 cm (20 in) in length.

255

Other front-fanged snakes

Front-fanged snakes that have fixed fangs include the tiger snake, the taipan, kraits, and sea snakes. Unlike true vipers and rattlesnakes, these snakes cannot stab their prey with their fangs and must actually bite. The cottonmouth and its close relatives, the moccasin and the copperhead, are pit vipers and are thus members of the Crotalinae, the viper subfamily that includes the rattlesnakes.

BANDED SEA SNAKE

SEA SERPENT

Sea snakes include the world's most venomous snakes. Luckily, the banded sea snakes, of which five species live in coastal waters around New Guinea and Pacific islands, seldom bite in defence.

TIGER
SNAKE

TOXIC TIGER

The venom of southern Australia's tiger snake is highly toxic – just 3 mg is enough to kill a human. It feeds mainly on frogs, but also kills small mammals and lizards. The tiger snake is quick to attack if disturbed.

NEVER FATAL

The American copperhead is found in open woodland, where it feeds on mice, birds, frogs, and insects. Contrary to popular belief, its bite is never fatal, although this has not stopped the widespread killing of these snakes.

*Copperhead
hibernate i
communal de*

COPPERHEAD

TURTLE EATER

The cottonmouth, also called the water moccasin, is an impressive-looking, heavy-bodied snake that lives in swamps and marshes in the US states of Alabama, Georgia, and Virginia. Its prey includes small turtles and young alligators.

COTTONMOUTH

Taipans shelter in mammal burrows, rock crevices, or under piles of forest litter

TAIPAN

DO NOT DISTURB

The taipan is a large, slender snake found in northern Australia. When not hunting, it seeks shelter and, whenever possible, it will retreat when disturbed. If cornered, however, it becomes fearsomely aggressive.

Prey consists of small mammals

Taipan is one of Australia's most dangerous snakes

COMMON KRAIT

The common, or blue, krait is a highly venomous snake found in the dry woodland plains and meadows of Bangladesh, India, and Sri Lanka. It hides during the day and at night hunts rodents, lizards, and other snakes.

FRONT-FANGED FACTS

• A cottonmouth uses its bright yellow tail as a lure to attract prey.

• A bite from a krait is fatal in over 75 per cent of cases.

• Some species of sea snake are considered to be a delicacy in the Far East.

S N A K E S

257

BIRDS

WHAT IS A BIRD?

BIRDS ARE DIFFERENT from all the other animals in the world because they have feathers – over a thousand of them. They also have two wings, a strong bill, no teeth, scaly legs and feet, and three or four toes with claws on the end. Most birds can fly, and they are the largest, fastest, and most powerful flying animals. Like us, birds breathe air, have a skeleton inside their bodies, and are warm-blooded. Unlike us, birds lay eggs.

JUVENILE
STARLING
FEATHER

ADULT
STARLING
FEATHER

FEATHERS
Birds' feathers are light, yet strong and flexible. The feathers of young birds are often a different colour from those of the adults.

STARLING
EGGS

EGGS
A bird's egg is a survival capsule which protects and nourishes a baby bird while it develops inside. When it is ready to hatch, the baby bird has to force its way out.

Secondary
flight feathers

Primary flight
feathers

Rump

Upper tail
coverts

Under tail
coverts

Tail

Wing
coverts

Ankle

STARLING

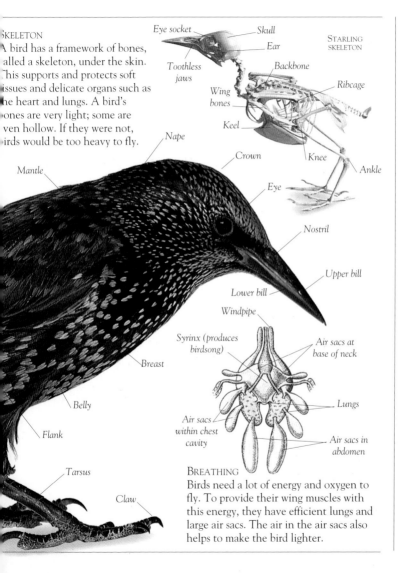

SKELETON

A bird has a framework of bones, called a skeleton, under the skin. This supports and protects soft tissues and delicate organs such as the heart and lungs. A bird's bones are very light; some are even hollow. If they were not, birds would be too heavy to fly.

Eye socket

Skull

Ear

Toothless jaws

Backbone

Wing bones

Ribcage

STARLING SKELETON

Keel

Knee

Ankle

Nape

Mantle

Crown

Eye

Nostril

Upper bill

Lower bill

Windpipe

Syrinx (produces birdsong)

Air sacs at base of neck

Breast

Belly

Air sacs within chest cavity

Lungs

Flank

Air sacs in abdomen

Tarsus

Claw

BREATHING

Birds need a lot of energy and oxygen to fly. To provide their wing muscles with this energy, they have efficient lungs and large air sacs. The air in the air sacs also helps to make the bird lighter.

261

BIRDS

Types of birds

The huge variety of birds alive today – over 9,000 species – evolved from reptile-like creatures that climbed trees about 150 million years ago. Reptile scales developed into bird feathers, although there are still scales on a bird's legs. Now, there are birds of all shapes and sizes, from huge ostriches to tiny wrens. Some of the main types of bird are shown here.

PIGEON

PIGEONS
Most pigeons and doves have rather small heads, plump bodies, dense, soft feathers and a powerful straight flight. They live all over the world.

ARCHAEOPTERYX
The first bird we know of lived about 150 million years ago. It is called *Archaeopteryx*, meaning ancient wing. It could not fly well, but had feathers.

ANCIENT BIRD FACTS

• Birds may be living descendants of the dinosaurs.

• *Archaeopteryx* had teeth.

• The first flying bird was a tern-like seabird called *Ichthyornis*.

• The heaviest bird, *Dromornis stirtoni*, was four times heavier than an ostrich.

ZEBRA FINCHES

PERCHING BIRD
Over half of the birds ali
today are perching land bir
Most are strong fliers ar
many sing we

PARROTS
Colourful, noisy, tree-
living birds of the
tropics, parrots
have powerful,
hooked bills.

GREEN-
WINGED
MACAW

DUCKS
These are broad-bodied
water birds with a wide, flat
bill, webbed feet, and
short legs set well
back on the body.

WOOD
DUCK

KING
PENGUIN

GOLDEN
EAGLE

PENGUINS
Flightless seabirds
of the Southern
Hemisphere
with wings
like flippers.

EAGLES
Powerful
birds of prey,
eagles have
broad, rounded
wings, strong
talons and a
hooked bill.

BLACK-
HEADED
GULL

GULLS
These stocky seabirds have a
heavy bill, long, pointed
wings, and webbed feet.

263

Bird senses

Birds rely mainly on their eyes and ears to find food or a mate, to fly, and to escape from danger. Their eyes are so large that there is not much room for them to move in the skull. Instead, birds have flexible necks and move the whole head to see things. Most birds have a poor sense of smell.

Large eyes to spot danger coming

SIGHT

A bird's huge eyes are often as big as its brain. Much of the brain deals with the information picked up by the eyes. Like us, birds see in colour, but they may have better eyesight than we have.

PIED AVOCET

The avocet uses its sense of touch to catch small water creatures.

TOUCH

Some birds, such as the avocet, have a well-developed sense of touch in the tongue and bill tip. Nightjars have bristles around their broad bills to help them sweep moths into their mouths as they fly at night.

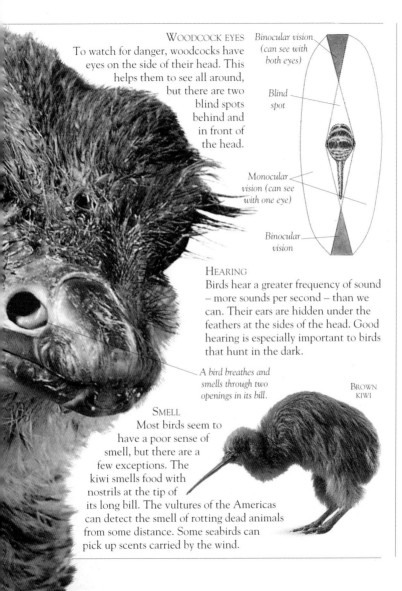

WOODCOCK EYES
To watch for danger, woodcocks have eyes on the side of their head. This helps them to see all around, but there are two blind spots behind and in front of the head.

Binocular vision (can see with both eyes)

Blind spot

Monocular vision (can see with one eye)

Binocular vision

HEARING
Birds hear a greater frequency of sound – more sounds per second – than we can. Their ears are hidden under the feathers at the sides of the head. Good hearing is especially important to birds that hunt in the dark.

A bird breathes and smells through two openings in its bill.

BROWN KIWI

SMELL
Most birds seem to have a poor sense of smell, but there are a few exceptions. The kiwi smells food with nostrils at the tip of its long bill. The vultures of the Americas can detect the smell of rotting dead animals from some distance. Some seabirds can pick up scents carried by the wind.

265

FEATHERS

A BIRD'S BODY is almost completely covered with feathers, although some birds have bare legs. Feathers keep the bird warm, give it shape, colour and pattern, and help some birds to fly. Some birds have special display feathers. Feathers carry out so many important jobs they need to be kept in good condition.

What is a feather?

There are three main types of feather – flight, body, and down. Feathers grow out of pits or follicles in a bird's skin, like the hairs all over our skin. They can be easily repaired because of the way the parts of the feather hook together.

Vane

Smooth, curved shaft for flight

Shaft or rachis

MACAW FLIGHT FEATHER

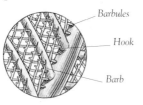

Barbules

Hook

Barb

BARBS AND BARBULES
Each side of a feather consists of parallel barbs, held in place by tiny hooks on side branches called barbules. There are many thousands of barbules on a flight feather.

FEATHER STRUCTURE
Feathers have a central shaft with a vane or web on either side. They are made of a strong, flexible material called keratin, which also forms our hair and nails.

FLIGHT FEATHERS

Found in the wings and tail, flight feathers provide a large area to push the bird through the air. Their special aerofoil shape lifts the bird in the air, and controls the way it twists and turns in flight.

PEACOCK DOWN FEATHER

Short shaft

REGENT PARROT FLIGHT FEATHERS

Long shaft

AFRICAN GREY PARROT BODY FEATHER

Inner fluffy part to keep bird warm

Quill

DOWN FEATHERS

The soft down feathers trap warm air next to the body and are very important in young birds. The barbs are long and soft and the barbules do not hook together so the feather stays fluffy.

FEATHER FACTS

• Swans have 25,000 feathers, sparrows 3,500, and humming-birds less than 1,000.

• The male crested argus pheasant has the longest and largest tail feathers at 173 cm (5.7 ft) long, 13 cm (5.1 in) wide.

• Feathers evolved from reptile scales.

• Grebes eat their feathers to help digestion.

BODY FEATHERS

Overlapping like tiles on a roof, body feathers act as a weatherproof jacket. The inner part has softer barbs and the barbules have no hooks.

267

Feather colour

The colours of bird feathers are produced in two main ways. One is by chemical pigments laid down in the feather when it is being formed. The other is by the structure of feathers and the way they reflect the light. Bird colours help individuals of the same species to recognize each other. They also help birds to attract a mate, threaten a rival, or camouflage themselves.

SHINING COLOURS
Peacock feathers are iridescent –
they change colours as they move.
This is probably caused by a
mixture of pigments and
reflection of the light.

*Male peacock
uses his colourful
feathers in a
courtship display*

FLAMINGO
FEATHERS

FOOD COLOUR
The colour of flamingo
feathers comes from a
pink pigment in the
shrimps and other small
water creatures which the
birds sieve from the water.

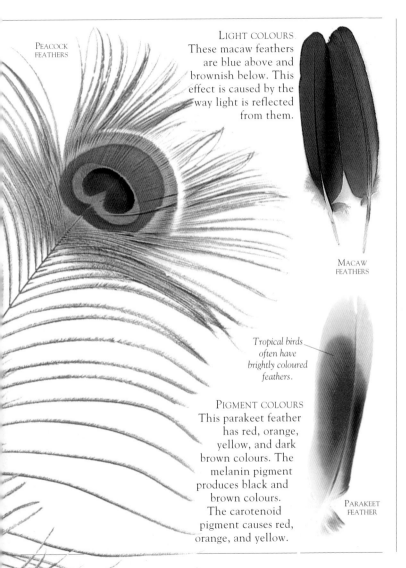

PEACOCK
FEATHERS

LIGHT COLOURS
These macaw feathers
are blue above and
brownish below. This
effect is caused by the
way light is reflected
from them.

MACAW
FEATHERS

*Tropical birds
often have
brightly coloured
feathers.*

PIGMENT COLOURS
This parakeet feather
has red, orange,
yellow, and dark
brown colours. The
melanin pigment
produces black and
brown colours.
The carotenoid
pigment causes red,
orange, and yellow.

PARAKEET
FEATHER

269

Looking after feathers

Birds must take great care of their feathers
and spend a few hours each day cleaning
and tidying their plumage.
They use the bill to
pull ruffled feathers
into shape, and
may also take
water or dust
baths. Many
birds spread
an oily liquid
over their
feathers to
keep them
waterproof.

YELLOW
CANARY
PREENING

PREENING
To preen its feathers, a bird draws
each one carefully through its bill.
This fits the barbs and barbules back
into place – like pulling up a zip – and
cleans and smooths the feathers.
Preening also removes parasites, such
as feather lice, which live on feathers
and eat them.

*Most birds use
their feet to
preen their head
feathers.*

*The oil used for preening
comes from a special
gland at the base of the
tail, on the rump.*

BIRD BATH
Many birds, like the blue tit below, bathe in water. They clean their feathers and skin, and get ready for preening. Most birds bathe and preen regularly. Some also take dust baths, perhaps to get rid of parasites.

NEW FEATHERS
A new feather is rolled up as a cylinder inside a thin, horny sheath. When it is fully developed, the sheath splits open and flakes away. The feather can then unroll and begin to grow to its full length.

Emerging adult feather

Fully grown tail feather

Young penguins lose their fluffy feathers

MOULTING KING PENGUINS

Horny sheath

ADULT KESTREL FEATHER

YOUNG KESTREL FEATHER

GROWING FEATHERS
At least once a year, most birds moult their feathers and new feathers grow to replace old ones. Moulting allows birds to replace worn or damaged feathers, and to change colour as they grow up or the seasons change.

271

HOW BIRDS MOVE

TO FIND FOOD and escape danger, birds walk, run, hop, swim, and wade. Most birds can also fly. They have light bones, powerful flight muscles, and an efficient respiratory system. A few birds cannot fly. Some of these flightless birds run very fast indeed.

Flight

In order to fly, birds flap their wings up and down. As the wings beat down, they push the air back, and the bird moves forwards. Air flows over and under the wings creating a lifting force.

TAWNY OWL

LIFT
Birds have curved wings made of feathers to push and steer them through the air. The inner part of a bird's wing can stay still to provide lift.

TAKE-OFF
A heavy bird, such as a swan, has to run along while flapping its wings to get enough lift for take-off. Smaller birds take off by jumping into the air and flapping their wings to create lift.

COMING IN TO LAND

To land, birds slow down in mid-air, then drop gently to the ground, onto a perch, or the surface of water, spreading out their wings and tail like brakes. Heavy birds land into the wind to help slow themselves down.

Strong legs to absorb impact of landing

Wings and tail spread to increase air resistance and drag

BLUE-AND-WHITE FLYCATCHER

CURVED WINGS

A bird's wing is an aerofoil shape – curved on top and slightly hollow underneath. The air flows faster over the top, creating low air pressure, while air pressure underneath stays much the same. The difference in pressure produces lift.

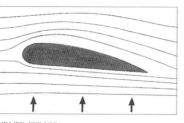

Finger-like feathers to push and steer through the air

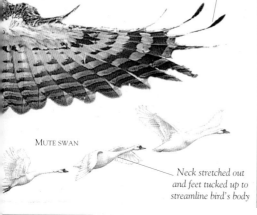

MUTE SWAN

Neck stretched out and feet tucked up to streamline bird's body

---

FLIGHT FACTS

• Common swifts may stay in the air for three years at a time without landing.

• Some hummingbirds beat their wings up to 90 times a second.

• Swans have been recorded flying as high as 8,230 m (27,000 ft).

• Peregrine falcons can reach speeds of 180 km/h (112 mph) when diving after prey.

273

Flight patterns

Different kinds of bird have differently shaped wings which they flap in patterns that suit their lifestyle. To save energy, some birds like seagulls and vultures soar on rising air, while smaller birds glide between flaps of the wings. Ducks and other heavy birds flap their wings all the time they are in the air. A few, such as hummingbirds and kestrels, can hover in one spot.

FLIGHT PATH
Small birds, like this minla, have a bouncing, undulating flight. Bigger birds such as cranes, ducks, and geese tend to fly in straight lines.

RED-TAILED
MINLA

Feathers sprea apart on upstro for air to slip through wing

Eagles thermalling

Hot air rising

Seabirds have powerful flight muscles.

GLIDING AND SOARING
Seabirds glide upwards on air currents rising from waves or over cliffs. Large birds of prey, such as eagles or vultures, also use natural currents of rising hot air to lift them higher into the air. These currents are called thermals.

GLIDING IN
A THERMAL

HOVERING

Hummingbirds can hover, move straight up or down, and even fly backwards. They do this by turning each wing in a circle, and using up and down wingbeats for extra power.

HUMMINGBIRD

Unlike other birds, hummingbirds have rigid wings with a swivel joint at the shoulder.

Between flaps, wings fold against body so bird can glide and rest

Feathers closed together on downstroke to push against the air

GLIDING
HERRING GULL

Tail used for steering and changing direction

Long, narrow wings for gliding

Feathers hug the body, creating a streamlined shape so air can flow past more easily

WING SHAPE

The size and shape of wings give clues to how a bird lives and helps with identification, especially if the bird is high in the sky.

Long and wide for soaring – buzzards and vultures

Long and narrow for gliding – fulmars and albatrosses

Wide and rounded for short, fast flight – pheasants

Narrow and pointed for fast flight – swallows and swifts

CASSOWARY
AND CHICK

Flightless birds

A few birds have given up flying altogether. Some of them are so good a swimming or running that they do not need to fly. Many flightless birds, such as ostriches, rheas, or emus are very large birds that can run faster than thei enemies, or can win a fight so easily that they do not need to fly away. Som flightless birds live on remote islands where there are few enemies from whic they need to escape.

DEFENCE
With powerful legs and dagger-like claws, birds such as cassowaries do not need to fly away. Cassowaries even attack people, lashing out with strong feet and sharp nails.

GALAPAGOS
CORMORANT

WING
Flightless birds usuall have small, weak wing which are not strong enoug for flight. The Galapag cormorant uses its wings t help it balance on land

FLIGHTLESS FACTS

• The flightless Stephens Island wren was wiped out by a cat within a year of being discovered.

• Ostriches are nearly seven times too heavy to fly. They have the biggest legs of any bird.

• The Inaccessible Island rail is the world's smallest flightless bird, about the size of a chick.

BIRDS IN DANGER
Many flightless birds, such as this kakapo, are threatened by people who introduce cats and rats to their island homes. Kakapos are too heavy to fly.

KAKAPO

GREATER
RHEA

FAST RUNNERS

Running away from danger can be just as good as flying. Rheas can sprint faster than a horse, reaching speeds of 50 km/h (31 mph), and are also good swimmers. Rheas are related to ostriches and emus and follow a similar lifestyle, but they live on the South American grasslands, rather than on the grasslands of Africa or Australia.

Fluffy wings used for display, not flight

Long neck to see over tall grasses

HUMBOLDT
PENGUIN

FAST SWIMMERS

Penguins are so well suited to their life in the sea that they are a different shape from most birds. They use their wings as flippers for swimming while their feet and tail steer like a rudder.

Large leg muscles provide power when running

Three strong toes on each foot for defence and for running fast

LEGS AND FEET

BIRDS USE their legs and feet for preening their feathers, as well as for moving about. The size and shape of their feet depends on where they live and how they feed.

Three toes point forward and one back.

String-li[ke] tendon[s].

PERCHING
Birds that perch can slee[p] without falling off a branch. They bend their legs, pulling the tendons tight and drawing in the toes. This locks their feet tightly rou[nd] the perch.

TAWNY OWL TALON

TALONS
Birds of prey, such as owls and eagles, have strong, sharp, curved claws called talons. They use these to catch and carry their prey.

Long toes that spread wide

WATTLED JACANA

Scaly skin along each toe

WIDE TOES
Some water birds, such as coots, have lobes of skin on each toe. These push aside the water for faster swimming and help to stop the coot sinking into mud.

COOT TOES

LONG TOES
Jacanas or lily trotters have very long, thin toes. These spread the weight of the bird over a bigger are[a] so it can "trot" across lily pads on the ponds and lakes where it lives.

ˢPEED
ᵒstriches have long legs and
ˢˢrong toes to run at speeds of up
ᵗ 70 km/h (43 mph). They only
ʰave two toes on each foot; most
ᵇi̇rds have three or four.

BLUE
FRONTED
PARROT

WEBBED FEET
Water birds, such as ducks,
geese, and flamingos have
webs of skin between their
toes. The webs work like
paddles when the bird is in
water. They are also useful
when the bird is walking on
soft, marshy ground.

GRIPPING TOES
The two outer toes of a
parrot's foot point
backwards, and the two
inner toes point
forwards. This
gives parrots a very
powerful grip for climbing
through the trees. It also
allows them to hold
food up to the bill.

*Two toes
forward, two
toes back*

LEGS OF
FLAMINGO

279

COLLARED
SUNBIRD SIPPING
NECTAR

FOOD AND FEEDING

BIRDS SPEND MUCH of their time
finding food, whether pecking at
berries and nuts, or snapping up fish or
small mammals. They rely mainly on their
eyes and ears to find food, and their bill or
claws to catch it. A few birds steal their food
from other birds. Some birds eat plants; others
eat animals or have a mixed diet.

Hunting and fishing

Meat-eating birds usually catch weak
or unfit prey. They may lie in wait to
ambush their quarry, or chase after it
through air or water. Most of these birds
hunt by day; a few, such as
owls, hunt at night.

GREAT WHITE
PELICAN

GOLDEN
EAGLE

BIRDS OF PREY
Most birds of
prey, such as this
golden eagle, soar
high in the sky to
search for food,
then swoop down to
seize and crush their
prey in their sharp talons. However,
nine out of ten attacks are unsuccessful
and the prey manages to escape.

*A pelican's bill can
hold more food than
its stomach*

UMBRELLA FISHING
Some birds have developed their own special techniques for catching food. The black heron shades the water with its wings. This cuts out reflections and makes it easier for the bird to see fish.

Great white pelicans eat about .2 kg (2 ½ lb) of fish a day.

SNAKE HUNTERS
Secretary birds are unusual because they search for their prey on foot. They have tough scales on their legs for protection from snake bite. They pin prey to the ground with sharp claws.

SECRETARY BIRDS

Sharp, hooked bill to pull and tear at food

EGYPTIAN VULTURE

FISHING IN GROUPS
Great white pelicans usually fish in groups. The birds gather in a circle on the water, lifting their wings and plunging their bills into the water to drive the fish into the middle of the circle. Then they scoop up the fish.

USING TOOLS
A few birds use tools to find and deal with their food. Egyptian vultures throw or drop stones on to ostrich eggs to break open the thick shells.

281

What birds eat

Birds have healthy appetites. They need to eat large amounts of food to give them enough energy to fly, keep warm, build nests, and lay eggs. Some birds eat only one kind of food, while others, such as starlings, crows, and jays eat almost anything. Birds such as vultures eat carcasses, the dead bodies of animals.

HELMET BIRD

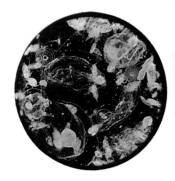

MICROSCOPIC SEAFOOD
A drop of seawater teems with tiny plants such as diatoms and animals such as crab larvae. This plankton floats about the oceans and is a vital part of the diet of many seabirds.

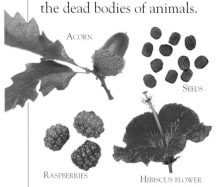

ACORN

SEEDS

RASPBERRIES

HIBISCUS FLOWER

FLOWERS, FRUITS, AND SEEDS
The sweet liquid called nectar produced by flowers is a high-energy food for birds such as hummingbirds. Many birds eat the fruits and seeds that develop when the flowers are pollinated.

GRASS

CABBAGE LEAF

CONIFER

GRASS AND LEAVES
A few birds, such as geese, ducks, and grouse, eat grass and leaves. These ca[n] be hard to digest and poor in nutrien[ts] so the birds have to eat a lot of this s[ort] of food to get the energy they need.

GROUND BEETLE

FLY

GRASSHOPPER

CRAB

SNAIL

COCKLE

EARTHWORM

[IN]SECTS

[A]dult insects are more abundant in [w]armer weather, but caterpillars and [gr]ubs survive colder periods buried in [soi]l or under bark. Insects are a body-[bu]ilding food, vital for young birds.

INVERTEBRATES

Invertebrates such as crabs and shellfish are an important source of food on the seashore, where there are few insects. Garden and woodland birds, such as thrushes, eat juicy earthworms.

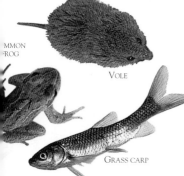

[CO]MMON [F]ROG

VOLE

GRASS CARP

NEST AND YOUNG

[VE]RTEBRATES

[Bir]ds that feed on vertebrates (animals [wit]h backbones) have to work hard for [the]ir meals. The animals they hunt do [the]ir best to run, swim or slither away, [an]d often succeed in escaping.

EGGS AND YOUNG

Some birds eat the eggs and helpless young of other birds. For example, skuas pounce on puffin and penguin chicks, and magpies often take eggs and young birds from the nest.

283

Bird bills

A bird uses its bill like a hand to carry out all sorts of tasks, from catching and holding food to preening its feathers and building a nest. Parrots also use their bills to help them climb. The size and shape of a bird's bill depends mainly on what it eats and where it finds its food.

YELLOW-HEAD[ED]
PARROT

FRUIT-AND-NUT EATERS
A parrot's bill deals wit[h] two different kinds of food. The hook at the t[ip] pulls out the soft parts [of] fruit, while the strong nutcracker at the base opens seeds. Parrots use their feet to hold food.

FLAMINGO

A flamingo dips its bill upside down in the shallow water.

FILTER-FEEDER
The flamingo has a very special bill. Sieve-like edges on the top bill filter out tiny plants, shrimps, and other invertebrates from the water. The bottom bill and the tongue move up and down to pump water through comb-like fringes on the sides of the top bill.

Bee-eaters beat sting[ing] insects against a bran[ch] to get rid of the sting

WHITE-THROATED
BEE-EATER

INSECT EATERS
Birds that feed on insects have thin, pointed bills to probe und[er] bark and stones. Birds that eat flying insects have wide, gapin[g] bills to scoop them up as they f[ly]

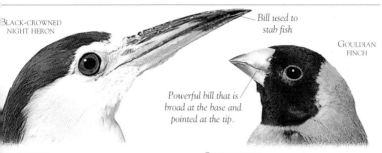

BLACK-CROWNED
NIGHT HERON

Bill used to
stab fish

GOULDIAN
FINCH

*Powerful bill that is
broad at the base and
pointed at the tip.*

[FI]SH EATERS

[A] dagger-shaped bill is characteristic of
[fis]h-eating birds, such as herons. Others,
[su]ch as cormorants, have a hooked bill
[wi]th which to tear the fish into pieces.

SEED EATERS

To crack open seeds, seed-eating birds
such as finches have pyramid-shaped
bills. The hawfinch's bill is so strong it
can even crush cherry stones.

[S]CARLET-CHESTED
SUNBIRD

*Flaps over
nostrils keep out
flower pollen*

[N]ECTAR EATERS

[N]early one-fifth of all the
[w]orld's birds feed on nectar.
[Su]nbirds and hummingbirds
[pu]sh their needle-like bills into
[flo]wers and lick up the sweet nectar.

*Powerful
hooked bill to
tear up food*

GOLDEN
EAGLE

MEAT EATERS

Often called birds of prey, these include
eagles, owls, and falcons. They use their
bills to pull apart animals they kill into
bite-sized chunks. Owls swallow small
animals, such as voles and mice, whole.

COURTSHIP

BEFORE MATING, male birds usually court the females. Some males grow more colourful or elaborate feathers for the breeding season. They may give singing or dancing displays. Some show off nest-building or hunting skills.

YELLOW-THROATED LAUGHING THRUSH

TERRITORY
Many birds nest in an area, or territory, that has enough food for their young when they hatch out. Male birds sing in their territory to attract a mate and keep away other males.

Laughing thrushes make loud, cackling sounds.

MALE PIN-TAILED WHYDAH

MALES AND FEMALES
Male and female birds of the same species often look different. The male is usually more colourful, but the dull colours of the female help camouflage her on the nest.

Female bird duller, with short tail

Long tail feathers used in display flight to impress females

FEMALE PIN-TAILED WHYDAH

MALE
PEACOCK

*Male's long
feathers make
flight difficult*

DISPLAY
The male
peacock spreads
out his long, colourful
feathers in a shimmering
fan to impress a female.
After the breeding season, the
long tail feathers fall out.

RED-CROWNED
CRANES

*The "eyes"
may hypnotize
the female.*

DANCING
Some birds dance together
before they mate. Cranes jump
up and down in the air with
their partners. Great crested
grebes perform a series of
dances, including head-shaking.

NESTS AND EGGS

ALL BIRDS LAY EGGS and most build nests to keep eggs and young safe and warm. Birds know instinctively how to build a nest, and female birds usually do most of the work. Nests vary from a shallow scrape in the ground and simple cup shapes, to more elaborate constructions.

NEST BOX

Building a nest

Birds use a wide range of nesting materials and may make hundreds of trips to collect material. Nest materials must both support the nest and keep the young warm. Nest boxes encourage birds to nest in gardens or woods with few natural tree holes.

WAGTAIL NEST

PEBBLE NEST
Oystercatchers lay their eggs in a shallow dip, or scrape, on the shoreline. Their eggs are difficult to see among the pebbles.

TWIGS
Most hedgerow and woodland birds use twigs and sticks to support their nests as these are readily available.

FEATHERS
Birds may use feathers a warm lining for a nes Hundreds of feathers li a long-tailed tit's nest.

To make the cup shape, birds turn round and round.

MOSS
Moss traps warm air in the nest and stops heat loss. It helps to keep both eggs and young birds warm.

STRING
Birds sometimes collect household materials when nest-building. Pieces of string have been found in many nests.

MUD
Some nests are lined with wet mud mixed with saliva and droppings. When it dries, it forms a hard and strong lining.

MUD NEST
Swallows and martins collect mud with their bills and build nests with pieces of mud stuck together with saliva.

Woodpeckers have chisel-like bills.

TREE NEST
Woodpeckers dig nest holes in rotten trees with their strong beaks. Many other birds use existing tree holes. The nests inside the holes are usually lined with grass or feathers.

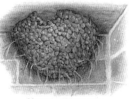

HOUSE MARTIN NEST

GRASS
Grass is a flexible nest material. It is used by many birds because it is easy to weave into differently shaped nests.

Unusual nests

From woven purses and saliva cups to mud ovens and compost heaps, some birds' nests are quite unusual and elaborate. They may be a strange shape, such as the trumpet-like weaver bird nests. Birds need a lot of practice to perfect the technique of making a complex nest.

PENDULINE
TIT NEST

Strong and lightweight basket

False entrance

WOVEN NEST
A male West African weaver bird knotted grasses to weave this nest. The entrance tunnel stops snakes and other enemies from getting inside.

PURSE NEST
The penduline tit weaves a hanging nest from grasses, leaves, and moss. A false entrance leads to an empty chamber and dead end.

THATCHED COTTAGE
Each colony of the sociable weaver bird of South Africa builds a huge "haystack" that is up to 4 m (13 ft) deep and 7.2 m (24 ft) across. Up to 300 pairs then build their nests under the protection of this thatched roof.

WEAVER
NEST

290

NEST FACTS

• Biggest nest ever found: a bald eagle's which was 2.9 m (9.5 ft) wide and 6 m (20 ft) deep.

• A bee hummingbird's nest is no bigger than a thimble.

• A mallee fowl's nest is a "compost heap" of rotting vegetation.

• A hammerkop nest may be made of over 10,000 sticks.

BASKET NEST
Reed warblers join their nest to several reed stems. This helps to hold the nest steady as the wind blows. The nest is made from grass, reed fibres, and feathers.

TAILOR BIRD ON NEST

Nest is joined to reeds

REED WARBLER NEST

SEWING BIRD
The tailorbird sews a pocket of leaves to support its nest. Its sharp bill makes a row of holes along the edges of the leaves. Then the bird pulls spider or insect silk or plant material through the holes to stitch the leaves.

BALTIMORE ORIOLE NEST

STRING NEST
Many birds that nest near people make use of artificial materials. This Baltimore oriole has used pieces of string in its bag-like nest, and has even joined the nest to a twig with string.

All kinds of eggs

Birds lay eggs because they would be too heavy to fly if they carried their young around inside them. Some birds lay one large clutch (set of eggs) in a season, while others lay several smaller clutches. Birds such as snowy owls lay extra clutches if there is plenty of food. No two eggs have exactly the same markings. The colour and shape depends on where the eggs are laid and how much camouflage they need.

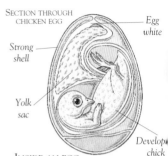

SECTION THROUGH CHICKEN EGG

Strong shell

Egg white

Yolk sac

Developing chick

INSIDE AN EGG

A bird's egg contains a developing bird – an embryo – plus a store of food and a supply of air. Pores in the shell allow air to pass through from outside. The egg white supplies proteins, water, and vitamins.

EGG FACTS

• One ostrich egg has the same volume as 24 hens' eggs.

• Cuckoos can lay eggs in a few seconds; some birds take 1-3 minutes.

• Nearly 80 species of bird lay eggs in the nests of other species.

• Grey partridges lay the largest clutches – up to 16 eggs.

• Most small eggs take under an hour to hatch.

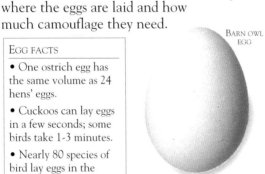

BARN OWL EGG

WHITE EGGS
Birds that nest in holes or burrows, such as owls or kingfishers, usually lay white eggs. They do not need to be camouflaged because they are hidden.

CURLEW EGG

SPECKLED EGGS
Birds that nest in the open, where there is little cover, usually lay patterned eggs. The camouflage colours hide the eggs from enemies.

PALE EGG   SPECKLED EGG   DARK EGG

DISGUISE
Female cuckoos lay their eggs in the nests of other birds such as dunnocks, robins, wrens, or meadow pipits. The foster parents raise the cuckoo chick as their own. The cuckoo's egg often looks similar to those of the foster parents.

COLOURS IN A CLUTCH
The three eggs above were laid by a single snipe but come from different clutches. In one clutch, the eggs usually look similar.

CUCKOO EGG

GUILEMOT EGG

EURASIAN ROBIN EGGS

BIG AND SMALL
Ostriches lay the largest eggs of any living bird. Each egg weighs about 1.7 kg (3.7 lb), and is as long as an adult human's hand. Hummingbirds' eggs, however, are only as big as peas.

PATTERNS
Common guilemot eggs show a variety of patterns and colours, possibly to help parent birds recognize them. The pear shape stops it rolling off cliff ledges.

HUMMINGBIRD EGGS

OSTRICH EGG

BIRTH AND GROWTH

PARENT BIRDS SIT on their eggs to keep them warm so that the chicks inside can develop properly. This is called incubation. After hatching, the parents work hard feeding the chicks, keeping them warm and clean, and protecting them from enemies.

Egg to chick

Most birds develop patches of bare skin, brood patches, to let body warmth through to the eggs they are

SWAN INCUBATING
EGGS IN NEST

incubating. Small birds incubate eggs for about two weeks, eagles for six or seven weeks, and albatrosses for up to 11 weeks.

First the chick pecks at shell to make a hole

Then chick cuts a circle

Chick pushes to widen crack

HATCHING
To break out of its shell, a baby bird chips away with a pointed "egg tooth" on top of its bill. This egg tooth disappears soon after hatching. Some clutches hatch together; others hatch at intervals of a few days.

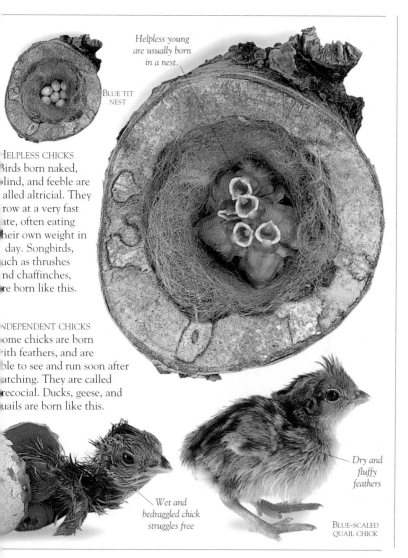

*Helpless young
are usually born
in a nest.*

BLUE TIT
NEST

HELPLESS CHICKS
Birds born naked,
blind, and feeble are
called altricial. They
grow at a very fast
rate, often eating
their own weight in
a day. Songbirds,
such as thrushes
and chaffinches,
are born like this.

INDEPENDENT CHICKS
Some chicks are born
with feathers, and are
able to see and run soon after
hatching. They are called
precocial. Ducks, geese, and
quails are born like this.

*Wet and
bedraggled chick
struggles free*

*Dry and
fluffy
feathers*

BLUE-SCALED
QUAIL CHICK

295

Growing up

Baby birds take a few weeks or a few months to grow up. They all rely on their parents to keep them warm and out of danger, and most chicks are fed by their parents as well. Small birds can make hundreds of feeding trips in a day; larger birds only two or three. Chicks that are born helpless grow faster than chicks that are born fluffy and alert.

HEN AND
CHICKS

EAGLE AND
CHICKS

BIRDS OF PREY
Eagles and other birds of prey tear up food for their chicks at first. As the chicks grow bigger, they learn to do this for themselves.

INDEPENDENT FEEDERS
Some baby birds, such as chickens, ducks, and geese, can feed themselves soon after hatching At first, they peck at anything then they watch their parents to find out what to eat.

PECKING SPOT
A herring gull chick pecks at a red spot on its parent's bill to make the parent cough up food. Herring gulls feed out at sea, so they swallow food to help them carry it long distances.

HERRING
GULL

CRECHE OF YOUNG
KING PENGUINS

Young penguins huddle
together for warmth and
protection while their
parents are away.

SAFETY IN NUMBERS

Young penguins cannot join their
parents in the water until they
have grown waterproof adult
feathers. The parent birds leave
them behind when they go to
sea to feed. When they
return, the adults cough up
partly digested fish for the
chicks, but there may be a
wait of days or even
weeks between meals.

JUVENILE
STARLING

A young starling
takes off unsteadily
for its first flight

FIRST FLIGHT

Baby birds have to learn how to fly
as quickly as possible to avoid
predators and other dangers. They
flap their wings while they are in the
nest to exercise their muscles, and make
them strong. Taking off and landing is
not easy – many young birds crash-land.

BIRDS

MIGRATION

NEARLY HALF the world's birds migrate – to find food and water, to nest, or to avoid bad weather. They navigate by

instinct, but use familiar landmarks, the Sun, the Moon, the stars, and the Earth's magnetic field to find their way. Migration journeys are often dangerous for birds and use up a lot of energy. Some small birds double their weight to provide enough fuel for travelling.

RED-BREASTED GOOSE

NESTING

This goose is one of many birds that migrate to the Arctic tundra to nest in the brief summer when there is plenty of food available.

MIGRATION ROUTES

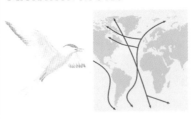

ARCTIC TERN

This is the champion bird migrant, flying from the Arctic to Antarctica and back each year. It spends summer in both polar regions.

AMERICAN GOLDEN PLOVER

This plover has the longest migration of all land birds. It breeds in northern Canada and flies to the Argentinian pampas for the winter

V-FORMATION

Flying in a V-shaped formation helps birds to save energy on a long journey. The birds following the leader fly in the "slipstream" of the bird in front. When the leader tires, another bird takes over.

SNOW GEESE
MIGRATING

Snow geese breed in the Arctic tundra and migrate to the Gulf of Mexico for the winter.

MIGRATION FACTS

• American golden plovers are fast migrants flying 3,300 km (2,050 miles) in 35 hours.

• The ruby-throated hummingbird travels 3,200 km (2,000 miles) across the Americas.

• Most migrating birds fly below 91 m (300 ft).

MOUNTAIN MIGRATION

Some birds migrate short distances. The Himalayan monal pheasant migrates up and down the mountains with the seasons, moving to warmer, lower slopes in winter.

HIMALAYAN
MONAL
PHEASANTS

SHORT-TAILED SHEARWATER

Between breeding seasons off southern Australia, this bird flies in a figure-of-eight route from Australia to the North Pacific and back again.

WHITETHROAT

This small warbler breeds in Europe in spring and summer, and then migrates to Africa just south of the Sahara Desert for the winter.

299

WHERE BIRDS LIVE

FROM BUSY CITIES to frozen polar regions, birds have adapted to a range of habitats on every continent. Where birds live depends on the food they eat and their nesting requirements, as well as their competitors and predators. In many parts of the world, where people live has had a destructive influence on the distribution of birds.

SEAS, CLIFFS, AND SHORES
Marine habitats are a huge feeding ground for many birds. They nest on shores around all continents.

DESERTS AND GRASSLAND
These dry, mainly hot habitats provide little shelter for birds. Food and water may be hard to find.

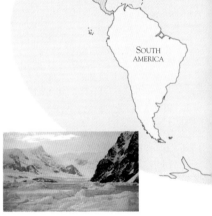

NORTH AMERICA

SOUTH AMERICA

POLAR AND TUNDRA
In the Antarctic, Arctic, and tundra, it is cold and windy. Birds breed there in summer.

RIVERS, LAKES, AND SWAMPS
Lakes and rivers are fresh water, while marshes and swamps are fresh or salt water.

FOREST AND WOODLAND
Conifers and broadleaved trees grow in temperate climates where there is usually rain all year.

RCTIC

EUROPE

ASIA

AFRICA

AUSTRALASIA

NTARCTICA

CITIES AND FARMLAND
Birds that have adapted to live near people can take advantage of the extra food and the less severe climate.

MOUNTAINS AND MOORLAND
Moorlands occur in cool, wet uplands. Mountains have a variety of habitats.

RAINFOREST
These are mostly hot, wet habitats near the Equator in the Americas, Africa, Southeast Asia and northeastern Australia.

CITIES AND FARMLAND

BIRDS HAVE LEARNED to live close to people, and eat the food we give them, as well as the plants, insects, or crops around our homes. Buildings, parks, wasteground, meadows, orchards, and hedgerows provide ample nesting places for birds.

KESTREL

HUNTING BIRDS
Most birds of prey do not like living near people, but kestrels and sparrowhawks hunt along roadsides and in parks.

HABITAT FACTS

• At night, a city is as much as 5°C (9°F) warmer than the surrounding countryside.

• Some starling roosts in cities may contain over one million birds.

• Only one in ten birds caught in the wild reaches the pet shop alive.

• The African red-billed quelea is the world's worst agricultural bird pest.

CITY BIRDS
Birds such as geese fly over cities on migration routes, or land to feed and roost in city parks. Starlings roost in city centres at night because it is warmer than the countryside.

CAGED BIRDS
Many people keep birds such as budgerigars, canaries, and parrots in cages. They like their colours, their company, and their songs. People breed birds to create colours never seen in the wild.

BLUE BUDGERIGAR

BARN
WALLOW
FEEDING
YOUNG

NESTS IN BUILDINGS

Window ledges, attics,
barns and even
chimney pots make ideal nesting places
for birds used to nesting on cliffs,
rocky hillsides or trees. Swallows
used to nest in caves, but now
many nest inside buildings.

NESTS IN HEDGEROWS

Hedgerows are small strips of
woodland where birds such as
the song thrush can nest safely.
Birds roost and feed in hedgerows.
They are an important refuge in
open areas of crops and grass.

SONG THRUSH

SONG THRUSH NEST

303

HOMES AND STREETS

MANY BIRDS HAVE LOST their natural fear of people and live near our homes and in our cities, despite all the noise and pollution. These urban birds change their diet or the places they nest to take advantage of our leftover food scraps, the artificial habitats we build, and the warm climates we create.

HOUSE SPARROW
By following people from country to country, the fearless house sparrow has spread from Europe and Asia over about two-thirds of the world's land surface. It nests in buildings close to people.

The male has a grey crown and black bib.

The house sparrow is friendly and intelligent.

BIRDS IN DANGER
Thousands of birds are taken from the wild every year. This has reduced numbers of some wild birds, especially parrots.

WHITE STORKS
In many parts of Europe, white storks are believed to bring good luck. They often nest on roofs and people may put up platforms to encourage them.

Upright black
crest and red
streak below eye

HOUSE CROW
The aggressive house crow is
always ready to grasp a tasty
morsel of food. It lives
near busy towns and
small villages in
India, as well as
in other parts of
Asia, often swarming
in large, busy groups.

Likes to perch on a
high branch to sing

RED-EARED BULBUL
The inquisitive red-eared
bulbul is not frightened of
people and is a common
species around the villages
of Asia. It has a pleasant
and varied song and is
often kept as a pet.

Pigeons are tame
enough to be fed
by hand.

PIGEON
The city pigeons of
today are descended
from the wild rock
doves which people
originally kept for food
and, later, for racing.
Pigeons have a strong
muscular part of the stomach
called a gizzard to help
them grind up seeds.

City pigeons
even travel on
underground
trains.

PARKS AND GARDENS

FROM TREES AND FLOWERBEDS to grassy lawns and garden ponds, parks and gardens contain a great variety of habitats for birds. People put up feeding tables, bird baths, and nesting boxes to encourage birds to live near houses. Unfortunately, pets such as cats often catch and kill garden birds.

BLACK-BILLED MAGPIE
This adaptable magpie visits suburban gardens. It eats a range of food, especially insects and small rodents, but also steals eggs and young from the nests of other birds.

Pale grey border

Red breast and face typical of robins

EURASIAN ROBIN
These birds are aggressive and males often set up territories in gardens. They sing loudly to keep away othe male robins. In winter, both males and females defend feeding territories.

BLUE TITS
These bold, lively birds often visit gardens in winter to feed on nuts, seeds, and leftover food scraps put out by people. They can easily land on nut feeders and often use the nest boxes that people build and put up for them.

Blue tits are agile, acrobatic birds.

Cone-shaped bill typical of a seed eater

WATERFOWL IN PARKS
The artificial lakes in parks make a welcome feeding, resting, and nesting area for geese, ducks, and grebes. Islands in the middle of lakes provide safe nesting places.

NORTHERN CARDINAL
These cardinals are frequent visitors to feeders in the backyards of North America. They often move around in pairs or family groups to feed on seeds that people leave out for them.

SUPERB STARLING
A common visitor to lawns, campsites, and hotels in East Africa, the superb starling is a tame bird, not frightened of people. It feeds mainly on the ground, pecking up seeds, fruit, and insects.

FIELDS AND HEDGEROWS

FARMLAND HAS TAKEN the place of woodlands, grasslands, and wetlands, but some birds have adapted to this habitat. They feed on the crops, and nest in the animal pastures, hedges, orchards, and farm buildings. However, numbers of farmland birds have been reduced by the removal of hedgerows and the use of poisonous pesticides.

GOLDFINCH
Flocks of goldfinches feed on weeds along the edges of fields. They are light enough to perch on thistle heads and eat the seeds.

FOLLOWING THE PLOUGH
Large flocks of birds, such as black-headed gulls, often follow a tractor ploughing a field. The birds feed on the insects and other invertebrates, such as worms, exposed by the plough.

Seagulls following the tractor

PHEASANT
The female common pheasant may nest in hedgerows, making a shallow scrape in the ground in which to lay her eggs. Pheasants wander over farmland, feeding mainly on grains, seeds, berries, and insects.

HOOPOE
In the Mediterranean, the reeds and grasses under the olive groves teem with invertebrates. Hoopoes probe the ground with long curved bills for worms and insects.

DUNNOCK
Sometimes called the hedge sparrow, the dunnock is not related to a sparrow at all – it just looks like one. Dunnocks nest in hedgerows, where they build cup-shaped nests.

The chicks are well camouflaged, like their mother.

The grey head and underparts help to tell the dunnock from a sparrow

FOREST AND WOODLAND

JAY

THIS KIND OF HABITAT provides birds with plenty of food and safe nesting places. A greater variety of birds live in the deciduous and eucalyptus woodlands than in the dark conifer forests, because of the warmer, wetter conditions.

FOOD AND FEEDING
Woodland birds feed on buds, berries, and seeds from the tre and shrubs. Some eat insects and small animals. Diets may vary with changes in season.

BIRDSONG
Most woodland birds, such as the nightingale, have loud songs and calls to attract mates, and establish breeding territories in the thick undergrowth.

PHEASANT WING

NIGHTINGALE

WINGS
Many woodland birds have short, broad, rounded wings t help them rise fast into the air and avoid twigs and branches. Pheasants can fly quickly fo short distance

Nests in holes
Holes in trees are safe and warm places for birds such as redstarts to raise a family. In the nesting season, the adults frequently fly in and out with food for the growing young.

MALE REDSTART

CAMOUFLAGED WOODCOCK

Forest facts

• The northern forest called the taiga is the largest in the world.

• There are over 600 species of eucalyptus in Australia.

• Up to half of all woodland birds nest in tree holes.

• The woodpecker family has existed for over 50 million years.

Camouflage
Many woodland and forest birds are well camouflaged to protect them from predators. The dull, mottled colours of this woodcock hide it against the decaying leaf litter of the woodland floor.

DECIDUOUS WOODLAND

IN THESE temperate woodlands, a great variety of birds can live together because they feed at different levels, sharing out available food. In warm weather, the birds nest, raise their young, and eat as much as possible. In colder weather, the leaves fall off the trees, and some birds migrate to warmer places.

Thick skull

Long, curved claws to cling to tree trunks

WOODPECKER SKULL

GOLDEN-FRONTED WOODPECKER
This thrush-sized woodpecker of the Americas hammers into decaying tree trunks to find insect larvae and make nesting holes. It licks up insects with its long, sticky tongue.

Strong, stiff tail feathers for support

LONG-TAILED TITS
Long-tailed tits flit about on the edges of woodlands, pecking insects and spiders off the leaves and bark. Outside the breeding season, the tits huddle in small groups at night to keep warm.

GREEN WOOD HOOPOE
These birds probe tree trunks with their long, curved bills searching for food. They live in noisy family groups in African woodlands.

Long bill is used to find insect grubs or eggs, and spiders.

The bill is broad at the base to catch insects.

SPOTTED FLYCATCHER
Perching on exposed branches, spotted flycatchers dart out to snap up passing insects. In cold weather, they migrate to warmer places, such as Africa, to find food.

Green wood hoopoes have high, cackling calls

WHIP-POOR-WILL
During the day, this well-camouflaged bird sleeps on the woodland floor. At night, it flies near the ground catching insects.

313

CAPERCAILLIE
The capercaillie is able
to eat pine needles. This
helps it survive through
the hard winter. Comb-
like fringes on its toes
stop it sinking into snow.

CONIFEROUS FORES

DARK CONIFEROUS FORESTS – the
taiga – stretch across the top of
the Northern Hemisphere, from
the tundra in the north to the
more open deciduous woodlands
farther south. The leaves stay on
the trees all year round, but
winters are bitterly cold and most
birds leave for warmer places. In
the short summer,
they feed on seed
berries
or insects.

SISKIN
The restless and acrobatic
siskin often hangs upside-
down to pull the see
out of pine and
larch cones.
Siskins are
social birds and
build nests high i
conifer trees, whe
the young cannot
easily be reache
by enemies.

*The siskin feeds
on the seeds of pine,
larch, alder and
birch trees.*

...ED CROSSBILL

...rossbills use their scissor-
...ke bills to lever apart the
...ales on the cones of pine,
...ruce, larch and other
...onifers to reach the seeds.
...arent crossbills cough up
...rtly digested pine seed to
...ed to their young.

PINE
CONES

Scales
opened by a
crossbill

Male and
...nale birds
...e similar
...n colour

WAXWING

These birds are named
after the red, wax-like
tips on some of their
flight feathers. Waxwings
eat berries or fruit, but
will also catch insects
when they can. They
migrate south in the
autumn in large numbers.

Waxwings
live in
large flocks

JUVENILE BALD EAGLE

Bald eagles live in forests
near water, where they hunt
for fish and waterbirds. They
do not grow the white
feathers on the head and tail
until they are four years old.

315

EUCALYPTUS WOODLAND

IN THE EVERGREEN eucalyptus woodlands of
Australia, there is food and shelter for a variety
of unique birds all year. The birds
help to pollinate the trees and
shrubs, and spread their seeds.
In the rainy season, waterbirds
gather in marshy areas on the
borders of these woodlands.

Strong, hooked beak characteristic of parrot family

MALLEE FOWL
These birds build a huge moun
of rotting vegetation covered
with sand to keep their eggs
warm. The male checks the
temperature with his bill.

Two toes in front and two toes behind

RAINBOW LORIKEETS
Noisy flocks of rainbow lorikeets feed
high in the trees. They crush the flowers
of eucalyptus and other flowering trees to
soak up the sticky mixture of nectar and
pollen with their fringe-tipped tongues.

Large, broad-
ised bill to
atch and
allow prey

Large head
and bill with
brown ear
patch

LAUGHING KOOKABURRA
Named after its very noisy,
chuckling calls, the laughing
kookaburra is a giant kingfisher that rarely
eats fish. Instead, it pounces on reptiles such as
snakes, small mammals, birds, and invertebrates.

317

Feathers are fanned out to make owl look frightening

OWLS

MOST OWLS SLEEP by day and hunt by night. Their sharp hearing and keen eyesight help them catch prey such as mice and small birds. Many owls roost in trees and have brown feathers for camouflage.

SCOPS OWL
Almost impossible to spot because of its superb camouflage, the scops owl eats large insects. It raises its feathers to defend itself from an enemy.

In a complete pellet, animal f and bones are stuck together

Owl mucus binds pellet together

OWL FACTS
- Order Strigiformes
- About 174 species
- Mainly nocturnal
- Birds of prey
- Eat birds, insects and small mammals
- Habitat: mainly woodland
- Nest in tree holes, or other birds' nests
- Eggs: white

OWL PELLETS
Once or twice a day, owls cough up pellets containing indigestible bits of their last meal, such as fur or bones. Pulling a pellet apart reveals what an owl has eaten.

BOOBOOK OWL
This small Australian owl gets its name from its double hoot. It feeds mainly on insects.

Large feet with hooked talons

318

BARN OWL

A heart-shaped face is the trademark of the barn owl, a bird so different from other owls that it has its own family. The disc of feathers on the face collects sounds like a radar dish. Barn owls make a haunting shrieking sound.

Owls catch and kill prey with their sharp talons.

"Ears" are only tufts of feathers

EURASIAN EAGLE OWL

The largest of all owls, eagle owls are powerful hunters, strong enough to attack hares and mallards. They have very loud hoots: male eagle owls can be heard hooting over 1 km (1/2 mile) away.

BARN OWL FEATHER

TAWNY OWL FEATHER

OWL FEATHERS
Soft, velvety feathers with fringes on the flight feathers muffle the sound made by the wings in flight.

Thick covering of soft feathers

RAINFOREST

TROPICAL RAINFORESTS are the richest bird habitats. They provide a wealth of food and safe nesting places, and a warm, wet climate all year round. Rainforest birds usually have short, broad wings to twist and turn easily when flying through the trees. This unique habitat is under threat from forestry, mining, dams, and farming.

CANOPY

UNDERSTOREY

FOREST FLOOR

BIRDS OF PARADISE
Male birds of paradise have ornate and colourful feathers to attract females. Some tail feathers are very beautiful, like these from a Count Raggi's bird of paradise.

LAYERS OF LIFE
The birds live at different levels in the trees. In this way, they share the available food and nesting places, so a huge variety of birds can live close together.

SPREADING SEEDS
Fruit-eating birds such as aracaris and parrots help to spread the seeds of rainforest trees. They feed on fruits and pass the seeds in their droppings.

Wide tail helps the aracari to balance on branches

CHESTNUT-EARED
ARACARI

Long bill with
serrated edge

Groups of crested
oropendolas hang
their woven nests
from tree branches.

NESTING
To keep their nests
out of sight and out of
reach of predators, rainforest birds nest
high in the trees or in dense thickets above
the ground. Some, such as parrots and
hornbills, nest in tree holes.

COLOUR
The bright colours of rainforest
birds like these macaws are
surprisingly hard to see among the
leafy trees. These birds are feeding
on mineral-rich soil.

HABITAT FACTS

• Since 1945, over half
the rainforests have been
destroyed; an area the
size of a soccer pitch is
cut down every second.

• Rainforests contain
over 50 per cent of all
plant and animal species.

• One-fifth of all the
kinds of birds in the
world live in the
Amazon rainforest.

321

UNDER THE CANOPY

BENEATH THE GREEN ROOF of the forest is the dark, cool understorey of smaller trees, shrubs, and climbing plants, and below this, the leafy forest floor. There is less food and warmth at these lower levels than up in the canopy, so there are fewer birds. Large birds such as trumpeters and cassowaries stalk across the forest floor. In the understorey, hummingbirds and jacamars flit through the branches.

HOATZIN CHICK

HOATZIN
Groups of hoatzins live along riverbanks in the rainforests of South America. They are poor fliers and make short flights through the trees.

Chick has claws on its wings for climbing

DOUBLE-WATTLED CASSOWARY
This huge cassowary melts into the forest if it senses danger. Males make loud, booming calls during courtship. The horny casque on its head is used to push aside forest undergrowth.

SUNBITTERN
This bird is named after the sunset colour on its wings, visible during its courtship display. At other times, it is well camouflaged by the mottled grey and brown colours of its feathers.

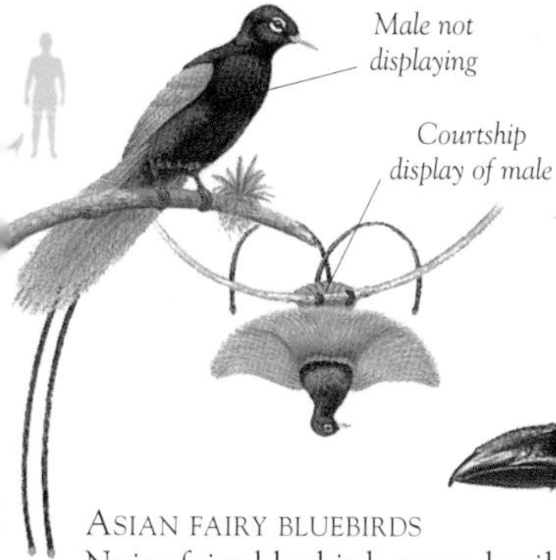

Male not displaying

Courtship display of male

BLUE BIRDS OF PARADISE

The male blue bird of paradise performs a dramatic upside-down display to show off his iridescent feathers to a female. He also makes a series of loud, vibrating notes. Females look after the young on their own.

These birds live in the middle or upper levels of the rainforest, rarely coming down to the ground.

ASIAN FAIRY BLUEBIRDS

Noisy fairy bluebirds move busily through the trees searching for fruit, such as figs. The metallic blue of the male is not easy to see in the shade of the trees.

...airy bluebirds ...n make sharp, ...histling calls.

IN THE TREETOPS

HIGH UP IN THE RAINFOREST CANOPY it is light
and warm and there is plenty of food, especially
fruits, seeds, and insects. Bird life includes large bird
predators such as eagles which patrol the treetops looking
for prey. Canopy birds, such
as parrots and toucans, climb
well and have strong feet for
grasping branches.

Bare, orange-yellow face and bill

HARPY EAGLE
The huge harpy
eagle is one of the most
powerful birds of prey. It
swoops into the canopy to
seize monkeys (like this
capuchin), birds, sloths, a
reptiles. It can fly very fas
through the branches.

LADY ROSS'S TURACO
This African turaco lives in small, no
groups, usually high in the canopy.
Although clumsy fliers, turacos are
good at running along tree branche
They make a great variety of
cackling and croaking calls.

OCO TOUCAN
his is the largest toucan, with
bill up to 19 cm (7½ in) long. The bill
hollow inside with supporting struts,
it is not as heavy as it looks.
he colours help it to recognize
her toucans and find a mate.

RANGE-BELLIED LEAFBIRD
his Asian leafbird helps to
ollinate the forest trees as it
eds on nectar. It also
reads the seeds of
ants in the
istletoe family
eating the
rries.

*This leafbird is
good at
mimicking other
birds' songs.*

*The casque is a thin layer
of skin and bone over
a honeycomb structure.*

GREAT INDIAN HORNBILL
The hornbills of Southeast Asia and
Africa look like the toucans of South
America because they live and feed in
a similar way. They are named after the
horny casques on their bills. No-one
knows what these bony growths are for.

325

BIRDS

PARROTS

MOST PARROTS are brightly coloured and live in tropical forests. They tend to fly about in flocks, making harsh, screeching calls. Many species are threatened by habitat destruction. There are three main groups: the lories, the cockatoos, and the parrots.

Narrow, tapering wings to fly fast through the trees

CANARY WINGED PARAKEE
This small parrot long tail helps i balance as it flies fas through the trees. Large parrots usually fly mor slowly. One parrot, th kakapo, cannot fly at al

CHATTERING LORY
The chattering lory spends most of its time high in the trees feeding mainly on pollen and nectar. Lories have a brush-like tip to the tongue which soaks up their liquid diet.

LESSER SULPHUR-
CRESTED COCKATOO
Cockatoos raise and lower their head crests when they are excited, frightened, or angry. They also do this when landing on a perch.

PARROT FACTS

- Family: Psittacidae
- About 330 species
- Diurnal
- Tropical land birds
- Eat fruits, seeds, nuts, and other plants; also some invertebrates
- Habitat: forest, scrub, grassland, and mountains
- Nest: usually tree hole, holes in banks or among rocks
- Eggs: white

ECLECTUS PARROTS
These parrots are unusual because the bright red female is such a different colour from the green male, whereas male and female parrots usually look alike. Eclectus parrots feed on fruits, nuts, and leaf buds.

Nutcracker bill to crush seeds and nuts

SKULL AND BILL
Parrots have broad, large skulls with a fairly big space for the brain – they are intelligent birds. The top bill curves sharply down, fitting neatly over the broad, bottom bill, which curves upwards.

Many parrots have green feathers to camouflage them in the leaves of the trees.

Two toes point forwards and two backwards to give a powerful grip.

RIVERS, LAKES, AND SWAMPS

WATERY HABITATS are home to a rich variety of birds, from ducks, coots, and rails to herons and storks. There is plenty of food for birds to eat, and safe nesting places in reeds and on riverbanks. Many birds rest and feed on lakes, marshes, and swamps during migration. But drainage schemes, dams, acid rain, and pollution from farms and factories threaten these habitats.

KINGFISHER DIVING

WEBBED FEET FOSSIL

Many waterbirds, such as Canada geese, have webbed feet to push the water aside as they swim. Long legs to wade in deep water, and long toes to walk over soft mud are other common features of waterbirds.

CANADA GOOSE FOOT

HUNTING FOR FISH

To catch fish, birds like this kingfisher dive into the water to seize their prey. Others, such as herons, stand still and catch fish that swim past. Another technique is to scoop up fish from the surface.

CATCHING FISH

Birds need strong bills and feet to hold slippery prey. Mergansers have serrated edges to their bill to help them keep a grip on fish they catch.

HOODED MERGANSER SKULL

NORTHERN
SHOVELER

FILTER FEEDING
Birds like the shoveler
filter tiny floating plants
and animals from water.
The shoveler has "combs"
on its bill to trap food.

CAMOUFLAGE
The dark, mottled colours of some
birds, such as the buff-banded
rail, help to
camouflage them
as they skulk
noiselessly through the reed
beds of marshes and swamps.

BUFF-
BANDED
RAIL

NESTING
Hiding a nest away from predators is a relatively
easy task in these habitats. Nesting materials
such as dried reeds are also easy to find. Some
birds even build floating
platforms of
vegetation for extra
security.

COOT
NESTING IN
REEDS

RIVERS AND LAKES

THESE FRESHWATER habitats are important for birds, especially in undisturbed areas free of pollution. Some birds prefer the still waters of ponds and lakes while others, such as dippers, are adapted to move in fast-flowing waters. Around the edge of the water are many places to nest and a variety of food for the young, including water insects.

GREY WAGTAIL
The busy grey wagtail patrols mountain streams, darting out to snap up flying insects in its long bill. It has sharp claws to grip slippery rocks and wet branches.

WESTERN GREBES
The courtship dance of the western grebe is long and unusual. During the dance, a pair stands up tall and races fast across the water with heads tilted forwards.

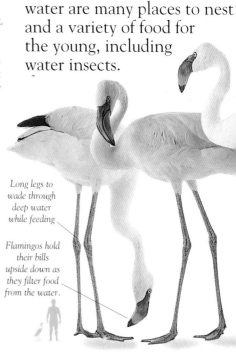

Long legs to wade through deep water while feeding

Flamingos hold their bills upside down as they filter food from the water.

At the last moment, the feet swing forward to grasp the fish.

OSPREY
The osprey is a powerful hunter, plunging feet first into water to snatch fish from near the surface. It sometimes goes right under before pulling up into the air again. Strong claws and spines under the toes help it hold slippery fish.

All flamingos have some black feathers in their wings.

WHITE-CROWNED FORKTAIL
These Asian birds live by rocky streams, perching on boulders wagging their long tails. They have a loud, high-pitched whistle to communicate above the noise of the water.

Lesser flamingos are the smallest of the six species of flamingo.

Crop

LESSER FLAMINGOS
Flamingos live in noisy colonies, sometimes containing thousands of birds. They nest on mounds of mud, and both parents feed the young on a rich "milk" produced in the crop.

331

SWAMPS AND MARSHES

WET, TREELESS GRASSLANDS, called marshes, and waterlogged forests, called swamps, are often given the name "wetlands". They can be fresh- or saltwater habitats. Fish-eating birds, such as egrets and pelicans, are common, but a lot of birds can feed together by eating different kinds of food at different levels in the water. Wetlands are often refuges for rare birds, as large mammal predators cannot easily hunt there.

SCARLET IBIS
Spectacular flocks of scarlet ibises feed, roost, and nest together in the tropical swamps of South America. Scarlet ibises feel in soft mud or under plants for insects, crabs, shellfish, frogs, and fish. Young scarlet ibises have grey-brown backs for a year while they mature into adults.

Long, thin, down-curved bill to probe for food

Slim body to slide easily through dense vegetation

BLACK CRAKES
These East African birds have long, widely spaced toes to sto[p] them sinking into the mud an[d] help them walk over floating water plants. Their short, thic[k] bills are not long enough to probe in mud, so they peck small invertebrates and seeds off the surface.

BEARDED TIT

Active and acrobatic bearded tits or reedlings fly low over reed beds on their rounded wings. They feed on insects in warm weather, and seeds in cold weather. Both parents build the nest in the reeds and share the care of their young.

WHOOPING CRANES

Among the world's rarest birds, the whooping crane spends the winter on the coastal marshes of Texas, U.S.A. In spring, it migrates to Canada to breed.

Male has black moustache

A bird's "knee" is really its ankle, so it bends backwards, just like a person's ankle.

BIRDS

DUCKS

WEBBED FEET and broad, flat bills are a distinctive feature of ducks. These birds are good swimmers and strong fliers. There are two main types of duck – dabbling ducks, such as the mallard, that feed on the surface, and diving ducks, such as the pochard. Many ducks migrate to avoid cold weather.

FEMALE

MALE

DOWN FEATHERS
Female ducks pluck down feathers from their breasts and use them to line their nests and cover the eggs to keep them warm.

Short legs set well back on body

MANDARIN DUCKS
These ducks live near ponds and lakes surrounded by woods, and nest in tree holes. The male is more colourful than the female, except when he moults his feathers once a year.

CAROLINA OR WOOD DUCK
Found in North America, Carolina ducks are related to Asian Mandarin ducks. The females look after the nest, eggs, and ducklings on their own.

The ducklings swim soon after hatching

DUCK FACTS
- Family: *Anatidae* includes ducks, swans, and geese
- About 152 species
- Diurnal
- Waterfowl
- Eat water plants and small water animals
- Habitat: ponds, lakes, rivers, or the sea
- Nest: platform near water, or in tree holes
- Eggs: white or pale

DIVING DUCKS
These ducks have shorter, rounder bodies than ducks that feed on the surface. Diving ducks, such as this pochard, can stay underwater for 30 seconds or more.

PLUMED WHISTLING DUCK
Whistling ducks live in the tropics and look more like geese than ducks. They feed mainly on the surface.

MALE MALLARD

Webbed feet used like paddles for swimming

Wide, flat bill to sift food out of water

MALLARDS
These ducks feed on the surface of the water or upend to reach plant and animal food below the surface. Mallards are the ancestors of most domestic ducks.

335

SEAS, CLIFFS, AND SHORES

SOME SPECIALLY adapted birds spend most of their lives gliding over the open oceans. But they nest on shores and in the safety of cliff ledges, usually in large colonies. The rich feeding grounds of estuaries attract huge numbers of waders and wildfowl, especially on migration.

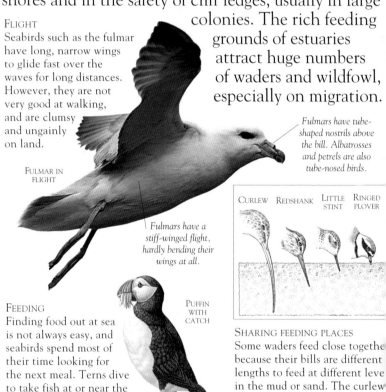

FLIGHT
Seabirds such as the fulmar have long, narrow wings to glide fast over the waves for long distances. However, they are not very good at walking, and are clumsy and ungainly on land.

FULMAR IN
FLIGHT

Fulmars have tube-shaped nostrils above the bill. Albatrosses and petrels are also tube-nosed birds.

Fulmars have a stiff-winged flight, hardly bending their wings at all.

CURLEW   REDSHANK   LITTLE STINT   RINGED PLOVER

FEEDING
Finding food out at sea is not always easy, and seabirds spend most of their time looking for the next meal. Terns dive to take fish at or near the surface. Other seabirds, such as puffins, swim deeper underwater.

PUFFIN
WITH
CATCH

SHARING FEEDING PLACES
Some waders feed close together because their bills are different lengths to feed at different levels in the mud or sand. The curlew's long bill reaches worms in deep burrows, while the ringed plover picks insects off the surface.

HERRING
GULL EGGS

Most seabird
eggs are more
pointed at one
end than the
other.

CAMOUFLAGED EGGS
Birds such as gulls or terns
have camouflaged eggs, as
they nest in the open on
beaches or dunes. The
spots and other
markings help the
eggs to blend into
the background so
predators find it
hard to see them.

GANNET
ON NEST

NESTING
Many seabirds nest in
tightly packed colonies
of thousands or even
millions of birds. The
vast numbers stimulate
them to breed at the
same time. Gannets
nest close together
in noisy, smelly
colonies.

HABITAT FACTS

• Oceans cover about
70 per cent of the
Earth's surface.

• The sea cools more
slowly than the land,
keeping coastal areas
warmer in winter.

• The tidal range in
open oceans is only
about 50 cm (20 in).

• In 1 sq m (10 sq ft)
of estuary there may be
over 1,000 worms.

SEAS, CLIFFS, & SHORES

337

ESTUARIES AND SHORES

APART FROM CLIFFS, other areas along the shoreline, such as dunes and beaches, provide nesting areas for seabirds. And where rivers meet the sea, the shallow, muddy waters of estuaries teem with a wealth of food such as fish, worms, and shellfish. Estuaries are particularly important in cold weather, when inland feeding areas are frozen.

PURPLE SANDPIPER
Stocky purple sandpipers migrate south in colder weather to feed on rocky shores. They search the shoreline for food, finding their prey by sight rather than by touch.

BLACK-NECKED STILT
This stilt has extremely long legs which allow it to feed in deeper water than other waders. It uses its long bill to take small creatures from water and mud.

On dry ground, the stilt bends its legs awkwardly to feed.

In flight, the stilt's legs stick out 18 cm (7 in) beyond the tail to counterbalance the head and neck.

SLEEPING
On an estuary, waders such as this dunlin feed when the can, and sleep when the tide comes in and covers their feeding grounds. They flock to the safety of high-tide roosts, such as small islands

INCA TERN

This South American tern often gathers in flocks of many thousands, and roosts on sandy beaches. Inca terns are graceful fliers, hovering over the sea, and dipping down to snatch food from the surface.

Inca terns may follow whales and seals to seize scraps of food.

GREAT BLACK-BACKED GULL

These huge gulls are fierce predators of seabird colonies on the coast. They have long, powerful wings for gliding.

RINGED PLOVER

As soon as the ringed plover stops moving, its colours make it hard to see among the pebbles on the beach. Females may pretend to be injured to draw predators away from eggs and young.

SEA AND CLIFFS

OVER THE OPEN OCEAN, seabirds search for food, also landing on the surface to rest and preen. Seabirds have waterproofed feathers, webbed feet for swimming, and sharp bills to catch slippery prey. Many nest on cliffs where eggs and young are safe from predators.

NESTING SPACE
To share the nesting sites on a cliff, the birds nest at different levels. Gannets, and kittiwakes nest near the top, and razorbills in the middle. Shags and cormorants nest lower down.

After fishing, the cormorant holds its wings open to dry.

GANNET SKULL
To catch fish, gannets plunge into the sea like torpedos from heights of up to 30 m (100 ft). They have a strong skull to withstand the impact when they hit the water with such a great force.

COMMON CORMORANT
The feathers of the common or great cormorant trap very little air, so the bird sinks in water more easily than other seab and can feed on bottom-living creatures.

340

A frigatebird robs a tropicbird of its fishy meal.

PIRACY AT SEA
Frigatebirds steal much of their food from other birds such as pelicans and gulls. They are speedy fliers and can swoop, dart, soar, and hover better than most other seabirds.

Nests of grass, seaweeds and mud sit snugly on narrow ledges.

KITTIWAKES
These small gulls nest close together in colonies consisting of hundreds of birds. They are named after their call. Unlike other gulls they are rarely found on land.

DESERTS AND GRASSLAND

IN THESE MAINLY HOT, dry habitats, birds may have to travel long distances to find food and water, or migrate to avoid dry seasons. Seeds and insects are the main sources of food, but some larger birds also feed on reptiles, small mammals, and dead animals.

Honeybees form the main diet of bee-eaters.

INSECT EATERS
Birds such as bee-eaters and warblers feed on the insects which are most abundant during a rainy season. In the dry season, insect eaters often have to migrate to find enough to eat.

ROADRUNNER

VARIED DIET
Food is often hard to find, so birds survive by eating any food they come across. Reptiles are a common source of food. This roadrunner has caught a lizard.

White-throat[ed] bee-eaters [fly] to wet[t] grasslan[d] in the d[ry] seaso[n]

WHITE-THROATED BEE-EATER

These birds are threatened by the caged bird trade.

SEED EATERS

Grass seeds are a vital source of food for many birds, such as these Australian Gouldian finches. When the grasses die back in the dry season, the finches migrate towards wetter areas on the coast.

GOULDIAN FINCHES

RUBBISH CLEARANCE

The carcasses of large grazing animals and human rubbish tips provide food for birds such as marabou storks and vultures.

BURROWING OWLS

NDERGROUND SHELTERS

keep out of the heat of e sun, burrowing owls rest d nest safe from enemies side burrows dug by small mmals like prairie dogs.

MARABOU STORK

HABITAT FACTS

• More than a quarter of all the land on Earth is covered in grass.

• Deserts have less than 25 mm (10 in) rainfall each year.

• In the deserts of Death Valley, U.S.A., temperatures can reach as high as 55°C (131°F).

• The African ostrich is the heaviest, tallest and fastest-running bird in the world.

DESERTS

BIRDS THAT LIVE in deserts have to get most of their water either from their food or by flying long distances. By day, they may rest in the shade of rocks, or inside cacti or underground burrows. Some come out to feed at night, when it is cooler. Many birds of prey survive in deserts on a diet of reptiles and small mammals.

SANDGROUSE
These birds are strong fliers and travel many kilometres to find water. The male birds carry water back to their chicks in their belly feathers.

Hooked beak typical of bird of prey

ELF OWL
The sparrow-sized elf owl nests in holes dug out by woodpeckers inside giant saguaro cacti. The spines of the cactus protect the eggs and young from predators. Elf owls hunt for insects in the cool of the night.

It is much cooler inside the cactus.

HARRIS' HAWK
A fearless hunter of birds, lizards, and small mammals, Harris' hawk sometimes feeds on carcasses, alongside vultures and caracaras. It is often found near roadsides in the desert regions of the Americas.

The female does not have orange cheek patches and her bill is a duller red.

The male has zebra-like stripes on the chest.

ZEBRA FINCHES

These lively little birds are common in the Australian outback. They nest after the rains when there are plenty of seeds and insects to feed to their young. They live in flocks of up to 100 birds, and several may nest together.

345

SCRUB AND BUSH

THE BIRDS OF these warm, dry, dusty habitats may roam widely in search of food, or follow the rains. The thorny bushes and shrubs often form dense thickets and these make safe nesting places. The berries that grow on the bushes and shrubs can be a useful source of food in colder weather.

Males have brighter markings on the face than the females.

COCKATIELS
These small cockatoos wander over the Australian bush count looking for fruits and grass seeds. They usually nest after rainfall at any time of year.

BLUE-CAPPED CORDON-BLEU
Small groups of cordon-bleus search the ground for grass seeds and insects in the thorn scrub of East Africa. They feed their young mainly on a protein-rich diet of insects.

Short, stubby bill to crush seeds

NDIAN GREY FRANCOLIN
These birds are common in southern
Asia because they are able to survive
in dry conditions. They usually live in
small family groups, and feed
on weed seeds and grain
crops. In warm weather,
they also eat
insects.

*Francolins try to
escape danger by
running.*

SCRUBLAND
The scrubland habitats of small trees and
thorny shrubs are halfway between
grassland and woodland. They include
the Mediterranean scrublands, the
Californian chaparral, and parts of the
Australian bush or outback.

EMU
Small flocks of flightless
emus roam widely through the
Australian bush in search of
seeds, berries, and insects.
The male looks after
the chicks for
up to 18 months.

WHITE HELMET SHRIKE
me and active white helmet
hrikes live in small flocks of
two to 20 birds. They hop
through the African bush
pping up insects and spiders
h their strong, hooked bills.

GRASSLAND

A VARIETY OF seed- and insect-eating birds live in grasslands, especially those birds that can adapt to living near people. Some birds follow herds of grazing animals to snap up the insects disturbed by their feet. Other birds feed on the animals when they die. Long legs enable birds such as ostriches and rheas to see over tall grasses and watch for danger.

Oxpeckers and giraffe

OXPECKERS

These birds pick ticks and insects off the fur of large African mammals such as giraffes and zebra. They cling to the mammal's fur with their sharp claws.

In breeding plumage, male is bright chestnut, with black head and throat

This weaver is a shy bird, with a fast, dashing flight.

CHESTNUT WEAVER

These weavers nest in dense colonies in the African grasslands. Out of the breeding season, both male and female are dull brown.

OSTRICH

Able to survive in very dry conditions, ostriches stride over the African savannah grasslands on their long legs, searching for leaves, seeds, and insects. They are threatened by hunting and habitat destruction.

*Bare head
and neck*

HOODED VULTURE
The bare head
and neck of the
hooded vulture allow it to
reach right inside an animal
carcass to feed without getting
its feathers dirty. Vultures fly
high, using their sharp eyesight
to spot carrion.

*Sometimes called
the ovenbird because
the nest looks like
an old-fashioned
baker's oven*

*Strong talons
cling onto branch*

RUFOUS HORNERO
There are few trees on the South
American pampas grasslands, so the
rufous hornero builds a huge mud nest to
protect its eggs and young. The nest is
made of mud and straw baked by the sun.

349

MOUNTAINS AND MOORLAND

MOORLAND TEND TO BE wet, boggy places while mountains can be very cold and windy. Only a few hardy birds live on mountains and moorland because of the harsh climate and lack of food, especially in the cold seasons. However, these habitats are important breeding areas for birds.

This shy, secretive bird rarely emerges from the bamboo thickets and dense forest where it lives.

SEASONAL MIGRATION
Hardy pheasants such as this Lady Amherst's pheasant live in the mountain forests of Asia. They move up and down the mountains with the seasons. Many pheasants are threatened by hunting.

Feathered feet to insulate against the cold

CAMOUFLAGE
In autumn, the ptarmigan grows new white feathers for camouflage. These tough birds bury themselves in snow to keep out cold, biting winds. In summer, their plumage is mottled grey-brown.

Colourful feathers and neck ruff

LADY AMHERST'S PHEASANT

NESTING
CURLEW

MOUNTAIN FORESTS
The warmer forests on the lower slopes of mountains provide many birds with plenty of food and nesting places. In colder weather, birds may move down to these forests from the upper slopes.

RUFOUS-
BELLIED
NILTAVA

These Asian flycatchers live in mountain forest above 1,000 m (3,000 ft).

ESTING PLACES
Vaders such as this curlew nest
n windswept moorland in
ummer. They hide their nests
nong grasses and bushes.
Their young feed on insects,
orms, frogs, and snails. In
inter, they move to the coast.

GROUSE
EGG

MOORLAND EGGS
Heavy blotches of colour help to camouflage the eggs of moorland nesters such as grouse and waders among the heather and bracken. The eggs are laid in a shallow scrape on the ground.

CURLEW
EGG

*Male has long
tail for display*

HABITAT FACTS

• The Appalachians were formed over 250 million years ago; the Himalayas formed only 40 million years ago.

• The world's longest mountain chain is the Andes at 7,250 km (4,500 miles) long.

• Some moorland is created by a change to a wetter climate; others by people clearing trees for farmland.

351

MOUNTAINS

IN COLD WEATHER, food is scarce on mountains, but these areas are undisturbed breeding areas for birds. Birds' feathers keep them warm when it is freezing cold, and efficient lungs enable them to get enough oxygen from the thin air. Many mountain birds are powerful fliers.

RAVEN
These large members of the crow family are mainly scavengers. They patrol the mountain slopes, searching for food with their sharp eyes.

WALLCREEPER
This nimble bird clings on to rock faces with its sharp claws, probing for insects with its slender bill. In cold weather, it moves to lower slopes where there are more insects for it to eat.

SWORD-BILLED HUMMINGBIRD
This hummingbird lives high in the Andes. It has a very long bill, which it uses to sip nectar from flowers.

SNOW, ICE, AND ROCK

GRASSY MEADOWS

CONIFEROUS FOREST

TEMPERATE FOREST

HABITAT ZONES
Mountains have a variety of habitats. There are warm, deciduous forests on the lower slopes, cooler coniferous forests higher up, and just below the snow-covered peaks, grasslands and scrub.

*The lammergeier is
also called the
bearded vulture.*

*Lammergeiers fly to
great heights and drop
bones on to rocks to
break them apart.*

LAMMERGEIER
Soaring over the
mountain slopes on
rising warm air currents, the
lammergeier searches the steep
slopes for the carcasses of animals
killed by the harsh climate. It drops
the bones onto rocks to smash them
open, then scoops out the marrow
with its long tongue.

ANDEAN CONDOR
The world's heaviest bird of
prey, the Andean condor, has
very keen eyesight and
long, broad wings. It soars
over the Andes looking
for dead, sick, or wounded
animals to feed on. There
is a ready supply of food
because of the
difficult living
conditions.

MOORLAND

THIS WATERLOGGED habitat of grasses and low-growing shrubs is found in cool, upland areas with lots of rain. It is an important breeding ground for waders and grouse. Predators such as hen harriers and golden eagles find many small birds and mammals to eat here, and there are plenty of insects breeding in the peaty bogs.

Golden plovers feed on insects, worms, and seeds.

Upper parts have golden colour all year round.

GOLDEN PLOVER
In late spring, golden plovers migrate to moorland to breed. They lay their well-camouflaged eggs in a shallow scrape in the ground.

STONECHAT
The restless stonechat perches on bushes and posts to watch for insects, worms, and spiders. It builds a nest of moss, grass, and hair, well hidden in bushes or thick grass.

PEREGRINE FALCON
These falcons stoop at an incredible speed to kill prey such as golden plover or pigeons with their talons. They pluck the feathers from prey before eating the flesh.

RED GROUSE
This bird is a distinctive sub-species of the willow grouse or willow ptarmigan. Many moorlands are carefully managed to keep a lot of these birds for shooting in the autumn grouse season.

Birds such as red grouse shelter, hide, and nest in heather.

Some stonechats migrate to warmer places in cold weather.

BIRDS

EAGLES

WITH THEIR SHARP eyes, huge wings, and strong legs and feet, eagles are the most powerful of the birds of prey. Females are usually larger than males. Many species of eagle are threatened by people hunting them, poisoning them, and destroying their habitat.

Light-coloured crown and neck feathers

Strong talo to grip an crush pre

COURTSHIP

During courtship, many eagles show off their amazing flying skills. A pair of bald eagles will tumble and spin through the sky, while trying to touch or grip one another's talons.

Courtship display of bald eagles

IMPERIAL EAGLE

Feathered legs are a characteristic of the imperial eagle, which belongs to a group called the booted eagles. It is widespread in parts of Asia, but rare in Europe.

GOLDEN EAGLE

These eagles are strong fliers, soaring high on outstretched wings to search for prey. They are named after the golden feathers on the top of the head and the back of the neck.

Primary flight feathers for power and steering

BATELEUR EAGLE

This eagle's name comes from the French word for "juggler" because of its aerial courtship display. It has long wings and a short tail. When it is excited or angry, its crest is raised.

Raised crest

A bald eagle's eyrie

EYRIE

Eagle nests are called eyries and bald eagles have made some of the biggest eyries in the world. They use the same nest year after year, adding more and more twigs and sticks each time they nest.

EAGLE FACTS

• Family: *Accipitridae* – includes snake eagles and booted eagles

• About 53 species

• Diurnal

• Birds of prey

• Eat a variety of animals, alive and dead

• Habitat: wide range

• Nest: mass of sticks in tree or on cliff ledge

• Eggs: white or marked with brown

357

POLAR AND TUNDRA

THE FROZEN POLAR REGIONS are the coldest and windiest places on Earth. Few birds can survive there all year round. Most migrate there to breed in the short summer months, when the sun shines 24 hours a day and there is plenty of food. These unique habitats are threatened by mining, tourism, and pollution.

TUNDRA LANDSCAPES

Around the edge of the Arctic Ocean lie the flat tundra lands, which have a frozen layer called permafrost under the ground. In summer, the soil above the permafrost thaws out, and lakes and marshes form on the surface.

Tundra means "barren land" in Finnish

Ice floating on water

Shoreline

Tundra with permafrost under the ground

Marshy tundra landscape in summer

MIGRATION

In summer, millions of ducks, swans, and geese, such as the barnacle goose, migrate to the tundra lands to feed and nest there. They eat new vegetation sprouting from the warm, moist ground.

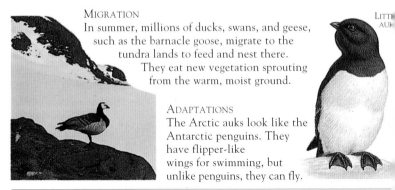

LITTLE AUK

ADAPTATIONS

The Arctic auks look like the Antarctic penguins. They have flipper-like wings for swimming, but unlike penguins, they can fly.

KEEPING WARM
Birds such as the eider duck cover their eggs with soft down which the female plucks from her own breast. This helps to keep the eggs warm until they are ready to hatch.

PENGUIN
FLIPPER

SWIMMING
Many birds of these habitats are good swimmers. Penguins have stiff, densely packed scale-like feathers on their wings to reduce the drag of the water against them when swimming.

EIDER DUCK NEST

LAPLAND
BUNTING

FACTS
• Antarctica has 90 per cent of all the ice on Earth and 70 per cent of all the water.

• Permafrost under the tundra can be up to 1,400 m (3,840 ft) thick.

• The Arctic is an ice-covered ocean surrounded by land – Antarctica is frozen land surrounded by ocean.

FOOD
The tundra summer is brief, but thousands of insects swarm over marshy pools. So birds like the Lapland bunting have plenty of food to collect for their young.

ARCTIC AND TUNDRA

AROUND THE NORTH POLE is a huge ice-covered ocean surrounded by tundra landscape. This region is called the Arctic. In summer months, gulls, auks, and terns feed on the fish at sea, and nest on the coast. The insects and seeds on the tundra are food for waders, ducks, geese, and small songbirds. Before winter, the birds fly south to warmer regions.

Male giving his mate a fishy gift during courtship

ARCTIC TERNS
After courtship, terns raise their young in the Arctic summer, then fly all the way to Antarctica for the summer there. They do an incredible round trip of 35,000 km (22,000 miles)

SNOWY OWL FOOT
SIZE OF LABEL

SNOWY OWL
The plumage of the snowy owl camouflages it against the Arctic landscape, as it glides over the ground lookir for prey. Feathers on its legs and feet help it to keep warm.

COMMON REDPOLL

This little bird can survive low temperatures. It eats a lot of seeds, and some small insects and their larvae in summer. Some redpolls nest in dwarf birches near the ground in tundra habitats.

Redpolls are named after their red forehead, or "poll".

EMPEROR GOOSE

This handsome, grey goose breeds along marshy shores in Alaska. Some birds may migrate south to northern California in winter.

Adults have orange legs.

In winter, the male snow bunting turns browner and looks more like the female.

SNOW BUNTING

Hardy snow buntings breed in the Arctic – farther north than any other perching bird. They usually hide their nest from predators in crannies in the rocks.

Snow buntings may burrow in the snow to escape intense cold.

361

ANTARCTICA

THIS VAST AREA of frozen land surrounded by ocean has little rain or snow, so the birds have little fresh water to drink, apart from melted snow. The only two land birds are sheathbills. All the others are seabirds, including albatrosses, petrels, and penguins, millions of which nest around Antarctic coasts in summer. The seabirds have dense feathers or layers of fat to keep warm, and are strong swimmers or fliers.

BROWN SKUA
With their hooked bills and strong claws, skuas are fierce predators of penguin eggs and chicks. In summer, they regularly patrol penguin colonies in Antarctica.

ADELIE PENGUINS
Adelies are one of the two species of penguin that nest on the rocky coasts of Antarctica itself. In spring, they march inland from the sea to nest on the ground in huge rookeries.

BLACK-BROWED ALBATROSSES
Albatrosses mate for life and reinforce the pair bond each year when they return to the nest. This pair is bill-touching and preening each other.

The only bird found in Antarctica that does not have webbed feet

SNOWY SHEATHBILL
A relative of pigeons, this bird scavenges around seal and penguin colonies as well as searching the shoreline for fish, invertebrates, and shellfish. Sheathbills live in small flocks, except in the breeding season.

IMPERIAL SHAGS
These impressive birds nest in large colonies on coastal ledges or among rocks. They have strong, hooked bills to grasp slippery fish. In the breeding season, they grow wispy crests.

BLACK-BROWED
ALBATROSSES

Nest is a big heap of mud and grass about 60 cm (24 in) high

BIRDS

PENGUINS

WITH THEIR SMOOTH, streamlined shape, and stiff, strong wings, penguins are expert swimmers. They dive to catch fish and squid with their spiky tongues. Dense, oily feathers, and thick fat under the skin keep them warm in the cold southern oceans. Penguins only come out of the water to moult and breed, some in colonies of thousands.

EMPEROR PENGUINS
These are the biggest penguins. They never come on land, but breed on the ice that floats around Antarctica in winter. Males incubate the single egg for about nine weeks.

Powerful, narrow wings for swimming

KING PENGUINS
The striking golden-orange ear patches of these birds are used for display during courtship. The markings also help them to recognize other king penguins. These large penguins can dive down as deep as 250 m (850 ft).

Stiff tail feathers used to support body on land

Male king penguin incubates egg against bare patch of warm skin

364

Porpoising
Adelie penguins

In water, penguins look dark from above and pale from below – this helps to camouflage them

et well ck on ly to act rudder

SWIMMING AND DIVING

In order to breathe while swimming fast, penguins leap in and out of the water. This technique is called porpoising. They can travel through water in this way at over 30 km/h (20 mph), using their stiff wings to push themselves along.

MACARONI PENGUIN

During their courtship displays, these birds shake their bright yellow head crests. The crests also help them to recognize other macaronis.

Spread flippers cool bird down

CHINSTRAP PENGUIN

These penguins are named because of the black line under their chin. They are noisy and quarrelsome birds.

PENGUIN FACTS

- Family: *Spheniscidae*
- About 18 species
- Diurnal and nocturnal
- Flightless seabirds
- Eat fish, squid, and small sea creatures
- Habitat: southern oceans, cool temperate islands, tropical shores
- Nest: stones, grass, mud, caves, or burrows
- Eggs: whitish

MAMMALS

MAMMALS

WHAT IS A MAMMAL?

ALL MAMMALS HAVE FUR or hair, a backbone for support, and are warm-blooded. Females give birth to live young and feed them with milk from their mammary glands – after which mammals are named. They are the most intelligent and adaptable of all animals and have come to dominate the animal world. There are over 4,000 different kinds of mammal, from enormous whales to tiny bats and shrews.

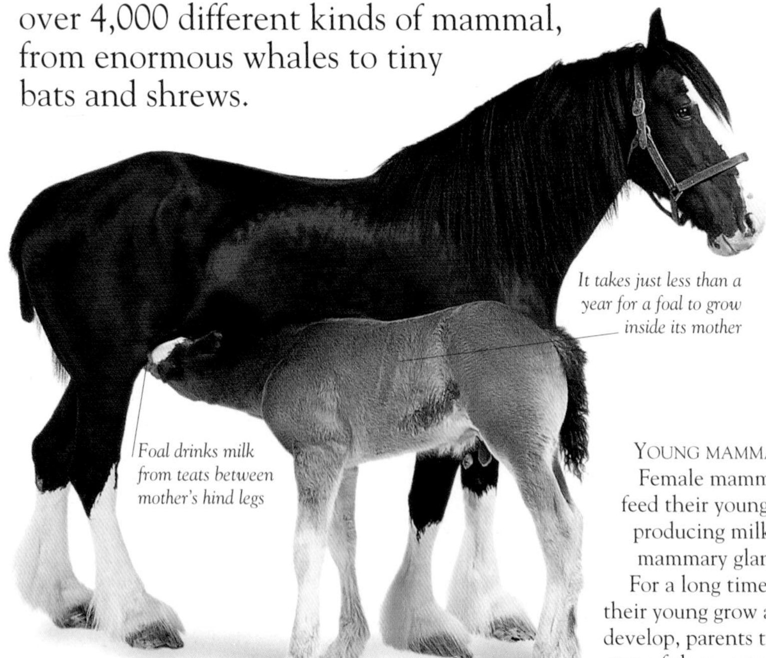

It takes just less than a year for a foal to grow inside its mother

Foal drinks milk from teats between mother's hind legs

YOUNG MAMMA
Female mamma
feed their young b
producing milk
mammary gland
For a long time,
their young grow ar
develop, parents tal
care of them, passir
on survival skil

HORSE AND FOAL

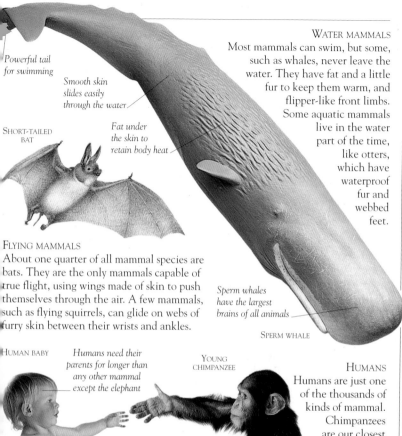

Powerful tail for swimming

Smooth skin slides easily through the water

SHORT-TAILED BAT

Fat under the skin to retain body heat

WATER MAMMALS

Most mammals can swim, but some, such as whales, never leave the water. They have fat and a little fur to keep them warm, and flipper-like front limbs. Some aquatic mammals live in the water part of the time, like otters, which have waterproof fur and webbed feet.

FLYING MAMMALS

About one quarter of all mammal species are bats. They are the only mammals capable of true flight, using wings made of skin to push themselves through the air. A few mammals, such as flying squirrels, can glide on webs of furry skin between their wrists and ankles.

Sperm whales have the largest brains of all animals

SPERM WHALE

HUMAN BABY

Humans need their parents for longer than any other mammal except the elephant

YOUNG CHIMPANZEE

HUMANS

Humans are just one of the thousands of kinds of mammal. Chimpanzees are our closest living relatives. Their body structure and behaviour is similar and we share 99 per cent of the same genes.

Humans are closely related to chimps, gorillas, and orang-utans

369

REPRODUCTION

MAMMALS REPRODUCE in three ways. Most of them, including humans, are placental mammals that nourish their unborn young inside the mother's womb through an organ called a placenta. Marsupial mammals begin developing in the womb but, when still very tiny, crawl out to finish growing in their mother's pouch, called a marsupium. The third and rarest kind are monotremes, the only mammals to lay eggs. All three types of mammal feed their young on milk.

Baby develops in mother's uterus

Baby, or foetus, facing head-down ready to be born

Placenta

Blood reaches placenta through umbilical cord

Muscles of uterus will contract to push baby out

PREGNANT WOMAN

PLACENTAL MAMMALS
The placenta is a disc-shaped organ that forms in the lining of the uterus after fertilization. The umbilical cord is attached to the placenta. This allows the baby to receive food, oxygen, and antibodies from its mother, and to pass waste products back into her blood.

Amniotic sac filled with fluid to cushion the baby

Mucus plug blocks cervix during pregnancy

FOETUS AT 36 WEEKS

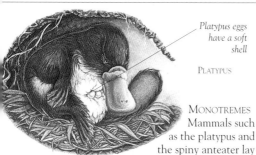

Platypus eggs have a soft shell

PLATYPUS

AMAZING FACTS

• At birth, a baby kangaroo would fit into a teaspoon.

• While a baby squirrel takes just 22–45 days to develop in its mother's womb, a young elephant takes as long as two years to be born!

• Female Norway lemmings can breed at just 15 days old.

MONOTREMES

Mammals such as the platypus and the spiny anteater lay eggs. The platypus incubates its eggs in a nest for about three weeks. During incubation, yolk in the egg nourishes the embryo. When they hatch from the eggs, young monotremes suck milk from their mother.

Mother's teat swells in the baby's mouth, keeping it attached for 1–2 months

Baby kangaroo, or joey, stays in the pouch for about six months

KANGAROO AND JOEY

MARSUPIALS

Young marsupials, such as kangaroos, spend only 12–30 days in the mother's uterus, and are born in an immature stage of development. They crawl into their mother's pouch to reach her teats for feeding on milk, and stay there until fully developed.

BIRTH AND GROWTH

MOST FEMALE MAMMALS give birth to live young. Seals, whales, and monkeys and apes have only one or two young at a time. Other mammals bear up to 10 or 15 babies in a single pregnancy. Mice can have a litter of 18! Most tropical mammals are born at various times of the year; in temperate and cold climates, births usually take place in spring and summer. Mammals tend to spend a lot of time caring for and educating their young.

HAIRLESS BABIES

Baby mice are born without hair or fur. Unable to see or hear, they are totally dependent on their mother. Fur starts to appear when they are one week old, and after ten days, their eyes open. The young are ready to leave the nest after two or three weeks.

Nesting material helps keep mice warm

NEW-BORN MICE

HAIRY BABIES

Kittens are born with their fur. The mother licks the fur, making it dry and fluffy so it traps body heat and keeps the kitten warm. Though new-born kittens are active, their eyes and ears are sealed, leaving them temporarily blind and deaf. They will be ready to leave their mother in eight weeks.

Mother cut through umbilic cord with her teet

Young hang upside down while their mothers go out to feed

Each female can recognize the cry of her own young

BAT ROOST

BAT NURSERY
Young bats are blind and hairless when they are born. They cling together in a nursery roost, clustered together for warmth, while their mothers go off to feed. Small species fly within about 20 days, but larger species, such as flying foxes, take three months to fly.

PARENTAL CARE
Some mammals, including primates such as gorillas, spend many years raising their young and teaching them how to hunt and feed. Mothers usually provide most of the care, but as in other social species, like bats, elephants, and lions, the care of infants may be shared among members of the group.

Gorillas teach their young life skills

GORILLA AND BABY

SKIN AND HAIR

A MAMMAL'S SKIN is a protective outer layer that, aided by hair, regulates body temperature. Hair, which is unique to mammals, grows as fur, whiskers, wool, prickles, and spines. It traps warm air and keeps out cold, heat, wind, and rain. Some mammals, like chinchillas, have thick, dense fur coats. Others, such as whales, have smooth skin with very little hair.

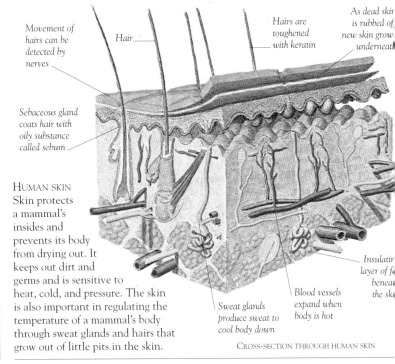

Movement of hairs can be detected by nerves

Hair

Hairs are toughened with keratin

As dead skin is rubbed off, new skin grows underneath

Sebaceous gland coats hair with oily substance called sebum

HUMAN SKIN
Skin protects a mammal's insides and prevents its body from drying out. It keeps out dirt and germs and is sensitive to heat, cold, and pressure. The skin is also important in regulating the temperature of a mammal's body through sweat glands and hairs that grow out of little pits in the skin.

Sweat glands produce sweat to cool body down

Blood vessels expand when body is hot

Insulating layer of fat beneath the skin

CROSS-SECTION THROUGH HUMAN SKIN

BOTTLENOSE
DOLPHIN

*Fatty blubber under
the hairless skin
smooths out
body contours*

WATERPROOF SKIN
Members of the whale
group, which includes
dolphins, have smooth,
tough, rubbery skin with few
hairs. This makes them more streamlined in
the water. Many seals have heavy, oily fur, which
traps bubbles of air and keeps them warm and dry.
Whales rely on their fat, called blubber, for warmth.

*Camels don't need insulating
layers of fat as they live
in hot deserts*

MOULTING
Many mammals moult,
or shed, their fur coats with
the changing seasons. This process is
triggered by changes in temperature or
light and enables mammals to grow thin
summer coats and thicker winter ones. Some
mammals, such as Arctic foxes, also change
the colour of their coat with the seasons.

*Fur looks
ragged when
camel moults
its thick
winter coat*

MOULTING CAMEL

*Teeth and limbs
are used to comb
and brush the fur*

KEEPING CLEAN
To keep their skin and fur clean and
free from parasites, mammals groom
by licking, combing, and nibbling
at their coats. Some, like elephants,
bathe every day. Social mammals
groom each other, which reinforces
the bonds between individuals.

RAT GROOMING

375

SENSES

MAMMALS PICK UP information about their surroundings, and communicate with each other through their senses of sight, hearing, smell, taste, and touch. They are the only animals that have external ear flaps. Most mammals see the world in black and white.

Some dogs are trained to sniff out drugs and explosives

SMELL
Vital for identifying individuals, food, and possible predators or mates, a sense of smell is highly developed in some insectivores, carnivores, (such as dogs) and rodents. In whales and higher primates, such as humans, it is much less developed.

BLACK LEOPARD, OR PANTHER

BEAGLE

A dog's sense of smell is a million times more sensitive than our own

Wet nose helps identify scents

CATS WHISKERS
Whiskers are long hairs that grow out of the skin, usually on the face. Some mammals have whiskers on their legs, feet, or back. Whiskers respond when they are touched, helping mammals to feel objects in the dark and gauge the width of narrow spaces

Long, sensitive whiskers

Horseshoe bat

Sound echoes bouncing off prey

Insect prey

Bats can detect insects as small as midges from a distance of 20 m (65.5 ft)

Large ears to pick up sound echoes

HOW A BAT USES ECHOLOCATION

ECHOLOCATION
Some bats and dolphins have a special sense called echolocation. They make high-pitched sounds that bounce off objects in their environment and return as echoes, which can reveal the location of the objects.

BUSHBABY

Large ear flaps funnel sound

Large eyes to spot prey

NIGHT SENSES
Many mammals are nocturnal and have sensitive eyes and ears to navigate and locate food in the dark. Bushbabies have huge eyes with pupils that open wide to let in as much light as possible. Their large ears swivel to track small flying insects.

377

MAMMALS

FEEDING AND DIET

MAMMALS MUST EAT regularly to maintain a constant body temperature, and small mammals need to eat more often than large ones. Most are plant eaters, but some eat meat and others have a more varied diet. Most mammals have three kinds of teeth: incisors and canines for biting and tearing, and molars for grinding. These develop from two sets of teeth – milk teeth when they are young, and adult teeth, which grow as the jaws become larger.

PLANT EATERS

Herbivores, such as cows, horses, camels, sheep, goats, and deer only eat plants. They have long jaws that hold rows of molar teeth which grind and crush tough plant material. Many have a hard pad instead of top front teeth.

Deep lower jaw to anchor large chewing muscles

Horny pad

Jaws move sideways as well as up and down

GOAT SKULL

Gap for tongue to curl around bulky plant food

MEAT EATERS

Carnivores, like lions, tigers, and wolves eat meat. Their jaws are shorter and more powerful than those of herbivores. Carnivores have special cheek teeth called carnassials, which have pointed edges that can slice meat or crack bones.

Carnassial teeth work together like shears

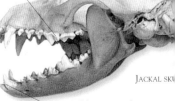

JACKAL SKULL

Powerful canine teeth

BEAVER

...ack part of
...oth wears away
...ore easily than
...e front, forming
...sloping, chisel-
...e edge

...VERGROWING TEETH

...odents, such as beavers, have four strong front teeth
...lled incisors that keep growing. They are continually
...orn down and kept sharp by constant use. The teeth
...pet rodents can grow too
...ng if they lack hard
...aterials to gnaw on.

...rved upper jaw to hold
...g lengths of baleen

Section cut away to show
baleen plates with fringes
facing inside the mouth

...OD STRAINER

...me whales, such as
...e humpback, grey,
...d blue whale,
...ve no teeth. Instead,
...ey have long, fringed
...tes hanging from their jaws.
...ey draw sea water into their mouths
...d spit it back out through the baleen
...nges, which trap food like a sieve.

BALEEN WHALE

BONES AND MUSCLES

ALL MAMMALS HAVE a skeleton, which is an internal
framework of bones that supports the body and
protects its delicate internal organs. As bones cannot
move on their own, they are pulled into different
positions by firmly attached groups of powerful
muscles, enabling mammals to move. Some mammals
have especially strong bones and muscles and can run
and swim faster than other animals.

INSIDE A GORILLA
This model of a female
gorilla's insides shows the
position of the bones and
muscles. The gorilla is
pregnant and the baby
inside its muscular
womb is almost
ready to be
born.

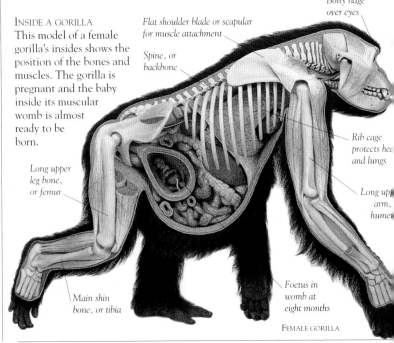

*Flat shoulder blade or scapular
for muscle attachment*

*Spine, or
backbone*

*Bony ridge
over eyes*

*Rib cage
protects hear
and lungs*

*Long up
arm,
humer*

*Long upper
leg bone,
or femur*

*Main shin
bone, or tibia*

*Foetus in
womb at
eight months*

FEMALE GORILLA

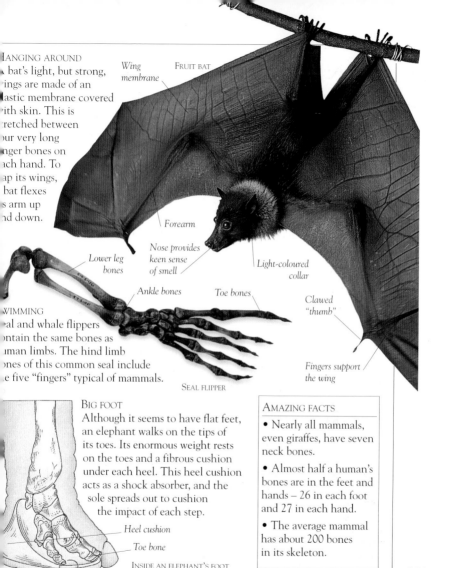

HANGING AROUND
A bat's light, but strong, wings are made of an elastic membrane covered with skin. This is stretched between four very long finger bones on each hand. To flap its wings, a bat flexes its arm up and down.

Wing membrane

FRUIT BAT

Forearm

Nose provides keen sense of smell

Light-coloured collar

SWIMMING
Seal and whale flippers contain the same bones as human limbs. The hind limb bones of this common seal include the five "fingers" typical of mammals.

Lower leg bones

Ankle bones

Toe bones

Clawed "thumb"

Fingers support the wing

SEAL FLIPPER

BIG FOOT
Although it seems to have flat feet, an elephant walks on the tips of its toes. Its enormous weight rests on the toes and a fibrous cushion under each heel. This heel cushion acts as a shock absorber, and the sole spreads out to cushion the impact of each step.

Heel cushion

Toe bone

INSIDE AN ELEPHANT'S FOOT

AMAZING FACTS

• Nearly all mammals, even giraffes, have seven neck bones.

• Almost half a human's bones are in the feet and hands – 26 in each foot and 27 in each hand.

• The average mammal has about 200 bones in its skeleton.

381

DEFENCE

PLANT-EATING MAMMALS, especially small ones, have many enemies. These include meat-eating mammals, humans, snakes, and birds of prey. To avoid detection herbivores might be camouflaged. Others bear weapons, from sharp claws and spiky coats to horns, armour, and terrible smells. Some find safety in numbers.

Horns are not shed each year, like a deer's antlers

Pointed tips of horns could injure a predator

ANTELOPE SKULL

Curved (annulated) horn

Joints between bones

Unlike antle horns are ne branched, b are curved a twis

PORCUPINE

HORNS, ANTLER
AND TUSKS
Used mainly to
fight other males
in competition fo
a mate or defend
a territory, horns,
antlers, and tusks a
also useful weapons
of defence. The
horns of antelope,
cattle, and sheep are
hollow structures made
of bone that has a
slightly softer covering.

SPIKE ATTACK
If threatened, a porcupine will turn its back, rattle its quills, grunt, and stamp its feet. If the enemy does not retreat, the porcupine runs backwards into its attacker, sticking quills into its skin.

ODOUR POWER

The skunk's striking black-and-white colour warns enemies to stay away. If this fails, a skunk will turn its back, stamp, and raise its tail. It squirts foul-smelling liquid, which burns the skin and takes a long time to wear off.

Skunk sprays smelly liquid from 3.6 m (12 ft) away

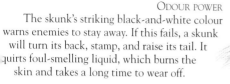

Body armour is impossible to penetrate

ARMADILLO

ARMOUR-PLATING

The body of an armadillo is encased in bony plates, or scutes, covered by horn. Some of the 20 armadillo species roll up into a ball when attacked, to protect their soft underparts.

Handstand warns enemy to watch out!

SPOTTED SKUNK

OKAPI

CAMOUFLAGE

Stripes break up a mammal's shape, making it hard to spot. The okapi, a close relative of the giraffe, lives in rainforests.

AMAZING FACTS

• Opossums play dead if attacked – predators prefer live animals.

• Zebra stallions kick lions, sometimes smashing their teeth.

• Only two mammals are poisonous: the male platypus has poison spurs on its back legs and the water shrew has poisonous saliva.

383

MAMMAL HOMES

BUILT IN TREES, under the soil, in riverbanks and lakes, or even in people's houses, mammal homes provide a safe, warm shelter that protects them and their young from the weather and from enemies. Mammals build their homes from natural materials, such as grass, leaves, sticks, and fur and use their teeth and limbs to shape them. Many of these homes, such as badger setts, are permanent, while others are built daily or seasonally.

Outer layer of
twigs and leaves

Cosy lining of grass, mo
leaves, bark, feathers, a
sheep's w

GREY SQUIRREL IN DRE

TREE HOUSES

As trees are exposed, they make windy homes. Squirrels build round, soccer-ball siz tree nests, called dreys, in which they rest, sleep, and raise their young. Most dreys are built in a new site each yea Winter nests are stronger than summer one and special nursery dreys are built for the youn

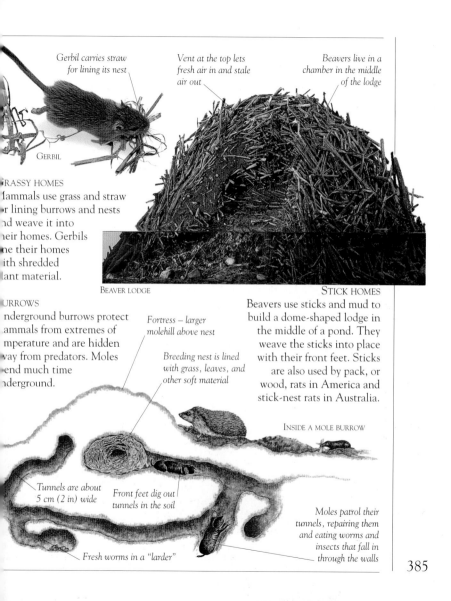

Gerbil carries straw for lining its nest

GERBIL

Vent at the top lets fresh air in and stale air out

Beavers live in a chamber in the middle of the lodge

GRASSY HOMES

Mammals use grass and straw for lining burrows and nests and weave it into their homes. Gerbils line their homes with shredded plant material.

BEAVER LODGE

STICK HOMES

Beavers use sticks and mud to build a dome-shaped lodge in the middle of a pond. They weave the sticks into place with their front feet. Sticks are also used by pack, or wood, rats in America and stick-nest rats in Australia.

BURROWS

Underground burrows protect mammals from extremes of temperature and are hidden away from predators. Moles spend much time underground.

Fortress – larger molehill above nest

Breeding nest is lined with grass, leaves, and other soft material

INSIDE A MOLE BURROW

Tunnels are about 5 cm (2 in) wide

Front feet dig out tunnels in the soil

Moles patrol their tunnels, repairing them and eating worms and insects that fall in through the walls

Fresh worms in a "larder"

WHERE MAMMALS LIVE

MAMMALS LIVE all over the world, from mountain tops and the icy poles to baking hot deserts. They can do this because they are warm-blooded, which enables them to keep a constant body temperature – even when their surroundings are extremely hot or very cold.

WOODLAND AND FOREST
There is plenty of food and shelter in these habitats, but mammals have to cope with seasonal changes that bring cold weather and less food.

- Woodland and forest
- Rainforest
- Grassland
- Deserts
- Mountains and polar
- Oceans and seas
- Rivers, lakes, and swamps

NORTH
AMERICA

ATLANTIC
OCEAN

PACIFIC OCEAN

SOUTH
AMERICA

AFRICA

RAINFOREST
The year-round warm, wet climate encourages a variety of mammals that live in the trees and on the forest floor.

RIVERS, LAKES, AND SWAMPS
Mammals in these habitats are often strong swimmers with waterproof fur and webbed feet.

OCEANS AND SEAS
These habitats form 70 per cent of the earth's surface. Some mammals breed on land; others never leave the water.

MOUNTAINS AND POLAR
With cold temperatures, strong winds, and little moisture, these habitats are home to some of the hardiest mammals.

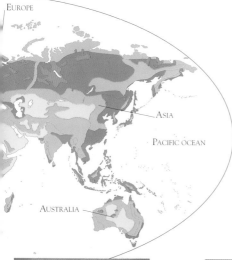

EUROPE

ASIA

PACIFIC OCEAN

AUSTRALIA

GRASSLAND
Small burrowers and herds of grazers live in both hot and cool grasslands, which occur where it is too dry for trees.

DESERTS
Desert mammals are specially adapted to survive dry conditions and extreme temperatures. Many store food and rarely drink.

MAMMALS

WOODLAND AND FOREST

PLENTY OF FOOD, shelter, and nesting places are to be found in woodland and forests. The main large herbivores are deer. Many small herbivores, such as mice and voles, live in the undergrowth, away from predators such as stoats and wolverines. Much of this habitat is protected, but some is still threatened by logging and pollution.

Powerful legs help pine martens climb

Long, bushy tail helps balance

FOOD AND FEEDIN
From nuts and berries to leaves and bar
food for plant eaters such as chipmunk
is adundant here and varies wit
the seasons. Small mamma
scurrying through falle
leaves are a major sourc
of food fo
predator

NIGHT HUNTERS
Many woodland mammals rest during the day, and become active at night, especially at dusk or dawn. The swift and agile pine marten is a hunter of birds and rodents, both in the trees and on the ground.

Chipmunks crack nuts with their strong front teeth

Cl

MOVING THROUGH THE FOREST
Some woodland mammals climb, glide, or fly up into the trees to find food or places to shelter and nest. Climbers, such as squirrels and koalas, have sharp claws for gripping, while gliding mammals can parachute from tree to tree. Only bats fly freely though the branches.

SUGAR GLIDER

Flaps of skin are spread along sides of body to glide between trees

WINTER SURVIVAL
Mammals survive the winter in many ways. Some, such as the sable, have a fur coat to keep warm, while others build up food stores ready for the hard times ahead. Larger mammals hibernate, or rest, during cold periods.

Sable is up to 45 cm (18 in) long

Thick fur coat

Even the soles of the feet are furry

Hedgehogs have up to 5,000 sharp, stiff spines

HEDGEHOG

HIBERNATING HEDGEHOGS
When a mammal such as a hedgehog or a dormouse hibernates, its body processes slow right down so it is only just alive. In this deep sleep, there is no need to waste energy finding food or keeping warm. A hibernating mammal relies on stores of food or body fat and a protected den to help it survive.

No spines underneath body

DECIDUOUS WOODLAND

IN TEMPERATE WOODLANDS, mammal lifestyles change
with the seasons. Young are born in spring, so they can
grow strong by the time winter comes. In summer and
autumn, mammals feed as much as possible to gain
stores of fat for winter's lean months. While larger
mammals spend the winter
resting in their burrows,
many small ones stay
active to keep warm.

*Meadow vole is
hard to see among
dead leaves*

UNDER COVER

Hidden in vegetation and leaf
litter, small mammals, such as
voles, depend on camouflage
for survival. As they must feed
frequently, many climb trees to
collect nuts and other food for
storage in underground chamber

SKILLED CLIMBERS

Leaping nimbly from branch to
branch, grey squirrels are masters of
life in the trees. They can balance
on the thinnest twigs and run up
and down tree trunks by climbing
with their sharp claws. Food is kept
in their twiggy nests, called dreys,
which are built high above ground.

*Squirrels eat
nuts and seeds*

*Bush
tail used fo
balance and signallir*

Badgers have keen senses of smell and hearing but poor eyesight

Black-and-white face markings break up the outline of the badger so it is hard to see in twilight

Long, strong claws for digging underground homes

Whiskers brush against surroundings to navigate in the dark

BURROWING BADGERS

A family of badgers lives in a system of underground burrows, called a sett, which may be hundreds of years old. Signs of an occupied sett include well-marked paths, piles of old bedding material, and dung pits.

AMAZING FACTS

• The largest badger sett had 50 underground chambers and 178 separate entrances!

• Grey squirrels carry acorns up to 30 m (100 ft) from an oak tree before burying them.

• Dormice in some countries hibernate for as long as nine months.

WOODLAND PREDATOR

Sharp claws

Ferocious hunters of small animals, weasels are slim enough to chase mice or voles right into their burrows. During the winter months in cold, snowy climates, weasels may grow a white coat, making it hard for both prey and predators to see them.

Weasels often stand up on their hind legs to look for signs of food and danger

391

CONIFEROUS FOREST

STRETCHING ACROSS northern Europe, Asia, and Nort America, coniferous forests provide year-round shelter for mammals. In the bitter winters, some mammals hibernate and others turn white for camouflage. To conserve heat, mammals that live here have thick fur coats and are larger than their southern relatives.

Powerful muscles give bear great strength

SLEEPY BEAR
In autumn, brown bears eat as much as possible to build up fat stores that keep them alive during the winter. In winter, females give birth to cubs, while males have periods of inactivity. Bears are not true hibernators – if it turns warm they wake up and begin feeding

Powerful jaws ar teeth allow the bear eat a variety of foo

Thick fur coat protects the bear against freezing temperatures

Strong claws for killing prey or digging for plant food

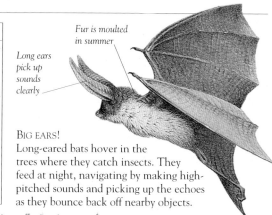

Fur is moulted in summer

Long ears pick up sounds clearly

BIG EARS!

Long-eared bats hover in the trees where they catch insects. They feed at night, navigating by making high-pitched sounds and picking up the echoes as they bounce back off nearby objects.

Thick fur keeps in heat

Powerful jaws give a crushing bite

PERSISTENT PREDATOR

As the largest member of the weasel family, the fierce wolverine can catch animals as large as caribou (reindeer) after pursuing them for 65 km (40 miles). Inuit peoples once prized wolverine fur for making parka coats because it can shed ice crystals.

Widespread toes help the wolverine to run over snow without sinking

Young have more distinct stripes than adults

WILD THING

The striped coat of the wildcat provides good camouflage as it stalks the forest. Wildcats live a solitary life, hunting at night. They are closely related to domestic cats.

393

EUCALYPTUS WOODLAND

AUSTRALIA'S HOT, DRY woodland provides food and shelter all year round. Most mammals here are marsupials (pouched mammals) that come out at night, using their sharp senses of smell and hearing to find their way around. Some, such as koalas and sugar gliders, live in the trees; others, including bandicoots, live on the forest floor.

POUCHED JUMPER

During the day, groups, or mobs, of grey kangaroos rest under the trees, but at night they search for plants to eat. Young kangaroos stay in the pouch for up to 11 months, longer than any other marsupial, suckling until they are 18 months old.

Large ears and eyes and keen sense of smell to detect signs of danger

AMAZING FACTS

• A baby kangaroo, or joey, is the fastest-growing animal. When born, it is thimble-sized, but it grows by 30,000 times in its lifetime.

• The common wombat is the largest burrowing marsupial. It burrows at 3 m (10 ft) an hour.

Fro limb have fi claw dig

Kangaroo graze w all four fe on the grou

Powerful back legs f bounding away fro enem

Tail helps keep balance

FUSSY EATERS

The tree-dwelling koala seldom comes to the ground, clinging to branches with its strong limbs and sharp claws. Koalas spend about 18 hours a day snoozing in the trees. When awake, they feed only on the leaves of 12 out of the 100 species of eucalyptus tree, eating about 1.5 kg (3 lb) of leaves each day.

A baby koala lives in its mother's pouch for six months, then spends another six months carried on her back

Koalas have a long intestine to help digest tough leaves

Tail can reach 20 cm (8 in) long

Numbats have about 50 teeth

TERMITE HUNGRY

One of the few mammals in these woodlands to be active during the day, numbats eat thousands of termites which they collect with their long, narrow tongue.

Striped coat camouflages numbat from predators such as eagles

NUMBAT

The name "devil" comes from its black colour and eerie call

LETHAL PREDATOR

The huge head and strong jaws of the Tasmanian devil allow it to crush and eat its prey, bones and all. Tasmanian devils live in dens under rocks or tree stumps and are mainly nocturnal. Their young stay in the pouch for 15 weeks and then are left in the nest or carried around on the mother's back until 20 weeks of age, when they are weaned.

Sensitive nose to sniff out prey

395

DEER

WOODS and forests, which provide plant food and shelter, are home to many kinds of deer. Their shy nature and camouflaged coats make them hard to spot. Sharp senses help to detect danger, and long legs allow a speedy retreat.

Sharp incisors to tear grass

MALE
MUNTJAC
SKULL

GRINDING TEETH
The narrow snout of the deer allows it to reach into small spaces to find food. Grinding molar teeth mash up tough plant material.

Long legs and broad hooves to move through deep snow, bogs, or lakes

Male moose have broad, flat antlers used to fight for females in the autumn

Overhanging top lip tears off leaves and branches

Flap of skin is known as the bell

Strong neck and shoulder muscles support heavy head and antlers

LARGEST DEER
Moose, or elk, are the largest deer, weighing up to 450 kg (1,000 lb) and standing 2 m (6.5 ft) tall at the shoulder. Unlike other deer, moose do not live in groups, and outside the breeding season are usually alone or with their young. In winter, moose eat woody plants but in summer, they wade into water for more tender vegetation.

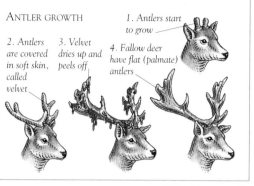

ANTLER GROWTH

1. Antlers start to grow

2. Antlers are covered in soft skin, called velvet

3. Velvet dries up and peels off

4. Fallow deer have flat (palmate) antlers

RED DEER AND FAWN

DEER ANTLERS

All male deer, apart from Chinese water deer, have a set of bony antlers on their head as a sign of strength and dominance. They shed and grow a new set of antlers each year. In the autumn rutting (mating) season, male deer use their antlers in pushing contests to win females.

ᴿOE DEER

ᵀhe reddish ᵇrown coat ᵒf the roe ᵈeer blends ᵢn well with ᵗhe summer ᶜolours of woods ᵃnd forests. In ᵂinter it grows ᵃ thick, dense, ᵍʳey-brown ᶜoat for ᶜamouflage ᵃnd warmth.

ᴹᴬLE ROE DEER

Antlers no more than 30 cm (12 in) long

Roe deer feed on grasses at dusk and dawn

AMAZING DEER FACTS

• Deer are the only animals in the world to have antlers.

• The American wapiti and the caribou have the longest antlers, at over 1.5 m (59 in) in length!

• The South American pudu is the smallest deer, only 38 cm (15 in) tall!

• Red deer are likely to live for over 30 years.

WOODLAND & FOREST

397

RAINFOREST

THE WORLD'S RICHEST habitat, rainforests provide a year-round warm, wet climate and a variety of food and resting places. Most mammals here are agile climbers that live in the trees, but large predators stalk the forest floor. Rainforests are being destroyed at an alarming rate.

Thin "wings" of skin run along the sides of the body

COLUGO, ALSO CALLED FLYING LEMUR

GLIDING IN THE TREES
Gripping with long toes, claws, or tails, gliding on skin flaps, or flying with wings, mammals move easily from branch to branch in search of food, mates, or to escape danger.

Canopy: monkeys, fruit bats, sloths, gliders

Understorey: jungle cats, tree kangaroos, lorises

Forest floor: peccaries, tapirs, okapis, elephants

LAYERS OF THE RAINFOREST
Mammals share the rich resources of the rainforest by living at various levels. In the trees, there are leave flowers, insects, fruits, and nuts on which to feed, whil the forest floor provides a feast of millions more insects, spiders, worms, and other invertebrates as well plant roots, shoots, and fun

FOREST ECHOES

Visual communication is difficult among thick tangles of vegetation, so many mammals, especially monkeys and apes, rely on sound or scent signals instead. They mark territorial boundaries by scent or shrill cries, and give out alarms and remain in contact with one another by calling.

Tail can be 90 cm (3 ft) long

HOWLER MONKEY

A tiger's stripes help it stalk its unsuspecting prey without being seen

Every tiger has a different pattern of black stripes on its face

Calls of the howler monkey can be heard up to 3 km (2 miles) away

Tigers live in the forests of South and Southeast Asia, and mark their territories with scent and droppings.

TIGER

WELL CAMOUFLAGED

Spots, stripes, and other markings on rainforest mammals help to camouflage them in the dappled forest light. They break up the animal's outline and blend it in with the background. Both predators, such as tigers, and their prey, such as deer, use camouflage. Young mammals are often better camouflaged than their parents.

IN THE TREES

HIGH UP IN the rainforest, tangled tree branches form precarious walkways. Mammals living here may be either good climbers or flyers that are able to move swiftly, or slow movers that can grasp branches well. Many tree-dwelling mammals come out at night to avoid predators such as cats, hawks, eagles, and snakes.

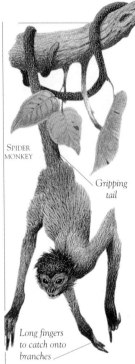

SPIDER MONKEY

Gripping tail

Long fingers to catch onto branches

JUNGLE ACROBAT
The strong tail of the spider monkey supports its weight, allowing it to reach fruits and leaves. The monkey uses its tail like an extra hand, making acrobatic leaps of 10 m (33 ft) through the branches.

LAZING IN THE TREES
Hanging upside down from branches in the rainforests of Central and South America, sloths spend 20 hours a day snoozing in the canopy. Their fur grows towards the spine so that rain runs straight off their backs. Green algae grow in the hair, camouflaging the sloth.

Claws hook around branches and only one limb is moved at a time

SLOTH

Nine neck vertebrae allow sloth to turn around more than other mammals

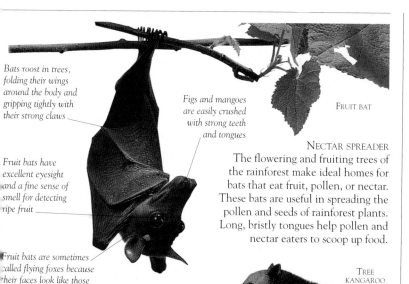

FRUIT BAT

Bats roost in trees, folding their wings around the body and gripping tightly with their strong claws

Figs and mangoes are easily crushed with strong teeth and tongues

Fruit bats have excellent eyesight and a fine sense of smell for detecting ripe fruit

Fruit bats are sometimes called flying foxes because their faces look like those of foxes

NECTAR SPREADER

The flowering and fruiting trees of the rainforest make ideal homes for bats that eat fruit, pollen, or nectar. These bats are useful in spreading the pollen and seeds of rainforest plants. Long, bristly tongues help pollen and nectar eaters to scoop up food.

TREE KANGAROO

Sharp claws for climbing

Feet are strong and wide, with rough pads for gripping branches

Doria's tree kangaroo lives in the cooler forests of New Guinea and has a warm fur coat

IN-THE-TREES FACTS

• Three-toed sloths are slow movers, with an average ground speed of just 1.83–2.44 m (6–8 ft) a minute.

• The tail of a spider monkey can be one-third longer than its body, at 90 cm (3 ft).

• Fruit bats are the largest bats, with wing spans as great as 2 m (7 ft)!

KEEPING A BALANCE

Living in northeast Australia and New Guinea, tree kangaroos have long tails that help them to balance on the branches. They do not hop like other kangaroos. Small groups of tree kangaroos live and sleep together in the same tree but they usually come down to feed.

401

ON THE FOREST FLOOR

THE RAINFOREST FLOOR is home to many
large mammals. Peaceful plant eaters,
such as elephants, and gorillas, feed on
leaves, while anteaters, pangolins, and
armadillos eat termites and other
invertebrates. Groups of peccaries
dig out roots, keeping a lookout
for predators, such as
jaguars and ocelots.

STURDY HERBIVORE
Consuming around 170 kg
(375 lb) of fibrous plant matter
a day, elephants need to have
tough stomachs. Their trunks
are also vital for reaching
understorey plants while
standing on the forest floor.

FOREST FLOOR FACTS

• The armadillo's front
claws, used for digging
up prey, are larger than
any other animal's.

• You can tell an
Asian elephant from
an African one by its
smaller ears and shorter
tusks. Its dome-shaped
forehead also contrasts
with the African
elephant's rounded one.

Long trunk
reaches up to
pick fruit or
tear down
branches

Trunk is a
long nose
and top lip
joined
together

Teeth have
sharp ridges
for grinding
up tough
plants

Adult bull
elephant stands
3 m (10 ft) tall

Flat sole spreads
out to carry the
massive weight

AFRICAN ELEPHANT

402

SHY ANTELOPE
Rabbit-sized royal
antelope, which live in
African rainforests, are
one of the smallest
hoofed mammals.
They are timid,
coming out at night
to feed on leaves. Royal
antelope can slip away
silently or leap as high
as 3 m (10 ft) into the
air to escape predators
such as birds and snakes.

*Females do not
have horns*

ROYAL ANTELOPE

*Protective horny
plates*

CHAMPION DIGGER
Massive claws on its front feet
enable the giant armadillo to
smash its way inside rock-hard
termite mounds. It also digs
for other insects, worms, and
spiders, and eats snakes.

GIANT
ARMADILLO

*Each ocelot has
different fur
markings*

RARE PAINTED LEOPARD
The ocelot or painted leopard
lives in the rainforests of
Central and South America.
Hunting at night, the ocelot
has large eyes to navigate
through the dark forest,
and its spotted coat gives
camouflage as it creeps up
on prey. Ocelots are rare
because of forest destruction
and hunting for their fur.

403

JUNGLE APES

TROPICAL RAINFORESTS are home to all the world's apes, including gibbons, chimpanzees, gorillas, and orang-utans. Unlike monkeys, apes do not have tails. Gorillas and chimpanzees spend much of their time on the ground, while gibbons and orang-utans swing through the trees. Apes usually live in families, and feed by day.

HANGING AROUND
Lar gibbons are mainly vegetarian and live in small groups in Asian rainforests. Gibbons are confident, skilled climbers, that can run upright along branches and swing effortlessly through the trees.

Lower spine is short and inflexible and rib cage is solid to avoid distorting the trunk while swinging

Arms are longer than legs

OUR CLOSEST RELATIVES?
This chimp is investigating a toy brick. Chimps are intelligent, communicating by sound and gesture.

AMAZING APE FACTS

• Male gorillas weigh about 135–175 kg (298–386 lb), but a zoo gorilla once weighed in at 310 kg (683½ lb)!

• Some apes can live to be over 50 years old.

• About 99 per cent of human genes are the same as a chimpanzee's.

GIBBON SWINGING
THROUGH TREES

Arms are twice as
long as legs, with
an armspan of
about 2 m (6 ft)

Flexible hook-like
hands quickly grasp
branches or prey

Hand-over-
hand swinging
movement is
called brachiation

"Rowing" movements
with its legs help
gibbon propel itself
through the air

GENTLE GIANT

This male gorilla is the head of
a family group that wanders
through the forest eating fruit and
ferns. Females and young climb trees,
but males rarely
do as they are
so big and
heavy.

Mature male
gorillas have
silvery grey hair
on their backs
and are called
"silver-backs"

Fatty
throat
pouch

Long,
powerful
arms

FIVE-YEAR-
OLD MALE

KING OF THE SWINGERS
In the forests of Borneo
and Sumatra, shy orang-
utans live a solitary life,
except in the breeding
season. Males are much
heavier and larger than
females, and mature males have
wide cheek flaps on their faces.

MALE GORILLA

405

GRASSLAND

LYING BETWEEN wet forests and dry deserts, grasslands fall into two categories– tropical, such as African savanna, and temperate, such as prairie or steppe. Grassland mammals include plant-eating herds, small burrowers, and the predators that feed on both these groups.

Prairie dogs live in colonies of thousands in underground tunnels

PRAIRIE DOG

Horns measure up to 40 cm (16 in)

Strong, grinding teeth for eating tough grasses and leaves

Long legs and sharp hooves to run swiftly away from danger

THOMSON'S GAZELLE

BURROWERS
To avoid the heat and cold, and to escape predators and fires, many small mammals burrow underground. Their burrowing mixes the soil and encourages plant growth. Most live off grass.

GRAZERS
The most common large grassland herbivores are grazers – grass-eating mammals like antelope, bison, and horses. Grasses, which sprout again when the tops are bitten off, produce a continuous supply of food. Grazers, such as Thomson's gazelle, live in herds of up to 10 for protection against predators.

HUNTERS

Most large hunters – like lions, cheetahs, leopards, and hyenas– are found on the African savanna. Since they hunt in groups, lions and hyenas can prey on animals much bigger than themselves. Cheetahs hunt alone but can run fast enough to catch swift antelopes.

CHEETAH → THOMSON'S GAZELLE

LION → WILDEBEEST

HYENA → ZEBRA

Fur tufts on ears can be 4.5 cm (1¾ in) long

Caracal is a Turkish word meaning "black ears"

Sharp teeth for tearing prey apart

A swipe of the paw can kill a bird in mid-air

GRASSLAND CATS

Cats, big and small, are common grassland hunters. Small cats, like caracals and servals, have longer legs than forest cats and rely on speed and surprise to catch their prey. Cats overpower prey with a vicious bite from their powerful jaws, which are armed with sharp, dagger-like teeth.

Short, dense fur keeps caracal warm at night and cool by day

CARACAL

PAMPAS AND STEPPES

Coat turns white and thickens in winter

Nostrils can be closed during sand storms

SAIGA ANTELOPE

THE VAST PLAINS known as pampas in South America and steppes in Europe and central Asia have hot summers and cold winters. Many small mammals, such as cavies on the pampas and mole rats on the steppes, live underground. Herds of wild grazers have mostly been replaced by domesticated cattle and horses.

STEPPE GRAZERS
The saiga antelope's long nose helps to warm the air it inhales during cold winters on the steppes. Huge herds of saigas once roamed the steppes; they are now a protected species.

As anteaters have no teeth, food is mashed up by hard ridges in the mouth and a muscular stomach.

Tongue pushes out 150 times a minute

MANED WOLF

GIANT PREDATOR
Insects are the main grazers of the pampas, and make a tasty meal for the giant anteater. Anteaters feed mostly on ants and termites, ripping open nests with their big claws and licking the insects with their sticky tongues.

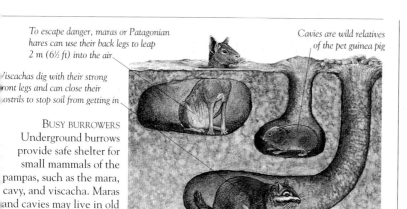

To escape danger, maras or Patagonian hares can use their back legs to leap 2 m (6½ ft) into the air

Cavies are wild relatives of the pet guinea pig

Viscachas dig with their strong front legs and can close their nostrils to stop soil from getting in

BUSY BURROWERS
Underground burrows provide safe shelter for small mammals of the pampas, such as the mara, cavy, and viscacha. Maras and cavies may live in old viscacha burrows in groups of up to 40.

Maned wolves run fast but usually ambush prey rather than chase after it

LONG-LEGGED HUNTER
The maned wolf, which is actually a large fox, has long legs to help it to see over tall grasses. If it is threatened, its mane stands up to make it appear bigger and more frightening. The maned wolf lives alone and hunts at night for cavies and other small mammals and birds.

AMAZING FACTS
• A giant anteater's tongue is about 60 cm (24 in) long.
• Saigas were overhunted for their horns, which were used in Chinese medicines. Now, they are protected and their numbers have increased.

MAMMALS

African Savanna

THE HUGE GRASSLANDS of Africa are called savannas. They are home to the last great herds of mammals, such as elephants and antelope, and their predators, including hyenas and large cats. There are two main seasons – wet and dry – and many grazers migrate regularly in search of fresh grass to eat.

*Meerca
sit up o
their hin
legs
watch f
dange*

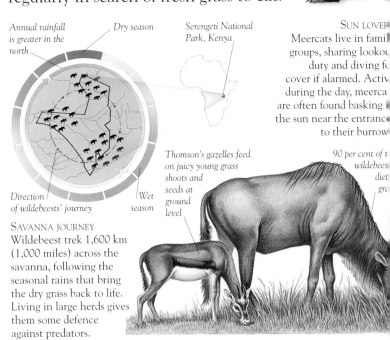

Annual rainfall is greater in the north

Dry season

Serengeti National Park, Kenya

Direction of wildebeests' journey

Wet season

SUN LOVER
Meercats live in famil
groups, sharing lookou
duty and diving f
cover if alarmed. Activ
during the day, meerca
are often found basking i
the sun near the entranc
to their burrow

Thomson's gazelles feed on juicy young grass shoots and seeds at ground level

*90 per cent of t
wildebees
diet
gr*

SAVANNA JOURNEY
Wildebeest trek 1,600 km (1,000 miles) across the savanna, following the seasonal rains that bring the dry grass back to life. Living in large herds gives them some defence against predators.

Large, rounded ears

Giraffes can reach leaves up to 6 m (20 ft) above the ground

Only four toes on front foot

EFFICIENT PREDATORS

Living in packs of 6 to 30, African hunting dogs are nomadic animals, roaming a wide area in search of prey. By hunting together, the dogs can bring down prey larger than themselves, even wildebeest. The pack shares a kill.

Many savanna animals have patterned skin for camouflage

Zebras feed on tough, grass tops and also dig for roots

SHARING FOOD

Various mammals live together on the savanna, sharing resources. Giraffes feed on the highest leaves; zebras crop the top of the grasses; wildebeest eat the medium-length grasses; and Thomson's gazelles nibble grass close to the ground.

AMAZING FACTS

• Hyenas have jaws so strong that they can crunch through bones.

• Young wildebeest can run very soon after they are born.

• African hunting dogs may start to feed on their prey while it is still alive.

411

MAMMALS

GRASSLAND CATS

INTELLIGENT, POWERFUL hunters with sharp senses, grassland cats, both big and small, have strong claws and teeth and a rasping tongue to scrape meat off bones. The spotted coats of leopards, cheetahs, and servals, and the tawny-coloured fur of caracals and lions, provide camouflage in the golden grasses. Lions are the only big cats to live in social groups.

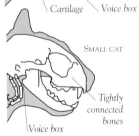

Loose bones

BIG CAT

Cartilage   *Voice box*

SMALL CAT

Tightly connected bones

Voice box

Male lion's mane makes him look fierce and protects his neck during fights

MALE

TO PURR OR ROAR?
Most big cats can roar, but little cats can only purr. The skull and voice box of a big cat, such as a lion or tiger, are loosely connected, allowing them to roar. In cheetahs and mountain lions, these connections are tighter, so the bones cannot vibrate.

412

Streamlined body   Flexible spine

At top speed, all four feet are lifted between strides

Tail helps balance when sprinting

Claws are made of keratin, like human nails

Long legs for fast running

Exposed claws grip the ground

RELAXED

EXTENDED

FAST CAT

Cheetahs hunt by day, stalking and attacking prey with a short burst of speed. They can reach 96 km/h (60 mph) in just three seconds!

KING OF THE CATS

Lions live in groups called prides, made up of 5 to 15 related adult females and their young and 1 to 6 adult males. Males defend the pride while females hunt and care for the young. Lions are the only cats to hunt together, share prey, and help rear each other's cubs.

CAT CLAWS

All cats, except cheetahs, can draw in their claws. This allows the cat to creep up on prey. A cat has four claws on its back paws and five on its front.

Male and female lions look more different than the two sexes of any other cat.

FEMALE

AMAZING CAT FACTS

• Lions sleep or doze for up to 20 hours every day.

• A lion's roar can be heard up to 5 km (3 miles) away.

• A cheetah can only run at top speed for 60 seconds, or it overheats.

• Adult lions eat as much as 18 kg (40 lb) of meat in one meal.

DESERTS

VERY LITTLE RAIN falls on the world's deserts. Most of them, such as the Sahara, are scorching hot all year round, although they get very cold at night. Some, such as the Gobi, have freezing winters. Many small desert mammals are nocturnal, burrowing by day to protect themselves from the extreme heat. Most desert mammals can survive with very little water. Their fur keeps out heat as well as cold.

LARGE MAMMALS
There are few large desert mammals because there is not enough food and water to keep them alive. Only a few kinds of specialized mammals, such as addax, camels, gazelle, antelopes, and kangaroos, manage to survive. They often have to travel long distances in search of water.

Both sexes have thin spiral horns, but the female's are thinner

The addax gets as much moisture as can from food

Addax travel around the African deserts in herds searching for food and water

Wide-spreading feet stop addax from sinking into the sand

ADDAX

DESERT DEFENCE

By coming out at night, small mammals avoid predators as well as the heat of the day. The light colour of their fur helps them to blend in with the sand and rocks. Small mammals can leap out of the way of predators.

EGYPTIAN SPINY MOUSE

Tail can be shed if grabbed by predator

Hair in ears keeps out dust and sand

Fur has stiff hairs to put off predators

ARABIAN SPINY MOUSE

BIG EARS

Some desert mammals, such as fennec foxes and jackrabbits, have large ears that work like radiators to give off heat and keep them cool. The African fennec fox looks very like the North American kit fox, because they have both adapted to survive in the same habitat.

Soles of feet are covered with long hair for walking on scorching sand

FENNEC FOX

DESERT BURROWERS

Most burrowing mammals, such as mulgaras, stay underground until the heat of the day has passed. The sand is much cooler a little way below the surface. The mammals' breath creates a moist atmosphere in the burrow, reducing the amount of water evaporating from their bodies. Many small mammals store food in their burrows to last them through lean times.

MULGARA

Mulgaras never drink and excrete concentrated urine to preserve water.

415

HOT DESERTS

TEMPERATURES IN THE deserts of western North America, Australia, and the African Sahara are scorching during the day, but because there are no clouds to retain the heat, they drop to freezing at night. There are few plants to provide shelter from the extreme temperatures. Most mammals avoid the daytime sun. Others have large ears or light coats to lose heat, and some pant to cool down. The dew that forms at night may provide much needed moisture.

Blood flow in ears is regulated to control heat loss or gain

COOLING SYSTEM
The long ears of the North American jackrabbit have many blood vessels close to the skin's surface. Heat passes from the blood to the air around the ears, helping to cool the jackrabbit down.

Streamlined shape and smooth, silky fur help the mole slide easily through the sand

MARSUPIAL MOLE

Marsupial moles are blind

BLIND TUNNELLER
The Australian marsupial mole uses its long claws to tunnel through sand. Its nose is protected by a horny shield. The burrows are not permanent – the sand is soft and tunnels collapse quickly.

Large ears to listen for prey and keep cool

UNSINKABLE CAT
Thick fur on the soles of the sand cat's feet prevent it from sinking into the soft sand. Sand cats shelter in a burrow or under scrub vegetation during the day and hunt at night. They don't drink, getting all the water they need from their prey.

Yellow-brown coat blends into desert background.

SAND CAT

NO SWEAT
Like all rodents, kangaroo rats conserve water by not sweating and by producing only a small amount of urine and dry droppings. Kangaroo rats are nocturnal and travel long distances looking for food. When they find seeds they carry them in their cheek pouches.

Big ears to listen for danger

Long tail helps to balance while hopping and running

Strong back legs for leaping away from predators

KANGAROO RAT

AMAZING FACTS
• Jackrabbits can bound at 56 km/h (35 mph).

• The kidneys of a kangaroo rat are four times more efficient than those of a person.

• Lions once lived in the Sahara but died out due to hunting by man and increasing dryness.

417

COLD DESERTS

CENTRAL ASIA'S COLD DESERTS, such as the Gobi desert, are particularly difficult habitats for mammals. Besides great swings in temperature between day and night, there are freezing winters of -40°C (-32°F). Some mammals, such as Bactrian camels and dwarf hamsters, rely on their thick coats to keep warm. Small mammals survive desert conditions by spending a lot of time in burrows.

Coat is thicker in winter

MIGRATOR
Also called the Asiatic wild ass, the onager can run away from enemies at a speed of 65 km/h (40 mph). It migrates to find fresh grass and water.

Even the soles of the feet are hairy

Some turn white in winter for camouflage in the snow.

Camels can close their nostrils to prevent sand getting in.

HAIRY HAMSTER
As they forage for seeds and nuts, dwarf hamsters push food into their cheek pouches and then carry it underground for storage. Dwarf hamsters have very thick fur to help them survive the extreme climate. They stay in their burrows for much of the time.

DESERT JUMPER

In the darkness of the desert night, jerboas emerge from their burrows to feed on seeds, shoots, and insects. Jerboas are like tiny kangaroos, able to jump away from enemies on their strong back legs. Their long tail helps them to balance when they jump and supports their body when they rest.

Large ears and eyes to sense danger.

Back legs are four times as long as the front legs

WALKING WATER TANK

The thick fur of a two-humped Bactrian camel holds in body heat during the bitterly cold Asian winters. These camels moult their fur in spring when the weather gets warmer. Camels have long, thick eyelashes to protect their eyes from sharp grains of sand.

Humps store fat, which can be broken down to provide energy and water.

Fur is moulted in spring.

Webbed feet with thick pads prevent the camel from sinking into the sand.

AMAZING CAMEL FACTS

• A camel can drink up to 60 litres (13 gallons) of water in minutes.

• Camels do not sweat until their temperature reaches 40.5°C (105°F) – a high fever in a human.

• A 500-kg (1,100-lb) camel stores more than 50 kg (110 lb) of fat in each hump.

419

MOUNTAINS AND POLAR

LONG, COLD WINTERS, fierce winds, intense sunlight, and cold, dry air, with little moisture are the main features of mountain and polar regions. Mammals in these habitats rely on thick fur coats or layers of fat to keep warm. Some of these mammals' coats change colour seasonally, for camouflage. To escape the extreme winter cold, many polar mammals migrate to warmer habitats.

Vicuñas have thick fur and can run at up to 47 km/h (29 mph)

VICUÑA

MOUNTAIN CLIMBERS
Large plant-eating mammals living on mountains have to keep moving to find food and avoid predators and bad weather. These herbivores include wild mountain sheep and goats, as well as the vicuñas and alpacas of South America. Sure-footed and agile, these mammals have sharp, pointed hooves that grip on steep, slippery slopes.

About 600–700 sensitive whiskers to help find food

POLAR OCEANS
In polar regions, the sea is often warmer than the air. It is also very rich in food. Some mammals migrate to polar oceans for the summer months, while others live there all year round.

Fatty blubber more than 10 cm (4 in) thick

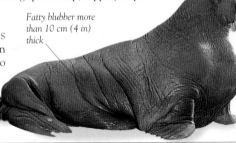

ARCTIC FOX IN
SUMMER COAT

TUNDRA CAMOUFLAGE
In the Arctic tundra – the frozen lands
around the edge of the Arctic – mammals
may change colour with the seasons. The
Arctic fox, snowshoe hare, and stoat, for
example, turn white in winter for camouflage
against the snow. In the summer, when the
snow melts, their coats change to brown or
grey to blend with the landscape.

*Chest and belly stay
a pale, greyish white*

*Hollow hairs trap
warm air near
the body*

*Furry paws act
like snowshoes*

*Two
layers of
thick fur keep
the bear warm*

KEEPING WARM
Thick layers of fur
and fat insulate
polar mammals
against the cold, and
blubber acts as a food
store for hard times. In
winter, small mammals,
such as marmots, hibernate
in burrows, while
female polar bears
give birth to their
cubs in cosy dens dug in the snow.

*Non-slip soles
to grip the ice*

POLAR
BEAR

ARCTIC TUNDRA

AROUND THE EDGE of the icy Arctic ocean is a flat, treeless region called the tundra, where the sub-soil is always frozen. Some mammals, such as musk oxen, are hardy enough to live here all year round. Others, including caribou, or reindeer, cannot stand the harsh climate and migrate here only for the summer months.

Long, curved horns for defence against wolves

Two-layered coat keeps out the cold

MUSK OX

ARCTIC WOLF

SHAGGY COAT
Musk oxen have long, woolly coats lined with underfur that is eight times warmer than sheep's wool. Some hairs in the outer coat are more than 1 m (3 ft) long. Musk oxen have sharp hooves for digging through snow or ice to find food.

SIBERIAN
LEMMING

BIG FEET
The wide hooves of the
caribou, or reindeer,
help it to walk on deep
snow without sinking
in. Caribou breed on
the tundra, moving
south for winter.

FAST BREEDERS
When food is plentiful, lemmings
nibble shoots and roots and breed
fast. In some summers, lemming
populations "explode", forcing
thousands to wander great
distances to find food.

*Thick,
waterproof
fur turns
grey-white
in winter*

*Sensitive ears
track sounds
from 3 km
(2 miles)
away*

Big feet

CARIBOU

*Long,
powerful legs
to run great
distances
after prey*

CAMOUFLAGED PREDATOR
Arctic wolves have thick
fur, which turns white in
winter. This allows them to
blend into the background
and creep close to prey,
such as musk oxen. Pack
hunting enables wolves
to kill larger prey
than if they
hunted alone.

AMAZING FACTS

• Wolves can leap up
to 4.5 m (15 ft) and can
even jump backwards!

• Musk oxen have
longer fur than any
other mammal.

• Adult caribou munch
their way through 4.5 kg
(10 lb) of food a day!

MOUNTAIN TOPS

MAMMALS ARE SCARCE on mountain tops. Many have adapted like Arctic mammals. To cope with the cold and wind, they have thick, shaggy fur coats to keep warm and may move up and down the mountain with the seasons. Some small mammals, such as marmots, hibernate in winter after building up layers of fat in the summer. The internal organs of mammals on high mountains may also differ from those in the lowlands. Many have developed large hearts and lungs to help them get enough oxygen from the thin air at high altitudes.

BATHING MACAQUE
To keep warm in winter, these monkeys from the mountains of northern Japan take hot baths in volcanic springs.

Thicker fur grows in winter

RARE HUNTER
The snow leopard, or ounce, hunts wild sheep and goats at up to 5,500 m (18,000 ft) high in the Himalayas. It roams its huge territory alone. The snow leopard is rare as it has been hunted for its thick fur.

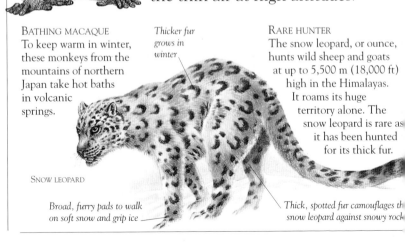

SNOW LEOPARD

Broad, furry pads to walk on soft snow and grip ice

Thick, spotted fur camouflages the snow leopard against snowy rock

FURRY CHINCHILLA

High up in the Andes mountains, chinchillas huddle in rocky holes. Many have been hunted for their coats, so they are rare in the wild. Chinchillas eat plants, holding food in their paws.

Bushy tail is 15 cm (6 in) long

Soft, dense fur coat

CHINCHILLA
Summer coat is short and smooth; winter coat is long and dense with soft underfur

AMAZING FACTS

• The yak is the highest-living large mammal, grazing at 6,000 m in the Himalayas.

• Chamois can live for two weeks without food.

• According to legend, yetis, or abominable snowmen, live in the Himalayas, but no-one has proved they exist.

CHAMOIS

Both sexes have horns

SURE-FOOTED CHAMOIS

The chamois has a very good sense of balance and can jump up to 9 m (29 ft) up sheer rock faces in the mountains of southern Europe and western Asia. Chamois browse on plants, moving down from the peaks in winter.

Hooves have a hard, thin edge for gripping rocks

Shock-absorbing legs and spongy hoof pads for extra grip on steep or slippery slopes

MOUNTAINS & POLAR

425

MAMMALS

OCEANS AND SEAS

LIVING NEAR THE SURFACE of the world's oceans and seas are a variety of marine mammals that come to the surface regularly to breathe. Some, such as whales and dolphins, never leave the water, while others, such as seals, return to land to mate and have their pups. Sea mammals are streamlined, with modified limbs and tails for swimming and thick fat, or blubber, to keep them warm.

FURRY WARMTH
Unlike other marine mammals, the sea otter has no blubber for insulation. Instead it relies on thick, waterproof fur for warmth. An adult may have as many as 800 million hairs, which help provide buoyancy in the water.

SEAL GROUPS
Seals fall into three main groups. True seals, such as the one below, swim with their back flippers and have no visible ear flaps. Eared seals, like the sea lion on the right, swim with front flippers. Walruses are the third group.

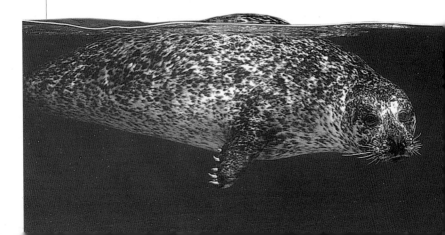

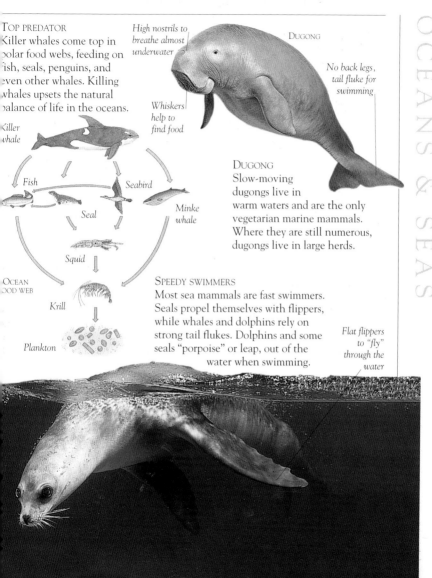

TOP PREDATOR

Killer whales come top in polar food webs, feeding on fish, seals, penguins, and even other whales. Killing whales upsets the natural balance of life in the oceans.

Killer whale

High nostrils to breathe almost underwater

DUGONG

No back legs, tail fluke for swimming

Whiskers help to find food

Fish

Seabird

Seal

Minke whale

Squid

OCEAN FOOD WEB

Krill

Plankton

DUGONG

Slow-moving dugongs live in warm waters and are the only vegetarian marine mammals. Where they are still numerous, dugongs live in large herds.

SPEEDY SWIMMERS

Most sea mammals are fast swimmers. Seals propel themselves with flippers, while whales and dolphins rely on strong tail flukes. Dolphins and some seals "porpoise" or leap, out of the water when swimming.

Flat flippers to "fly" through the water

OCEANS & SEAS

POLAR OCEANS

HARDY WHALES AND SEALS, such as beluga whales, and ringed seals, survive in polar oceans all year round. Many other sea mammals migrate to these cold waters in summer, when food is plentiful. This surge in sea life is fueled by the vast numbers of tiny creatures called plankton, which form the basis of food webs that include fish, whales, squid, seals, and seabirds.

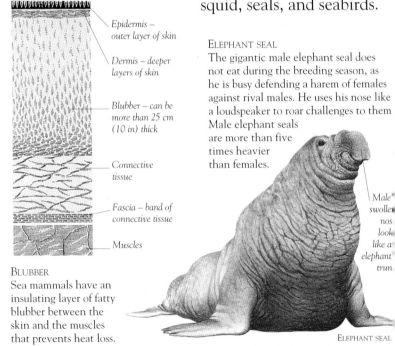

Epidermis – outer layer of skin

Dermis – deeper layers of skin

Blubber – can be more than 25 cm (10 in) thick

Connective tissue

Fascia – band of connective tissue

Muscles

BLUBBER
Sea mammals have an insulating layer of fatty blubber between the skin and the muscles that prevents heat loss.

ELEPHANT SEAL
The gigantic male elephant seal does not eat during the breeding season, as he is busy defending a harem of females against rival males. He uses his nose like a loudspeaker to roar challenges to them Male elephant seals are more than five times heavier than females.

Male swollen nose looks like an elephant trunk

ELEPHANT SEAL

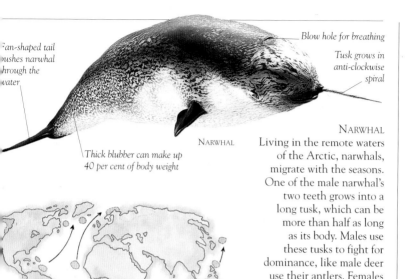

Fan-shaped tail pushes narwhal through the water

Blow hole for breathing

Tusk grows in anti-clockwise spiral

NARWHAL

Thick blubber can make up 40 per cent of body weight

NARWHAL

Living in the remote waters of the Arctic, narwhals, migrate with the seasons. One of the male narwhal's two teeth grows into a long tusk, which can be more than half as long as its body. Males use these tusks to fight for dominance, like male deer use their antlers. Females do not usually have tusks.

MAP OF WHALE MIGRATION

SUMMER FEEDING PLACES
WINTER FEEDING PLACES
MIGRATION ROUTE

WHALE MIGRATION

In summer, many whales travel to the cold polar waters of the Arctic and the Antarctic to feed. In winter, when the sea freezes over, the whales swim back to warmer waters in the tropics to mate and have their young. They eat little in the winter, using up the energy stored as body fat during the summer feast at the poles. Migrant whales include grey, blue, and humpback whales.

AMAZING FACTS

• Grey whales travel more than 20,000 km (12,000 miles) during migration.

• The elephant seal can survive without food for about 100 days.

• Male humpback whales sing the longest and most complex songs in the animal kingdom.

WHALES AND DOLPHINS

GIANT WHALES and smaller dolphins travel the oceans of the world, mating and giving birth in the water. They dive deep into the ocean, surfacing frequently to breathe air through a blow hole on the top of their head. Whales and dolphins have large, complex brains, live in groups, and communicate over vast distances using sound, which travels well through water. There are at least 80 species of whale, which fall into two main groups: toothed whales and baleen whales.

GREY WHALE

Scratches from other whales or collisions with boats

The grey whale is half the size of the gigantic blue whale

BALEEN WHALE
Blue, fin, grey, and humpback whales are all kinds of baleen whale, which are larger than toothed whales. They feed by straining fish and plankton from the water, using fringed plates of horny baleen which hang from their great arched jaws like curtains.

BLUE WHALE

An elephant could stand on a blue whale's tongue!

Grooves allow throat to stretch whale can gulp huge amounts of water

mooth,
treamlined body
hape cuts through
he water fast

Powerful muscles
pull tail flukes up
and down

PORPOISING
To breathe while swimming fast, dolphins sometimes leap in and out of the water, or porpoise. Some hurl themselves 7 m (23 ft) into the air. Spinner dolphins spin around as many as seven times in a single leap!

Flippers and fins are used
to steer and change direction

COMMON DOLPHIN
SWIMMING SEQUENCE

Stubby dorsal fin

Underneath the whale's fat,
r blubber, are powerful
uscles

Powerful tail flukes push
the whale through the water

BLUE WHALE
The world's largest animal, the blue whale grows 32 m (100 ft) long and can weigh 200 tonnes (197 tons) – as much as 40 rhinoceroses! It can eat up to 4 tonnes of krill (shrimp-like crustaceans) every day. The blue whale, which was once widely hunted, is now very rare.

Rows of sharp, cone-shaped
teeth snap up penguins, sea
lions, fish, and squid

KILLER WHALE
Orcas, or killer whales, live and hunt in groups called pods. They have stronger teeth than dolphins and feed on a great variety of prey – even attacking other whales and dolphins. Orcas, sperm whales, and dolphins are categorized as toothed whales, which are smaller than baleen whales.

SKELETON
OF A
KILLER
WHALE

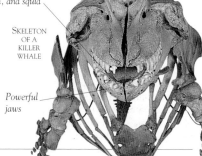

Powerful
jaws

RIVERS, LAKES, AND SWAMPS

RIVERS, LAKES, AND SWAMPS provide inviting
environments, rich in food and nesting places, that
attract a wide range of mammals. These animals
are often strong swimmers, gliding through
the water to find food or escape danger. Some,
like otters or river dolphins, spend most or
all of their time in the water. Others, like
raccoons, visit freshwater habitats to feed.
These freshwater ecosystems are often
threatened by drainage or pollution
from industry, towns, or agriculture.

BAIKAL SEAL

FRESHWATER SEAL
Living in and named after Siberia's largest lake, th
Baikal seal is the only seal that lives in fresh water
About 70,000 seals live in the lake, feeding on fish
and resting on lake shores and islands. Ancestors
of Baikal seals may have migrated to the lake from
the Arctic along a river during one of the ice ages.

UNDERWATER LIFE
Otters are well
adapted for swimming
underwater. They have
waterproof fur, webbed
toes, and a long tail that
acts as a rudder. Cubs are
taught to enter the water
but instinctively know
how to swim.

*Ears and nostrils can
be closed under the water*

*Otters swim b
undulating their boc
and tail and pushin
with their back fe*

*Thick, flesh
muscul
t*

Front legs steer

OTTER

FISHING FOR FOOD
Fish are an important source of food for water mammals. The fishing cat of southern and Southeast Asian marshes and swamps can flip fish out of the water with its slightly webbed paws. It also dives into the water after fish and catches them in its sharp teeth.

FISHING CAT

Open mouth that shows off huge teeth is a display of threat.

Eyes, nose, and ears stay above the water's surface when hippo is underwater

HIPPOPOTAMUS

RARE MAMMALS
Large mammals are not common in watery habitats – the hippos and antelope of African lakes and swamps are an exception, as are the manatees of western Africa, the Amazon, and the Everglades. More common small mammals include muskrats, mink, beavers, and capybara.

RIVERS AND LAKES

MANY MAMMALS MAKE their homes in safe freshwater lakes, ponds, and rivers. Homes can be hidden away in riverbanks or lakesides, and beavers have even learned to build their homes in the middle of lakes where predators cannot reach them. Some freshwater mammals use sound or electric fields to find food in muddy water.

PLATYPUS

BOTTOM FEEDER
Feeding mainly along the bottom of lakes and rivers, the platypus probes the mud with its sensitive bill for small aquatic animals such as worms, insects, and crayfish. Platypuses, which have no teeth, crush food between horny, ridged plates inside their bill. They nest in burrows.

Webbed feet with claws for burrowing

Underwater, the platypus can shut its eyes and ears to keep water out

AMAZING FACTS

• The platypus can detect electric fields given off by its prey.

• Strong enough to take the weight of a rider on horseback, the largest beaver dam measured 700 m (2,296 ft) long!

• Using its sharp front teeth, a beaver can fell a small tree in 10 minutes!

EXCELLENT SWIMMERS
Muskrats have webbed hind feet and long, flattened tails, which they use as a rudder. They feed mainly on water plants, but also eat fish and frogs. Muskrats dig burrows or construct homes from plants.

Waterproof fur

MUSKRAT

434

Long, slender snout to probe for shrimps

Dolphin is about 2.4 m (8 ft) long

RARE DOLPHIN
The rare Chinese whitefin dolphin is one of the few that lives in fresh water. As it has poor eyesight, it relies on sonar, or echolocation, for hunting fish.

CHINESE
WHITEFIN DOLPHIN

Strong, powerful, muscular tail

UNDERWATER HOME
Beavers make dams in rivers to create ponds around their homes, called lodges. Lodges protect beaver families from predators such as wolves, bears, and coyotes, which cannot dig through the walls or swim into the entrances.

Walls of lodge are made of sticks and mud

Adult beavers bring leafy twigs home, which they store underwater for eating in winter, when food is scarce

Floor of the lodge, where the beavers rest and sleep, is 15 cm (6 in) above water

The lodge has several underwater entrances

BEAVER
LODGE

Webbed feet and broad, paddle-shaped tail, which acts as a rudder

Young beavers swim within hours of birth

435

MAMMALS

SWAMPS

WATERLOGGED, FORESTED AREAS, swamps can be fresh or saltwater and are more extensive in tropical than in temperate areas. At different times of year, the water level in swamps may rise and fall, affecting the lives of the mammals who live there. These mammal inhabitants may swim through the water, wade through the mud, or live high up in the trees. For the few that can survive the variable water level and muddy conditions, food and shelter are plentiful.

Nose goes red if monkey is angry or excited

Long 76-cm (30-in) tail for balance

PROBOSCIS MONKEY

BIG NOSE
The agile proboscis monkey leaps through the branches of mangrove trees in the swamps of Borneo. The male is much larger than the female and has a long nose, which makes his honking calls of danger louder.

UNSINKABLE ANTELOPE
The long hooves and flexible ankles of the sitatunga antelope allow its feet to splay, preventing it from sinking into mud. The sitatunga swims well and often hides underwater.

436

WINGED HUNTER
The graceful fisherman bat detects its prey by echolocation, then uses its huge, powerful wings to swoop down into the water and catch it.

Sharp claws snatch fish and insects

AMAZING FACTS

• The nose of the male proboscis monkey can reach 17.5 cm (7 in).

• Fisherman bats are superb swimmers, using their wings as oars.

• Manatees munch through 75 kg (165 lb) of vegetation a day.

• Manatees can live for as long as 50–60 years.

Large, rounded tail pushes manatee through the water at speeds of 25 km/h (15 mph)

For breathing, only the tip of the snout is above the surface

SHY PLANT EATER
Manatees, often called sea cows, are shy, rare animals that feed at night mainly on sea grasses. Florida manatees of the Everglades swamps reach a maximum size of 3.9 m (12 ft 10 in) and weigh 1,660 kg (3,650 lb).

MANATEE

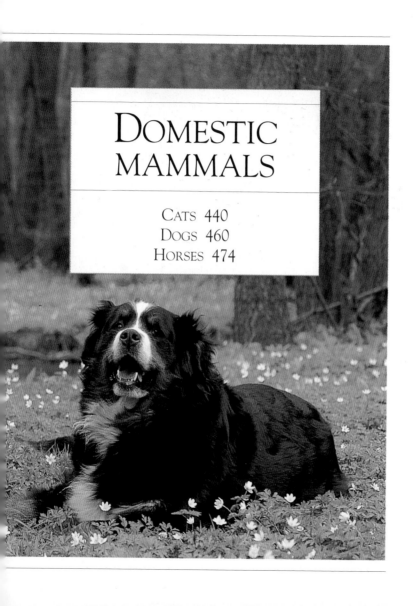

DOMESTIC MAMMALS

DOMESTIC MAMMALS

WHAT IS A CAT?

CATS ARE NATURE'S most efficiently designed hunting carnivores. They have powerful bodies, superb vision, and razor-sharp teeth and claws. Most cats are self-reliant, stalking their prey alone in dusk or darkness. One species has also succeeded in living with people, and is now kept as a pet around the world.

AFRICAN LION

ANCIENT EGYPTIAN CAT

Short, rounded head

Sandy-brown coat for camouflage

Cats lived near settlements, where they could easily find food.

Strong front legs and muscular neck for catching prey

Sharp claws are kept sheathed when not in use

HISTORY OF THE DOMESTIC CAT
Wall paintings show that cats were being tamed in ancient Egypt before 2500 B.C. Although the Egyptians forbade the export of their cats, they still spread to ancient Greece by 500 B.C. They were also recorded in India before 100 B.C.

TYPICAL MAMMAL

Like other mammals, cats are warm-blooded and have a skeleton and a four-chambered heart. The female gives birth to live young and produces milk to feed her kittens.

MOTHER AND KITTEN

CAT FACTS

• Cats survive on any meat or fish they can catch. When hungry, even the largest cats will eat insects.

• Australia and Antarctica are the only continents with no native cat species.

• Except for tigers, most wild cats attack people only if they are too old to catch their usual animal prey.

Loose skin for freedom of movement

Flexible backbone increases length of stride as cat runs

Tail is one-third the length of the body

Back legs are powered by the largest muscles in the cat's body

Long, dark hair at tip of tail is used for signalling

THE HUNTER

Virtually everything about a cat, including the domestic cat, is designed for hunting. Cats are lithe, intelligent, and strong, and react with lightning speed. A cat approaches its prey using stealth and camouflage, then overpowers its victim. Lions are the only cats that hunt in groups.

441

CAT ANATOMY

ALL CATS ARE AGILE and athletic predators. Their bodies are powerful and flexible, specially designed for running, jumping, and climbing. Some types of cat even excel at swimming. Superb hunters, cats first swiftly chase and then overpower prey with their strength. Sharp teeth are used to finish off the catch.

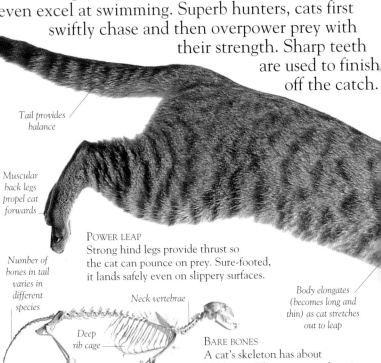

Tail provides balance

Muscular back legs propel cat forwards

Number of bones in tail varies in different species

POWER LEAP
Strong hind legs provide thrust so the cat can pounce on prey. Sure-footed, it lands safely even on slippery surfaces.

Neck vertebrae

Deep rib cage

Front legs are shorter than hind legs

Body elongates (becomes long and thin) as cat stretches out to leap

BARE BONES
A cat's skeleton has about 250 bones. The seven vertebrae in the neck are shorter than in most other mammals, and the spine is very flexible. This is a domestic cat skeleton, but the skeletons of the larger cats are similar.

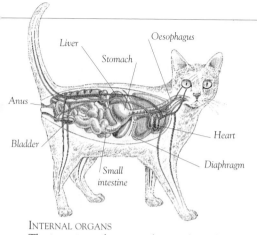

Oesophagus

Liver

Stomach

Anus

Bladder

Small intestine

Heart

Diaphragm

INTERNAL ORGANS

The intestines of a cat are short and simple since they need to digest only meat and not plants. Most of the nutrients from the food are absorbed in the small intestine.

Powerful jaw muscles attach to side of skull

Incisor, or biting, teeth

Canine teeth to kill prey

Carnassial teeth to tear prey apart

Front legs take most of the impact of landing

Pads on the feet help cushion the cat as it lands

CAT SKULL

A cat's skull is large compared to the size of its body. The eye sockets are big to allow for good range of vision. The jaws are short and strong. All of a cat's teeth are sharp and scissor-like for tearing and cutting, rather than flat, like a human's, for crushing.

443

Eyes and ears

As predators, cats depend on their highly developed senses of sight and hearing to find prey. The majority of cats hunt at night, so they need to be able to see in near darkness. A cat can see about six times better than a person can at night. However, a cat's colour vision is not as developed as ours. Cats also rely on their acute hearing to pinpoint the exact location of prey. Sounds inaudible to humans, or even dogs, can be detected by cats.

SOUND DETECTORS
The serval, a cat from the African savannah, has large, mobile ears. It can pick up the high-pitched calls of rodents hidden in the grass.

THE OUTER EAR
A cat's outer ear acts like a funnel, channelling sounds to the eardrum. Each ear can rotate to locate sounds precisely.

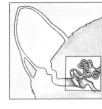

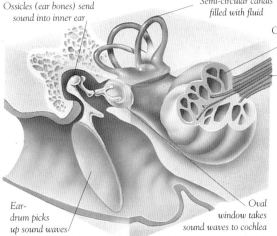

Ossicles (ear bones) send sound into inner ear

Semi-circular canals filled with fluid

Cochlea changes vibrations into nerve impulses

Auditory nerve takes signals to brain

THE INNER EAR
Sound waves vibrate the eardrum, which then moves the ossicles. The vibrations change to electrical impulses and travel down the auditory nerve to the brain. Here they are deciphered into meaningful sounds.

Ear-drum picks up sound waves

Oval window takes sound waves to cochlea

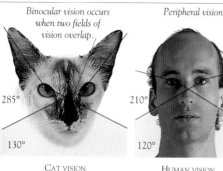

Binocular vision occurs when two fields of vision overlap.

285°

130°

CAT VISION

Peripheral vision

210°

120°

HUMAN VISION

THROUGH A CAT'S EYES
Cats can see at a wider angle around their heads than people can. This means that cats can be alert to movements to the side or slightly behind them. Binocular vision allows them to see images as three-dimensional, as well as to judge distance and depth very accurately.

PUPILS IN DARKNESS

PUPILS IN DAYLIGHT

UPIL DILATION
t night, the cat's pupils
nlarge to let in more light. In
·right light, some cats' pupils
·arrow to slits; others contract
· small circles.

·EEING IN THE DARK
·ats see well in semi-darkness.
·his is because of a "mirror" of
·ittering cells (called the
·*petum lucidum*) behind
·e retina. These cells
·flect light back, making
··jects clearer in the dark.

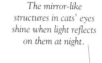

The mirror-like structures in cats' eyes shine when light reflects on them at night.

In the dark, the pupils dilate to become almost round.

Smell, taste, and touch

Cats have extremely acute senses. They rely on smell to identify the things around them, and on touch to feel their way around, particularly in the dark. Another sensory device cats possess is the Jacobsen's organ, located in the roof of the mouth. This structure seems to respond to both smell and taste, and helps the cat to detect scents that their nose cannot – for example, when a female is ready to mate.

The senses of smell and taste tell the cat if this toad is edible.

Cats never eat anything without carefully sniffing it first.

SENSE OF SMELL
A cat's nose contains some 19 million smelling nerves, compared to a human's 5 million. Cats are especially sensitive to rancid odours, such as meat that has gone off. They normally seek out fresh meat rather than scavenge dead animals.

ENTICING CATNIP
Many cats, especially tom (male) cats, find the smell of catnip irresistible. This garden herb contains a chemical that relaxes cats, or can make them roll around. About 50 per cent of cats do not react to catnip at all.

TOUCH-SENSITIVE HAIRS

Whiskers are specialized, stiff hairs with highly sensitive nerves in their roots. They help a cat like this leopard to familiarize itself with its surroundings. A cat uses its whiskers to gauge if it can fit through a gap.

The cat's saliva leaves its scent.

Cats groom each other to spread their scent, and also to show affection.

CAT COMMUNICATION

Cats use smell to communicate far more than people do. They recognize the familiar scents of their companions. Because their skin is covered in touch-sensitive nerves, cats also communicate by grooming each other.

Characteristic lip-curling known as flehmening

FLEHMENING

The curious way that a cat curls its upper lip is called flehmening. It does this to draw smells into the Jacobsen's organ in its mouth. Male cats flehmen to detect the scent of nearby females. The Jacobsen's organs of the lion and tiger are more sensitive than those of domestic cats.

447

Paws and claws

A cat uses its paws for everything from gentle grooming to fierce fighting. To aid a cat in one of its most important skills, running, the bones of the feet have evolved so that a cat permanently walks on its toes. In the wild, injuries to the paws can prove fatal, as these can prevent a cat from hunting successfully.

CLAWS FOR CLIMBING
Most cats are masterly climbers, and can make even a vertical ascent with ease. Coming back down is more problematic, since the claws curve the wrong way to grip when descending. Cats awkwardly make their way down a tree backwards.

Claws dig in to anchor the cat

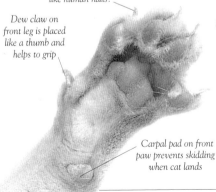

Claws are made of keratin, like human nails.

Dew claw on front leg is placed like a thumb and helps to grip

Carpal pad on front paw prevents skidding when cat lands

SPECIALIZED FEET
A cat has furless pads of tough leather on the underside of its paws. These pads enable the animal to stalk silently, and they cushion the impact of landings. Pads also help the cat to "brake" suddenly in mid-run. The cheetah has unique grooved pads to improve its control when running

SCRATCHING ITS MARK

This jaguar, like other cats, scratches trees to keep its claws clean and sharp. Scratching also marks a cat's territory. A cat leaves behind its scent from glands between its toes, while the scratches themselves show the cat has been in the area.

HUNTING WEAPONS

Watching a cat play will reveal many of its hunting techniques. Cats use their front paws to swipe at, scoop up, rake, or grip their catch. Playing with toys is one way domestic cats practise these moves. Pets tend not to use their claws ferociously against their owners.

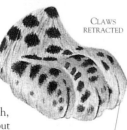

Claws extended to grasp toy

This 3-week-old kitten is already beginning to develop its hunting skills.

RETRACTABLE CLAWS

When a cat rests, ligaments keep its claws protected under extensions of the toe bones. The claws are only extended when needed. A cheetah, however, has its claws out permanently so it can grip the ground when it runs.

CLAWS
RETRACTED

CLAWS
EXTENDED

Relaxed cat with claws retracted out of sight

Ligaments slacken to unveil claws when necessary

449

CAT MOVEMENT

NORMALLY GRACEFUL and controlled, cats can also react with a sudden burst of energy. Balance, strength, speed, and quick judgement help cats to chase and seize elusive prey. The only physical quality cats lack is endurance. The cat is a particularly talented leaper, able to jump four and a half times its body length and land on a chosen spot with great accuracy.

A kitten extends its paws and claws to prepare for landing.

JUMPING

Cats can leap vertically when necessary. The caracal and lynx are expert jumpers, leaping up into the air to swipe a bird as it takes off. With one paw, they can knock their catch to the ground.

Head outstretched as cheetah accelerates to its full speed

CHEETAH

Claws help a cat climb and maintain its balance.

Looking before leaping, to judge its distance from the ground

TERRITORIAL MOVEMENTS

One of a cat's main daily movements is to patrol and mark its territory. It will roar around looking out for other cats or potential prey. Cats climb both to survey their area and because a higher position gives them an advantage over competitors.

LEAPING

A cat's most characteristic movement is its leap, demonstrated here by a lioness. The back muscles flex and relax as the cat leaps, with the tail extended for balance. The powerful back legs lift the cat and are the last part of the body to leave the ground.

The lioness stretches her body forwards as she takes off.

Tail is turned up for balance

Slender, light body and long legs enable the cheetah to reach high speeds

The tail is more than half the length of the body. It swings to counterbalance the body during sharp turns.

When running, the front paws never touch the ground at the same time as the back paws.

RUNNING

Most cats can leap better than they run, but the cheetah is built for speed. Its backbone is extremely flexible, so when the front legs touch the ground, the back end springs forwards. In mid-stride the body stretches full out and all four legs leave the ground. At full sprint the cheetah can reach 96 km/h (60 mph).

Balancing and falling

Some types of cat spend a significant part of their lives in trees, moving confidently along even the narrowest branches. However, if it does fall, the cat has evolved a unique method of protecting itself. Its eyes, brain, and sensitive balance organs in the inner ear ensure that the cat always lands on its feet.

The head rotates first to align with the ground.

1 INSTANT REACTION
The inner ear instantly reacts if the cat is off balance. This warns the brain that it needs to begin to respond to the fall.

2 ROTATING RAPIDLY
The front of the body receives signals from the brain and twists to follow the head. The backbone is so supple that it can rotate 180°.

Front legs pull around to upright position

GEOFFROY'S CAT

This cat lives in the mountainous forests of southern South America.

LIVING THE HIGH LIFE
Many of the small wild cats hunt and sleep in trees. The Geoffroy's cat from South America uses its sharp claws, keen eyesight, good reflexes, and superb sense of balance to stalk mammals and birds in the treetops.

PERFECT BALANCE

This leopard looks precariously balanced, but it will easily secure its kill off the ground and away from scavengers. The leopard is one of the biggest members of the cat family that spends a lot of time in the trees. It is strong enough to drag up a carcass heavier than its own body weight.

FALLING FACTS

• One cat is known to have survived a record fall of 61 m (200 ft).

• From heights of 18 m (60 ft), cats travel at 64 km/h (40 mph) before they hit the ground.

• If the front legs cannot absorb the force of impact, the cat's chin crashes into the ground. This is likely to cause a jaw fracture.

Back end still recovering

Eyes checking where it will be landing

The back legs will help to absorb the force of impact.

3 READY FOR IMPACT
As the cat's front legs begin to stretch out to make contact with the ground, the back of the body is still swivelling round. The collarbones at the top of the front legs will act as shock absorbers when the cat lands.

Legs prepared to run when cat touches ground

4 Landing on its feet
Only seconds after losing its balance, the cat is well positioned to land safely. The head and soft underparts are protected from injury. The cat instinctively relaxes its body before impact, which prevents it from tearing its muscles or jarring its joints.

Front legs take most of the shock of the landing

453

HUNTING

VIRTUALLY ALL CATS hunt on their
own, so they must attack
with surprise and speed.
They stealthily approach
their unsuspecting prey
using any available cover.
When they are close enough
they suddenly pounce, seizing
their quarry in a deadly grip.

HOUSEHOLD HUNTER
The domestic cat is famed for its
prowess as a mouser. Some cats
also excel at catching lizards, birds
or insects. However, hunting is a
learned behaviour, so not all pet
cats make efficient hunters.

GROUP CHASE
Unlike most cats, lions hunt
in groups. This means they
can kill animals larger than
themselves. The lionesses of
the pride do nearly all of
the hunting. To improve
their chances of a kill,
they single out a weak-
looking animal,
surround it, and then
chase it down.

*Cat holds its body
and tail close to
the ground*

FATAL BITE

This leopard pins down its victim to stop it from escaping. Then it bites through the neck of its catch to sever the spinal cord. If a cat cannot eat its kill all at once it will drag the carcass under cover to protect it from scavengers.

Spotted coat pattern keeps the animal camouflaged

FRUSTRATED KILLER

Domestic cats will play with a toy as if it were a prey animal. They creep up on the object, then bite and shake it. Wild cats sometimes toy with their quarry before killing it.

Mature cats play occasionally, but not as often as kittens.

ASIAN LEOPARD CAT

SILENT STALKER

Except for the cheetah, cats can manage only short bursts of speed. They must steal quite close to an animal before they bound forwards. Approaching slowly and silently, the stalking cat is alert to every movement. When it is within striking distance it springs on its prey without warning.

The cat runs forwards in this position, then stops and crouches down.

455

FUR TYPES

SLEEK AND FINE, or long and luxurious, a cat's fur is its finest feature. The coat insulates a cat in hot or cold weather, carries its scent, and is sensitive to touch. Fur type is often suited to where a cat lives, although the wide variation of coats in domestic breeds is due to selective breeding by people.

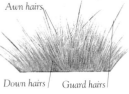

Awn hairs

Down hairs   *Guard hairs*

A CAT'S COAT
There are three kinds of hair in a cat's coat, although not every breed has all three. The longest are the coarse outer guard hairs. In wild and domestic cats, these carry the fur pattern. Slightly shorter awn hairs lie beneath. Short, soft down provides insulation.

Persians have thick down and up to 10-cm (4-in) long guard hairs.

BRITISH SHORTHAIR
This breed is typical of short-coated cats. It has a short, dense, crisp coat. The thick, plush fur stands out from the body like a rug.

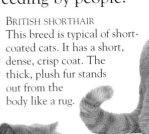

Coat is about 5 cm (2 in) thick

PERSIAN LONGHAIR
Persian cats have the longest and densest fur of any cat breed. The hairs are silky and fine, giving the cat a very fluffy appearance – even the paws are tufted. In warm summer months the cat moults, which makes its coat look shorter.

Fur is especially curly on back and tail

CORNISH REX

The unusual fur of the Rex breeds is wavy and crimped. All of the hairs in a Cornish Rex's coat are short and curly. The coat is made up solely of down and awn hairs, both of which are very soft to the touch. The fur is fine, so Rexes can be susceptible to the cold.

WILD CAT FUR

Wild cats have coats of two layers: warm down hair underneath and a resilient outer coat. In cold climates, cats have thicker fur. The Pallas's cat from Asia has the longest coat of any wild cat. It was once mistakenly believed to be the ancestor of domestic cats with long hair.

Longer fur on underside for warmth when lying on cold ground

PALLAS'S CAT

AMERICAN WIREHAIR

This cat's fur is distinctively wiry and springy. Every hair, including those in the ears and on the tail, is crimped, or even coiled. The Wirehair's fur is of medium length and very frizzy. It feels like lamb's-wool to the touch.

Wiry coat makes pattern look raised

"HAIRLESS" SPHYNX

Although the Sphynx looks bald, it has traces of fur on its tail and a light covering of down on its body. It also has very short eyebrows and whiskers. This breed's lack of hair means that it is vulnerable to sunburn.

Coat is like suede

Colours and patterns

Cats come in a huge variety of colours and patterns. Many have distinctive markings that originally evolved to help cats in the wild stay hidden from their prey. Domestic cats often come in more conspicuous colours because they have little need for camouflage. Breeders have achieved some very striking colour and pattern combinations.

SEAL TORTIE POINT SIAMESE

CORNISH REX TORTOISESHELL

CHARACTERISTIC MARKINGS

Siamese cats have a characteristic pattern of darker areas on the tail, legs, ears, and face. These markings are described as points. Young kittens develop their points as they mature.

TORTOISESHELL

For genetic reasons, tortoiseshell patterns occur almost entirely in female cats. Tortoiseshell fur is a combination of black and red.

COLOUR RANGE

Some cats have unpatterned coats of one pure, solid colour. There are many varieties, some simply paler versions of the basic colours. Here the typical darker colours are shown above their lighter variants, with white shown on its own.

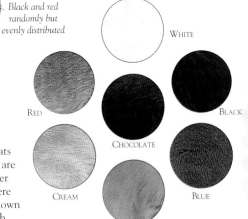

Black and red randomly but evenly distributed

WHITE

RED

BLACK

CHOCOLATE

CREAM

BLUE

LILAC

TABBY MARKINGS

This cat's spotted coat exemplifies the dark markings typical of tabbies. In different tabby cats, the patterning might be stripes, spots, or patches. These patterns are left over from the natural camouflage markings of wild cats. Tabby patterning is very common in feral cats (domestic cats that live in the wild).

SILVER SPOTTED BRITISH SHORTHAIR

Black spots are striking against a silver background

WILD CAT PATTERNS

The stripes or spots of a wild cat's coat are vital because they help the animal blend into its surroundings. Patterns camouflage a cat by breaking up the outline of its body shape. The markings of wild cats vary so considerably that the shape of the patterns is one way to distinguish the species. Individual cats of the same species also have slightly varying patterns.

Each individual ocelot has a different pattern.

Golden coat with black markings

OCELOT

Markings break up cat's outline in forests

Bold, ringed black spots

JAGUAR

Unique striped markings

Named after its cloud-like pattern

Grey-brown coat with marbled markings

TIGER

CLOUDED LEOPARD

459

WHAT IS A DOG?

THE DOMESTIC DOG, called *Canis familiaris* in Latin (from the word *canis* meaning dog), is one of 35 existing species of canids – meat-eating animals that evolved for the pursuit of prey across open grassland. The dog family ranges from the tiny Fennec Fox to the large Grey Wolf.

Insulating fur

Excellent hearing

Strong jaws and large canine teeth to catch and hold prey

Powerful muscles for speed and endurance

GREY WOLF

GREY WOLF
The Grey Wolf, one of two existing wolf species (the other is the endangered Red Wolf of southeastern US), is the ancestor of the domestic dog. It was once the most widespread mammal, apart from humans, outside the tropics.

JACKAL
The jackals of Africa, southeastern Europe, and Asia, have an undeserved bad name. Jackals are good parents to their young and do not scavenge as much as is supposed. Their diet ranges from fruit to small gazelle.

JACKAL

RED FOX

RED FOX
The Red Fox, like all foxes, is a small canid with a slender skull, large ears, and a long, bushy tail. Its coat comes in three colours – a flame red, a blackish silver, and the intermediate, "Cross" fox.

460

Dogs are social animals that adapt to their surroundings easily

PACK INSTINCT

Unlike more specialized carnivores, such as cats, which tend to hunt alone, most canids hunt in packs. Pack members also have a strong instinct to guard pack territory. Such instincts helped domestication, as canids readily adopted a human family as their "pack".

EVOLUTION

About 50 million years ago, in the Eocene epoch, *Miacis*, a small, weasel-like mammal with a well-developed brain, was the forefather of all canids, as well as more distantly related carnivores.

By the Miocene epoch, 42 different types of dog-like canid had emerged. Tomarctus had the beginnings of modern canine tooth anatomy.

Hesperocyon was a long-bodied, short-limbed canid living in the later Eocene epoch. Fossils have been found in North America.

Miacis had the distinctive teeth of a canid, and also spreading paws, indicating adaptation to life in the trees.

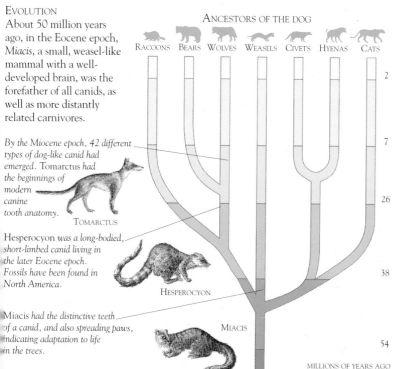

ANCESTORS OF THE DOG

RACOONS BEARS WOLVES WEASELS CIVETS HYENAS CATS

TOMARCTUS

HESPEROCYON

MIACIS

2

7

26

38

54

MILLIONS OF YEARS AGO

461

DOMESTICATION

DOGS WERE FIRST DOMESTICATED from wolves over 10,000 years ago in the Middle East and accompanied people across the world. Human-dog contact may have evolved as wolves scavenged around human settlements and when cubs were raised as pets. The dog's potential as a guard and hunting companion was soon realized.

Early Asian dogs migrated and interbred with North American wolves

EARLY HUNTING SCENE
Ancient cave paintings depict dogs assisting the hunt, as followers of human "pack" leaders.

The Carolina Dog may be descended from half-wild dogs brought across the Bering Straits by Asian peoples 8,000 years ago

MEXICAN HAIRLESS

The Chihuahua is possibly the oldest breed on the American continent. It may have been introduced to Mexico by traders from China

MEXICAN HAIRLESS
This primitive dog, descended from the Indian wolf, has much in common with the Chinese Crested Dog of mainland Asia, and may be related.

Wolves did not migrate to South America; dogs were brought here by early traders

PHARAOH HOUND
This oldest-recorded breed graces the tombs of ancient Egyptian pharaohs. It was probably a descendant of the Phoenician hound – the Phoenicians traded dogs throughout the Mediterranean.

PHARAOH HOUND

DOG OWNERSHIP FACTS
• Over 200 million dogs are kept as pets worldwide.

• North America has the largest number of pet dogs (60 million); followed by France (10.8 million), and Russia (10 million). Japan and Britain each have around 7 million dogs.

Sheepdogs originated in Europe more than 1,000 years ago

Mastiff-type dogs were domesticated in the Stone Age and later used in battle by the Greeks

The Greyhound is portrayed on 8,000-year-old Mesopotamian pottery

Wolf-like dogs similar to spitzes, such as the Elkhound and Siberian Husky, originated in Arctic regions

DINGO
The Dingo was brought to Australia 4,000 years ago. It is now a feral dog (a domesticated dog that has reverted to the wild).

DINGO

BASENJI
The Basenji's roots lie lost in the mists of antiquity. This non-barking African breed has remained more or less pure for thousands of years. It is depicted on Egyptian tombs.

BASENJI

463

DOG ANATOMY

THE BASIC DESIGN of the dog is that of a
highly developed carnivorous mammal
of the chase. Over the
centuries, humans have
modified dog anatomy
to exploit particular
talents, and for
aesthetic appeal.

Insulating coat

Loin

Brush, or tail

Croup

Flank

Stifle

Lower thigh

Knee

Hock

Pastern

INTERNAL
ANATOMY

Trachea

Backbone

Kidney

Bladder

Tongue

Heart

Stomach

Duodenum

INTERNAL ORGANS

The organs of the dog are essentially the
same as those of humans, and function in
the same way. Although its attitude to
food is that of a hunter-scavenger, the
dog is not a pure carnivore, tending
toward an omnivorous diet. Its digestive
system can cope with anything from fruit
and nuts to shellfish and raw meat.

PAWS

A dog's paws carry pads that act as
shock absorbers, provide a good grip
when running, and contain sweat
glands. The claws, unlike those of
most cats, cannot be retracted.

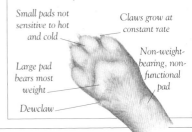

Small pads not
sensitive to hot
and cold

Claws grow at
constant rate

Non-weight-
bearing, non-
functional
pad

Large pad
bears most
weight

Dewclaw

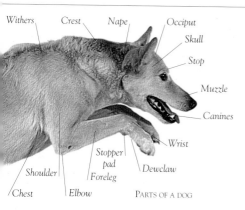

Withers Crest Nape Occiput Skull Stop Muzzle Canines Wrist Stopper pad Dewclaw Foreleg Shoulder Chest Elbow

PARTS OF A DOG

CLASSIC DESIGN

The classic canine design is seen in most wild or feral dogs and many domesticated mongrels: a lithe body, long legs, a long tail for balance and communication, efficient prick ears, and excellent vision – all ideal features for a resourceful hunting animal with plenty of stamina.

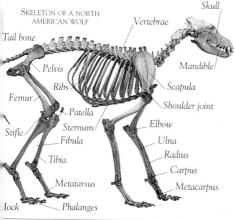

SKELETON OF A NORTH AMERICAN WOLF

Skull Vertebrae Tail bone Pelvis Ribs Femur Patella Stifle Sternum Fibula Tibia Metatarsus Hock Phalanges Mandible Scapula Shoulder joint Elbow Ulna Radius Carpus Metacarpus

TEETH

An adult dog has 42 teeth, including four stabbing, canine or "dog" teeth and four molar teeth called carnassials that are designed to shear through tough flesh.

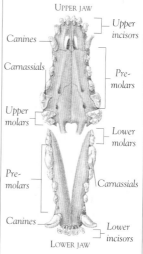

UPPER JAW

Canines Carnassials Upper molars Pre-molars Canines

Upper incisors Pre-molars Lower molars Carnassials Lower incisors

LOWER JAW

THE SKELETON

The basic dog framework provides strength, flexibility, and speed. However, selective breeding has resulted in some breeds possessing weak areas. Extra-long spines can lead to "slipped-discs"; flattened skulls to breathing troubles; and short legs may result in knee injuries.

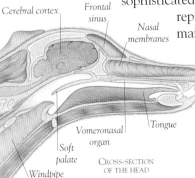

DOMESTIC MAMMALS

More on anatomy

All predatory animals depend on their sight, hearing, and sense of smell to catch prey. A dog's sense organs are some of the most sophisticated in the animal kingdom. Dogs' reproductive systems follow the basic mammalian pattern, but with some distinct features in the male.

Cerebral cortex
Frontal sinus
Nasal membranes
Vomeronasal organ
Tongue
Soft palate
Windpipe

CROSS-SECTION OF THE HEAD

SMELL AND TASTE

Dogs are marvellous smellers, in fact about one million times better than humans. Their long noses contain "smelling membranes" about 40 times larger than ours. Taste is not as important, as dogs "gobble" rather than "savour" food.

SIGHT

Dogs' eyes are more sensitive to light and movement than ours but they can often "miss" creatures that stand very still. Yet shepherds claim their working dogs will react to hand signals at a distance of 1 km (0.6 miles). Dogs are not totally colour-blind, but see mainly in black, white, and shades of grey. The anatomy of a dog's eye is very similar to ours.

Lacrimal gland
Pupil
Cornea
Iris covers anterior chamber
Lower eyelid
Third eyelid
Lens
Sclera
Retina
Optic nerve

CROSS-SECTION OF THE EYE

DOG'S EYE VIEW 250°–290°
HUMAN'S EYE VIEW 210°

VISION

A dog has a wider field of vision than a human because its eyes are set towards the sides of its head. Its carnivorous, hunter ancestors needed lateral vision.

HEARING

Dogs have excellent hearing. Equipped with large external ears served by 17 muscles, they can prick and swivel these sound receivers to focus on the source of noise. They can register high-pitched sounds of 35,000 Hz (vibrations per second), compared to humans' 20,000 Hz. This greater hearing range assists in tracking down quarry.

Ear turns to detect sound

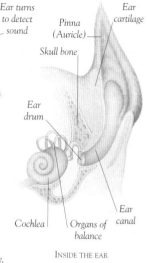

Pinna (Auricle)
Ear cartilage
Skull bone
Ear drum
Cochlea
Organs of balance
Ear canal

INSIDE THE EAR

HANGING EARS

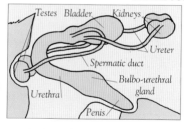

POINTED EARS

EAR TYPES
Hanging ears protect the ear when hounds hunt through vegetation. Erect ears trap sound waves most effectively.

REPRODUCTIVE ORGANS

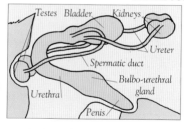

Testes *Bladder* *Kidneys*
Ureter
Spermatic duct
Bulbo-urethral gland
Urethra
Penis

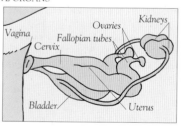

Vagina *Ovaries* *Kidneys*
Fallopian tubes
Cervix
Bladder
Uterus

MALE
The dog's penis contains a bone, through which the urethra passes, and a bulbo-urethral gland that swells up, thereby "tying" the dog and bitch together during sexual intercourse.

FEMALE
The female has a typical mammalian arrangement: vagina, cervix, uterus, Fallopian tubes, and ovaries. When a bitch is neutered, the ovaries, Fallopian tubes, and uterus are surgically removed.

LIFE CYCLE OF DOGS

ON AVERAGE, a dog's life span is about 12 years, though some breeds live a lot longer than others. In terms of ageing, the first year of a dog's life equals 15 human years, the second equals nine years and thereafter each dog year counts for four human years.

GETTING ACQUAINTED

Exploratory sniffing before mating begins

THE "HEAT" PERIOD
The female is called the bitch. She becomes sexually mature at 8–12 months old. Twice a year, she goes into "heat", usually for 18–21 days. This is when ovulation occurs.

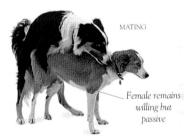

MATING

Female remains willing but passive

MATING
The male is sexually active all year and is attracted to the scent of a female in "heat". When a female is ready to mate, she draws her tail to one side. The transmission of sperm is completed within a minute but the couple remain "locked" together for half an hour.

DEVELOPMENT OF A PUPPY

7 DAYS
At this age the puppy only sleeps or suckles. Its eyes and ear canals are closed, but it responds to its mother's touch.

14 DAYS
The eyes are opening but they cannot focus properly for another 7 days. Between 13 and 17 days the puppy begins to hear.

3 WEEKS
At 3 weeks the puppy can focus its eyes and move around. Its nails should be trimmed to prevent it from scratching its mother.

1. *The yolk sac provides nourishment to the embryo for the first few days*

Yolk sac

Embryo

2. *By the third week of pregnancy, the embryo has a developing head, eyes, and limbs*

3. *By mid-pregnancy, all the internal organs are developed*

Most puppies will emerge head first in diving position

PREGNANCY

Pregnancy lasts an average of 63 days. Swelling of the mother's tummy is noticeable from the fifth week onwards. The breasts enlarge, the teats become bigger, and milk can often be produced 5–6 days before labour begins.

4. *At six weeks, the skeleton has developed*

BIRTH

When the puppies are ready to be born the mother may stop eating and find a nest site. She often gives birth to the first pups within two hours of the first contractions. After each puppy is born she may rest for minutes or for hours. Each pup's placenta is usually expelled within 15 minutes.

Mother sits contentedly while puppies suckle

Puppies huddle together for food and security

BONDING WITH MOTHER

10 DAYS
The puppy begins to play. Teething starts at 3–5 weeks. It should receive its first worming dosage.

6 WEEKS
Milk teeth are present, but the puppy is still weaning, and it should not be separated from its mother.

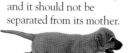

8 WEEKS
Mother and pup can be separated now, and the puppy should receive vaccinations against major diseases.

DOG BEHAVIOUR

DOGS EXHIBIT A BROAD RANGE of behaviour patterns that spring from their origins as social, hunting animals. Ear and tail movements are obviously expressive, but all patterns are vital rituals that express a dog's relationship with its environment.

SCENT GLANDS

Distinctive scents are produced by sebaceous glands in the dog's anal sacs (anal glands) that are passed on to faeces, and by sweat glands in the hind paws. These scents lay down sniffable information that only dogs can interpret.

SCENT MARKING

A dog marks out territory via deposits of urine or faeces, or by scratching the ground with its hind legs.

Dog shows interest in a scent

HOWLING

Howling is an ancient form of dog communication. Wild dogs and wolves howl to let other pack members know where they are and, in some cases, to inform strangers that they are in possession of territory. It can also be a sign of distress or loneliness.

DIGGING

Dogs inherit their love of digging from their ancestors who stored food in the ground in order to survive when hunting was poor. It leads well fed dogs to bury bones and dig them up late

AGGRESSION

Aggression can indicate possessiveness of prized objects, territory, or animals. It can be directed at outsiders who are not members of the home pack. Fear and pain also cause aggression.

DOMINANCE

Dogs asserting their dominance make eye contact, with tail raised and ears erect, and often place their neck on the other dog's shoulder. Size, though helpful, does not necessarily affect dominance.

Tail carried high indicates boldness

PLAY BOW

The play bow, often exhibited by puppies, is a clear request to human or fellow dog to meet on friendly terms. Indicating total lack of aggressive intent, it is usually an invitation to play.

Body is lowered to ground

SUBMISSION

Submissive individuals in the canine hierarchy reveal their position by their crouched postures, and by rolling onto their backs, looking away and appearing meek and defenceless.

Human pack leader offers food

Dog pack leader shows authority by rising above other dogs

HIERARCHY

Packs of wild canines have leaders to exercise authority and coordinate activity. This is usually, but not always, a male. Gatherings of domestic dogs behave in the same way.

INTRODUCTION TO BREEDS

AMONG DOMESTICATED ANIMALS only the dog has been selectively bred to produce such a wide variety of types. Worldwide, there are over 500 different breeds. National kennel clubs differ in the way they group breeds so, for the purposes of this book, general categories have been used.

GUNDOGS

Gundogs were developed to pick up the air scents of game and also be good sporting companions. They are highly responsive and amenable workers. Field trials are held regularly to test working skills.

IRISH RED-AND-WHITE SETTER

BORDER COLLIES HERDING SHEEP

CHOW CHOW

SPECIAL DOGS

This is a miscellaneous collection of breeds. Many, such as the Chow Chow, are highly distinctive, and some have specialized in particular types of work. Most make good companions; many popular pets fall into this category.

HERDING DOGS AND GUARD DOGS

These dogs were bred to protect and herd livestock, work as guards, pull and carry loads, or assist police and armed forces. Most of these dogs are happiest when they have access to open spaces and a job to do

HOUNDS

These athletes with sensitive noses and sharp eyes were the first dogs used by humans. They helped their (much slower) masters by hunting down animals, such as deer, for food.

FOXHOUNDS

TERRIERS

Developed from hounds to tackle small, burrowing animals, terriers are generally small, short-legged, stocky animals with alert and spirited temperaments. No group of dogs is more expert at tunnelling than terriers.

NORFOLK TERRIERS

TOY DOGS

These breeds' main function is to be loyal, decorative, and friendly companions. Many are useful for raising the alarm and nipping intruders' ankles. Small and dainty, they play a vital role in people's lives.

PEKINGESE

MONGRELS

Most dogs in the world are mongrels or "cross-breed" dogs that have interbred at random. Apart from their individual endearing qualities, they are often better-tempered, less disease-prone, and more adaptable than pure-breds.

DOGS

473

WHAT IS A HORSE?

SOME 60 MILLION YEARS AGO the first horses ran on
the plains of North America. The modern horse has
single-hooved feet and a greater length of leg than its
earlier ancestors. Like all mammals, horses suckle
their young, and as herbivores, their natural
food is grass. They are
social creatures,
and prefer to live
in groups.

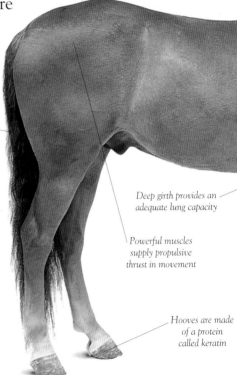

*Long tail helps
to keep flies off
the body*

HORSE FACTS

• Horses are measured
from the ground up to
the withers, which is
the highest point of the
shoulders.

• In 1910, North
America had about 20
million domestic horses.

• There are over 150
officially recognized
horse and pony breeds.

• Most modern horse
breeds have been
deliberately created to
do a specific task.

*Deep girth provides an
adequate lung capacity*

*Powerful muscles
supply propulsive
thrust in movement*

*Hooves are made
of a protein
called keratin*

Long hair on the back of the neck is called a mane

Horses have an excellent sense of hearing

Withers

Long head and neck allow horse to graze while standing

It takes over two years for a horse foal to take on adult proportions

Long legs developed to run from danger

HORSES AND HUMANS

As this cave painting shows, early humans hunted horses for their meat and skin. By keeping horses in herds, these essential items became more readily available. Eventually, horses were used for riding and pulling carts, and later they were bred to perform all kinds of work.

BORN TO RUN

Both wild and domestic horses give birth to fully developed offspring. This is because in the wild the young foal must keep up with its mother and the herd, as well as escaping from predators.

MAIN HORSE TYPES

MOST MODERN HORSES are thought to be descended from four types which inhabited Europe and Asia over 6,000 years ago. Their features can still be seen in some breeds today. Domestication led to the variety of modern breeds and their spread across the world.

Broad forehead with straight profile

Lean with narrow body

PONY TYPE 1
This hardy pony looked similar to today's Exmoor breed of Great Britain. It lived in northwestern Europe.

HORSE TYPE 1
Originating from central Asia, this horse lived in dry, arid conditions and resembled the modern Akhal-Teke.

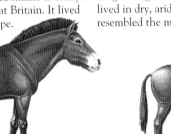

Small head

PONY TYPE 2
Similar to Przewalski's horse, the Type 2 was powerfully built with a heavy head. The breed roamed over northern Eurasia.

HORSE TYPE 2
Living in the hot deserts of western Asia, this slim horse was possibly the ancestor of the Arab and Caspian.

SPREAD OF INFLUENCE
Many of today's light
horses can trace their
ancestry to three main
breeds: Arab, Barb,
and Spanish.
Their influence
spread across
several continents
from the Middle
East, right through
Europe, and later,
on to North and
South America.

NORTH
AMERICA

EUROPE

ASIA

AFRICA

SOUTH
AMERICA

KEY TO MAP
ARAB ▉ BARB ▉ SPANISH

Heavy horse

Light horse

THREE MAIN GROUPS
The various breeds are
placed into three main
groups: ponies, light
horses, and heavy horses.
They are categorized
according to their size and
proportions. Ponies and
light horses can be found
living wild in parts of the
world today, but heavy
horses are entirely
domesticated.

Pony

477

BODY AND CONFORMATION

A HORSE'S BODY IS perfectly designed for its way of life. The neck is long so it can stoop to graze, and long, muscular legs allow it to run away from danger. The proportions of a horse's body, or conformation, may vary according to the group or breed.

Points

The external features of a horse are called the points. Each point has a different name and together they make up the horse's conformation.

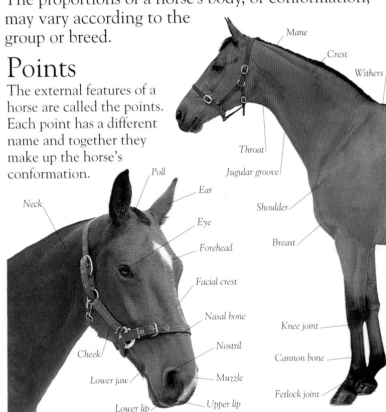

Mane

Crest

Withers

Throat

Jugular groove

Shoulder

Breast

Poll

Ear

Eye

Forehead

Facial crest

Nasal bone

Nostril

Muzzle

Upper lip

Neck

Cheek

Lower jaw

Lower lip

Knee joint

Cannon bone

Fetlock joint

PROPORTION

In a perfectly proportioned horse, certain measurements of the body should all be equal. Those shown in blue should correspond to each other, as should the lines drawn in both red and grey.

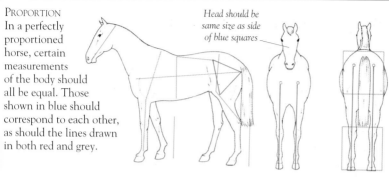

Head should be same size as side of blue squares

FRONT AND REAR LIMBS

When viewed from the front, a line from the shoulder should pass through the centre of the knees, fetlock, and foot. A straight line should also pass through the rear legs.

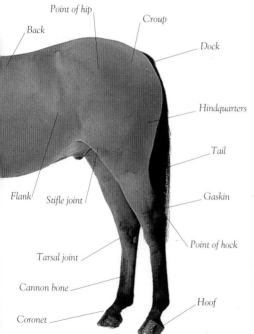

Point of hip
Croup
Back
Dock
Hindquarters
Tail
Gaskin
Flank
Stifle joint
Point of hock
Tarsal joint
Cannon bone
Hoof
Coronet

ANATOMICAL FACTS

• The body and head of a horse are streamlined and this helps to reduce wind resistance.

• A long neck and well-sloped shoulders may indicate that the horse is fast and good for riding.

• Large eyes usually show not only that the horse has good vision, but also a calm nature and intelligence.

Skeleton and muscles

The framework of the horse consists of a skeleton, made up of a number of connected bones that are moved by muscles. Along the spinal, or vertebral, column, which runs from the head to the tail, is the spinal cord – the connection between the horse's brain and body. When a horse wants to move, it sends a message from its brain down the cord via nerves to signal the appropriate muscle.

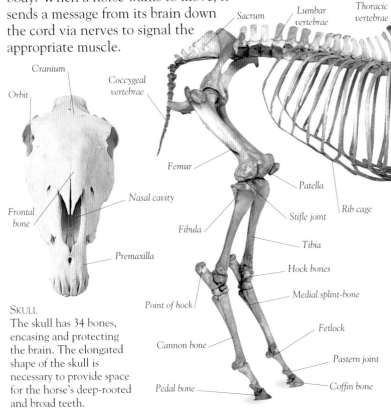

Sacrum

Lumbar vertebrae

Thoracic vertebrae

Cranium

Coccygeal vertebrae

Orbit

Femur

Patella

Nasal cavity

Frontal bone

Stifle joint

Rib cage

Fibula

Tibia

Premaxilla

Hock bones

Medial splint-bone

Point of hock

SKULL
The skull has 34 bones, encasing and protecting the brain. The elongated shape of the skull is necessary to provide space for the horse's deep-rooted and broad teeth.

Cannon bone

Fetlock

Pastern joint

Coffin bone

Pedal bone

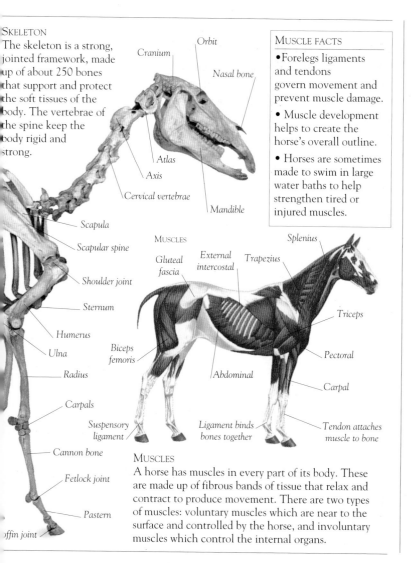

SKELETON
The skeleton is a strong, jointed framework, made up of about 250 bones that support and protect the soft tissues of the body. The vertebrae of the spine keep the body rigid and strong.

Orbit

Cranium

Nasal bone

Atlas

Axis

Cervical vertebrae

Mandible

Scapula

Scapular spine

Shoulder joint

Sternum

Humerus

Ulna

Radius

Carpals

Suspensory ligament

Cannon bone

Fetlock joint

Pastern

offin joint

MUSCLE FACTS

• Forelegs ligaments and tendons govern movement and prevent muscle damage.

• Muscle development helps to create the horse's overall outline.

• Horses are sometimes made to swim in large water baths to help strengthen tired or injured muscles.

MUSCLES

Gluteal fascia

External intercostal

Splenius

Trapezius

Triceps

Biceps femoris

Pectoral

Abdominal

Carpal

Suspensory ligament

Ligament binds bones together

Tendon attaches muscle to bone

MUSCLES
A horse has muscles in every part of its body. These are made up of fibrous bands of tissue that relax and contract to produce movement. There are two types of muscles: voluntary muscles which are near to the surface and controlled by the horse, and involuntary muscles which control the internal organs.

HORSES

481

Patterns and markings

Individual horses can be identified by body markings, which can be either natural or acquired. Natural markings are often areas of white hair on the head, legs, and hooves. Acquired markings are the result of branding or injury. Branding has been done for more than 2,000 years and can help to identify the horse if it is stolen.

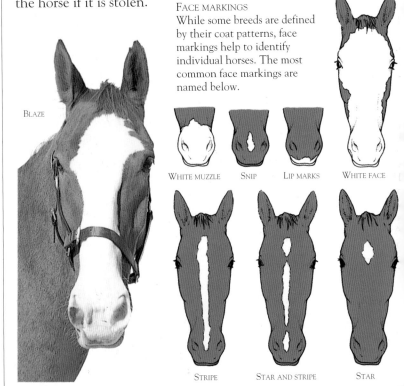

BLAZE

FACE MARKINGS
While some breeds are defined by their coat patterns, face markings help to identify individual horses. The most common face markings are named below.

WHITE MUZZLE

SNIP

LIP MARKS

WHITE FACE

STRIPE

STAR AND STRIPE

STAR

ERMINE

SOCK

STOCKING

ZEBRA

LEG MARKINGS

These markings are often white. They are called ermine if they are just above the hoof, a sock if they extend below the knee, and a stocking when extending above the knee. Zebra markings are dark rings.

HOOF MARKINGS

The blue hoof is made of hard blue horn and is most often associated with ponies. Hooves of black and white vertical stripes are seen on the Appaloosa and other spotted horse breeds.

BLUE HOOF

STRIPED HOOF

DORSAL STRIPE

This mark extends from the tail to the withers. It is found on primitive horses such as the Tarpan, and is associated with dun-coloured coats.

IDENTITY MARKINGS

Artificial markings help identify ownership and sometimes breed. Brand marks are applied by a hot iron rod which stops the hair growing back. Freeze marks are frozen on in a similar way.

BRAND MARK

FREEZE MARK

483

FOOD AND DIET

LIKE ANY ANIMAL, horses get their energy from food. They are herbivores, which means they only eat plants. In the wild, horses survive well on grass and herbs as long as grazing is plentiful. In the winter, when it is cold and there is less food, wild horses get out of condition, while in the summer they put on weight.

FIRST SOLID FOOD
Young horses are able to eat their first solid food from about six weeks.

Oesophagus takes food to stomach

Most digestion takes place in the large intestine

Waste expelled from rectum

Teeth start to grind down food

Stomach holds food

Colon absorbs B vitamins

Rib cage

Small intestine absorbs energy from food

DIGESTIVE SYSTEM
This diagram shows a horse's digestive system. An adult heavy horse needs to eat about two percent of its body weight every day. This is about 12.5 kg (28 lb), almost twice as much as a pony eats each day.

TEETH AND JAWS

Grazing wears down the foal's milk teeth and by the time the horse is five, these are replaced by a set of 36 adult teeth. The incisors cut the food into small pieces, and the molars grind it down, ready for digestion.

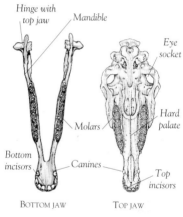

Hinge with top jaw

Mandible

Eye socket

Hard palate

Molars

Bottom incisors

Canines

Top incisors

BOTTOM JAW   TOP JAW

BALANCED DIET

Horses need a balanced diet, with enough vitamins and minerals to help them stay healthy and in condition. Horses should be fed little and often, and allowed constant access to fresh water.

Fruit and root vegetables must be chopped up lengthways so the horse does not choke

Feed bowl holds carrots, maize, linseed, nuts, chaff, and a slice of apple

Hay is grass that has been cut and dried

Bucket of clean, fresh water

FOOD DANGERS

• Plants like deadly nightshade, bracken, and ragwort may poison a horse if it eats them in any quantity. Pastures where horses are left to graze must be cleared of these plants.

• Horses should not graze in an area within 14 days of any spraying.

BEHAVIOUR

TODAY'S DOMESTIC HORSES show the same patterns of behaviour as their wild ancestors. The herd instinct still dominates, and horses prefer to be kept in groups rather than on their own. Much of their behaviour is linked to the way they communicate with other horses.

Horses sleep for only short periods at a time

SHIRE HORSE

SLEEPING
Horses are able to sleep standing up. In the wild, this increases their chances of escaping from predators.

EARS
The position of a horse's ears is an important indicator of its mood. If the ears point forwards, this shows curiosity. When the horse is uncertain, it keeps one ear forwards and the other backwards.

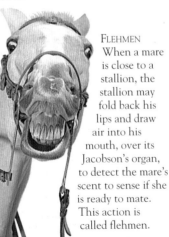

FLEHMEN
When a mare is close to a stallion, the stallion may fold back his lips and draw air into his mouth, over its Jacobson's organ, to detect the mare's scent to sense if she is ready to mate. This action is called flehmen.

MUTUAL GROOMING
Horses indulge in mutual grooming as a sign of a close relationship. They will gently nuzzle each other's backs, nibbling at the hair. Such sessions may last for several minutes at a time.

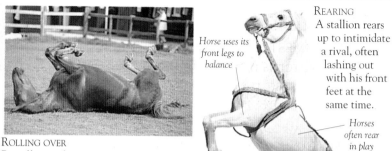

Horse uses its front legs to balance

REARING

A stallion rears up to intimidate a rival, often lashing out with his front feet at the same time.

Horses often rear in play

ROLLING OVER

By rolling, a horse can exercise the muscles in its back, and also clean its coat. Horses often roll when turned out to graze in a field.

Stallions rear naturally in the wild

Horses nuzzle each other to establish their relationship

SHETLAND PONY

BEHAVIOURAL FACTS

• Horses will call out to warn others of approaching danger.

• The tail is used as a fly swish rather than for communication.

• Repeated pawing at the ground with the hooves is often a sign of nervousness.

• A horse's ears are very mobile and can rotate independently 180° forward and back.

USES OF THE HORSE

IN SPITE OF THE SPREAD of mechanization, the horse still has a place in society. Today, horses can be found hard at work in cities, forests, and farmland. While traditional horse sports like racing and steeple-chasing remain popular, they are now being joined by leisure activities like trekking.

Working horses

Horses work in forests because they cause less damage than tractors. Farmers in developing countries also find horses easy to keep as they can live off the land. Though no longer used in war, horses are retained in many countries for ceremonial duties and the police horse has so far proved to be irreplaceable.

MULE TRAINS
Even in the late 20th century, it has been hard to find anything to replace the mule to transport goods over uneven ground. Mules are still used in many parts of the world.

London police horses undergo about 40 weeks of training

ROYAL ARTILLERY HORSE AND RIDER

CEREMONIAL DUTIES

Many countries still use horses for ceremonial duties. This dates from wars where horses were used as cavalry and to haul artillery.

POLICE HORSES

Mounted police can be seen in many cities today. Horses offer the rider a good view and mobility, and can move through crowds more easily than either motorcycles or cars.

Working cow ponies in the US tend to average 15 hands high (1hh=4in).

QUARTER HORSE

Average working life of a police horse is about 14 years

BRITISH POLICE HORSES AND RIDERS IN CEREMONIAL DRESS

HERDING CATTLE

Horses are still used to herd cattle and sheep in the Americas, the former USSR, Australia, and New Zealand.

HORSES

Horses for sport and leisure

Since the end of World War II, there has been a tremendous increase in the use of the horse for pleasure. Sports such as horse racing remain as popular as ever, and interest in horse events like show jumping and dressage has been heightened by television. Riding holidays are now a popular and relaxing pastime for many people.

POLO
Probably originating in Persia, polo has been played for 2,500 years. Modern polo is played by two teams of four using long mallets to hit the ball into the opposition's goal.

VERSATILE MORGAN
The American Morgan Horse, once favoured by the US cavalry, is shown in ridden and harnessed classes. It is also used for Western and pleasure riding, and jumping.

A hard hat protects the rider's head in case of a fall

Rider sits on the horse's centre of balance

Pony will cover 4.8–6.4 km (3–6 miles) in an hour

The use of plain snaffle bridles for recreational riding is almost universal

RACEHORSES

Horse racing has become a huge international industry. This statue in the Kentucky Horse Park, US, is of the famous racehorse *Man O' War*, or *Big Red*, who was beaten only once in 21 races. When he died in 1947, more than 1,000 people attended the funeral.

HORSE SPORTS FACTS

• The longest-running horse race is the Palio in Siena, Italy, begun in the 1200s and still run today. The winning horse attends a special banquet afterwards.

• The word polo comes from the Tibetan *pulu*, meaning ball.

• The first steeplechase was held in 1830 at St. Albans, England.

Riders learn to use aids such as the reins

Each rider keeps a pony-length away from the next

A novice rider is given a quiet, reliable horse

Riding school ponies are frequently cross-bred animals

RIDING HOLIDAYS

Those who want to ride occasionally or just for pleasure, can take riding holidays. These involve treks that last from a single day to a whole week. The distances covered each day can vary from 16–40 km (10–25 miles). Trips are always supervised and provide an opportunity to reach beautiful and inaccessible areas of a country.

Index

Acknowledgements

Contributors to this title include:
Editors: Elise Bradbury, Laura Buller, Alan Burrows, Bernadette Crowley, Alastair Dougall, John Mapps, Susan McKeever, Miranda Smith, Leo Vita-Finzi, Selina Wood, Sarah Watson.

Designers: Alexandra Brown, Sarah Crouch, Janet Allis, Tanya Tween.

DK India Team:
Managing Editor: Punita Singh
Managing Art Editor: Rachana Bhattacharya
Senior Editor: Sheema Mookherjee
Senior Designer: Sabyasachi Kundu
Designer: Sukanto Bhattacharjya
DTP Coordinator: Jacob Joshua
DTP Designers: Sunil Sharma, Umesh Aggarwal

PAGEOne: Melanie McDowell, Chris Stewart, Suzanne Tuhrim, Sophie Williams.

Dorling Kindersley would like to thank: Hilary Bird and Mark Lambert for indexing, Robert Graham for research and editorial support, Caroline Potts for picture library services, Natural History Museum, University Museum of Zoology, Cambridge, Thurston Watson for model making.

Photographs by:
Julie Anderson, Dennis Avon, Akhil Bakhshi, Simon Battensby, Geoff Brightling, Jane Burton, Peter Chadwick, Gordon Clayton, Geoff Dann, Philip Dowell, Mike Dunning, Neil Fletcher, Steve Gorton, Frank Greenaway, Steve Gorton, Marc Henrie, Kit Houghton, Colin Keates, Dave King, Bob Langrish, Cyril Laubscher, Ranald Mackechnie, Andrew McRobb, Ray Moller, Tracy Morgan, Stephen Oliver, Oxford Scientific Films, Nick Parfit, Tim Ridley, Bill Sands, Karl Shone, Steve Shott, Harry Taylor, Kim Taylor, Michael Ward, Jerry Young

Illustrations by:
Graham Allen, Janet Allis, Stephen Biesty, Joanna Cameron, Rowan Clifford, Karen Cochrane, John Davis, Ted Dewan, Gill Ellsbury, Samantha Elmhurst, Angelica Elsebach, Giuliano Fornari, Chris Forsey, Will Giles, Craig Gosling (Indiana University Medical Illustration Department), Tony Graham Nick Hall, Nick Hewetson, John Hutchinson, Mark Iley, Stanley Cephas

Johnson, Aziz Khan, Richard Lewington, Kenneth Lilly, Ruth Lindsay, Mick Loates, Janos Marffy, Malcolm McGregor, Sean Milne, Richard Orr, Maurice Pledger, Sandra Pond, Bryan Poole, Sally Alane Reason, Colin Salmon, Tommy Swahn, John Temperton, Simon Thomas, Kevin Toy, David Webb, Amanda Williams, Ann Winterbotham, John Woodcock, Debra Woodward, Colin Woolf, Dan Wright.

Picture credits:

t=top b=bottom c=center l=left r=right

The publisher would like to thank the following for their kind permission to reproduce their photographs:
Dennis Avon 286b, 323bl; 346bl; Professor Edmund D. Brodie Jr. 165cr; Lester Cheeseman 251c; Dr. Barry Clarke 23tr; John Holmes 175cl; Colin Keates 27cl; Dave King 25cr; Bob Langrish 487tl; Leszczynski 157cl **Ardea/**M Krishnan 257bl; Eric Lingren 238tl

BBC Natural History Unit/Galleria Degli Uffizi, Florence 168tl

Bridgeman Art Library/210tl, 233br

Centaur Studios/175bl

Bruce Coleman/231bc; Jen and Des Bartlett 258-259, 279tl; Erwin & Peggy Bauer, 216tl; Fred Bruemmer 203bl; John Cancalosi 236tl, 342bl; Eric Crichton 80cl; Gerald Cubitt 81br; Geoff Doré 81bc; M.P.L Fogden 154-

155; P.A. Hinchcliffe 60tr; Dr. M. T. Kahl 344tr; Jan van de Kam 338br; Stephen J. Krasemann 379tl; Gordon Langsbury 354-355b; 355r; Cyril Laubscher 290br; Werner Layer 366-367; Luiz Claudio Mango 307tr; George Mcarthy 287b;351tl; Michael McCoy 237tl; Rinie van Meurs 338 tr; Charlie Off 330bl; Dr. Eckart Pott 30-31, 133tc; Dr Sandro Prato 139tr; Hans Reinhard 99tl, 352cl, 361b, 365bc, 438-439; Hector Rivarola 349bl; Kevin Rushby 63tl; Dr Frieder Sauer 79br; Pacific Stock 142-143; Kim Taylor 51tr, 88cr, 94cr, 133tl, 272-273b, 302cr; 276c, 305b; 313cl; Norman Tomalin 106c

Mary Evans Picture Library/69ac, 151tr

FLPA/L Chance 237bl

Robert Harding/300cl; 301cr; 302cr; 353b; 475tr

Musée Nationale d'Histoire Naturelle/158tr 159tc

Naturhistoriska Riksmuseet/158c

Natural History Museum/Frank Greenaway 98cr; 99br, 16cr, 170cl, 170bl, 170br, 171tl, 172t, 172b, 173t, 173c, 173br, 177c, 179tl, 212bl, 212cl, 215cl, 216bl, 217t, 218b, 219t, 221tl, 223cr, 223br, 224tl, 225b, 226t, 226bl, 227br, 228b, 229t, 230–231, 230cr, 230b, 231c, 231t, 233t, 237tl, 241cr, 243br, 248r, 252bl, 256b, 437br

Nature Photographers/289tr; E.Lemon 300br; H. Miles 358bl; Paul Sterry 337br; 341r; 337br

Natural Science Photos/C Banks 221cr; 256tr, 256cl; M. Boulard 131bc; P. Bowman 92cl; M. Chinery 135cl; C Dani & I Jeske 209br, 221bl; Carol Farneti 106bl; Adrian Hoskins 95cr; G Kinns 246cl; JG Lilley 204c, 204b; Chris Mattison 227t, 246br; Jim Merli 176cr, 180bc, 188cl, 193tr, 255tl, 253t, 257tr; Pete Oxford 203tl, 205bl; Queensland Museum 253c; Richard Revels 92tr, 132cr, 252tr; C & T Stuart 249bl. P.H. & S.L. Ward 61cr, 137c; David Yendall 101tr

N.H.P.A/Stephen Dalton 437tl; Melvin Grey 271cl; Peter Johnson 362 bl; R & D Keller 373tl; Peter Parks 153br, 282tr; Philippa Scott 301tl; John Shaw 301br; 348r

Frank Lane Picture Agency/ E&D Hosking 281t; 303tr; 355tl; 362-363; 365cr;/ T&P Gardner; F.Polking 304br; Silvestris 328tr;/Roger Tidma 353t;/ Roger Wimshurst 307tr;/ W.Wisniewski 359br

Oxford Scientific Films/Doug Allen 364l; Larus Argentatus 274-275, 301bl; Kathie Atkinson 57tr; G.I. Bernard 101cl; Raymond Blythe 130bl; Densey Clyne 127tr; C.M. Collins 68bl; J.A.L. Cooke 79c, 134tl; David B. Fleetham 387tr; Michael Fogden 125tl; Peter Gathercole 67tr; Howard Hall 153t; 387cr; Stan Osolinski 166-167; Papilio 296br; Alan Root/Okapia 371cr

Mantis Wildlife Films/32cl; Peter O'Toole 68cr; James Robinson 76cr, 99br; Harold Taylor 83c; Steve Turner 81cr, 125tr; P & W Ward 124cr

Museum der Bildenden Kuenste, Leipzig/24cl

Planet Earth/K & K Ammann 387br; Andre Barttschi 321 bc; John R. Bracegirdle 386cl; Richard Coomber 436bl; Carol Farneti-Foster 449tr, 459tr, 386br; Daniel Heuclin 245bl; Gerard Lacz 217cr; John Lythgou 308b, 347tr; Mark Mattock 336cl; E Hanumantha Rao 244cl; Brian Kenney 232t, 236bl, 238bl, 255bl; Jonathan Scott 387bl, 387tl; Anup and Manoj Shah 451tr; Yur Shibbnev 311tl; Martin Wendler 239c

Premaphotos/K.G. Preston-Mafham 59tr, 67br, 71br, 73cl, 74br, 80br, 106br, 110bl, 123t, 123cr. Dr Bill Sands 70cr

Science Photo Library/Mark Deeble & Victoria Stone 213cr; John Downer 214br; Michael Fogden 215tr, 249tr; J.C Revy 114cr; Tui de Roy 186cr; Alastair Shay 247cr

Tony Stone Images/Mike Surowiak 101bc; 196cl; Maurice Tibbles 189c

Werner Forman Archive/14cl

Wild Images/Romulus Whitaker 193br; 214tr; Howard Hall 153 cl

Jerry Young/12c, bl, br

Zefa/J. Schupe 7tr; 447tr, 455t.